*Decorative detail*
*(Photo by Bernie Cleff)*

*West Rittenhouse Square, c. 1925. Charles J. Cohen notebooks (Historical Society of Pennsylvania)*

# HISTORIC RITTENHOUSE

*A Philadelphia Neighborhood*

*Edited by* **TRINA VAUX**

*Foreword by Thomas Hine*

BOBBYE BURKE
OTTO SPERR
HUGH J. McCAULEY
TRINA VAUX

*upp*

*University of Pennsylvania Press*
*Philadelphia   1985*

This book was prepared under the auspices of
Historic Rittenhouse, Inc. Major funding was
provided by the National Endowment for the Arts
and the Atlantic Richfield Foundation.

*Design by Adrianne Onderdonk Dudden*

*The "Inspection Checklist for Vintage Houses" on pp. 110–114
is reprinted with permission from* The Old-House Journal, *69A
Seventh Avenue, Brooklyn, New York 11217. Subscriptions
$16.00 per year.*

*Printed in the United States of America*

*Library of Congress Cataloging in Publication Data*

*Main entry under title:*

*Historic Rittenhouse, a Philadelphia neighborhood.*

 *Bibliography: p.*
  *1. Rittenhouse (Philadelphia, Pa.)—Buildings—Conser-
vation and restoration—Addresses, essays, lectures.
2. Architecture—Pennsylvania—Philadelphia—Conservation
and restoration—Addresses, essays, lectures.   3. Philadelphia (Pa.)—History—Addresses, essays, lectures.
I. Burke, Bobbye, 1929–               II. Vaux, Trina.*
*NA9053.C6H565 1985     363.6'9'0974811     84–10689*
*ISBN 0-8122-7938-7*

*ISBN 0-8122-1202-9 (pbk.)*

*To those who will determine the future of Rittenhouse*

# CONTENTS

The publication of *Historic Rittenhouse* has been a community endeavor in the sense that the book was conceived and written by four Rittenhouse residents and supported by hundreds of their neighbors. It is especially gratifying that the larger community of governmental agencies, local businesses and corporations, and cultural and professional institutions shared our confidence in its merits.

The University of Pennsylvania Press, and particularly its managing editor Ingalill Hjelm, lent invaluable assistance and brought the book to its final fruition. The support of the Atlantic Richfield Foundation confirmed our commitment to expand the scope and contents of *Historic Rittenhouse* beyond the "handbook" format and made possible publication of the book in its present form. The National Endowment for the Arts supported the initial concept for the project under its Architecture and Environmental Arts Program.

I wish to thank the Public Committee for the Humanities in Pennsylvania, whose joint grant to the Center City Foundation and the American Studies Program of Temple University encouraged me to see Rittenhouse in its historical perspective. Meredith Savery, former coordinator of the American Studies Program, helped me to articulate and refine the goals of the project: to find ways to accommodate change without sacrificing the continuity and sense of tradition that the physical environment of Rittenhouse affords.

Richard Tyler of the Philadelphia Historical Commission and Craig Schelter of the City Planning Commission encouraged our early efforts, as did Margy Ellin Meyerson, The Reverend Louis Temme, Edmund N. Bacon, Anne G. Tyng, F.A.I.A., and John F. Harbeson, F.A.I.A. Dennis Clark, George E. Thomas, Robert Ennis, Satoko Parker, Phillip Yanella, Jacqueline Saylor, and Mr. and Mrs. James Harper were always generous when asked to share their special knowledge of Rittenhouse architects, buildings, and people.

The dearth of publications on nineteenth-century Philadelphia made access to manuscripts, pamphlets, notebooks, and visual material vital. The following persons were indispensable guides to pertinent research materials: Peter Parker and Linda Stanley at the Historical Society of Pennsylvania; Alan Weinberg and Ward Childs at the Philadelphia City Archives; Sandra Tatman and Patricia Wright at the Athenaeum of Philadelphia; and Edwin Wolf 2nd and Kenneth Finkel at the Library Company of Philadelphia. Their intimate knowledge of their institutions' holdings made exciting "finds" possible.

The following people assisted by providing information for the Methods and Procedures chapters of the book, and also reviewed material and made suggestions as the book was in progress: Myra Harrison, at the Mid-Atlantic regional office of the National Park Service; William Watson and Brenda Barrett at the State Bureau for Historic Preservation; and Michael Scholnick of the Philadelphia Historic Preservation Corporation.

I wish to thank the members of the project team: Bernie Cleff, whose memorable photographs have provided a record of Rittenhouse that future generations will cherish; and Adrianne Onderdonk Dudden, whose book design inspired our best efforts to create a publication as informative as it is handsome. Architects Otto Sperr and Hugh McCauley have made urban design, architectural styles, and preservation of buildings understandable to the layperson. It is the reader who benefits from the love and respect with which they respond to the streetscapes and buildings of Rittenhouse. All the drawings in the book were done by Hugh McCauley except as noted otherwise. Jefferson Moak prepared with scholarly precision the list of architects who have worked in Rittenhouse. Mildred Blithe and Sarah Greenspan patiently and accurately typed through many drafts of the manuscript and responded to last-minute requests with forbearance.

Trina Vaux's contributions merit special recognition. She edited the other authors' sections so that each retains its distinctive view of Rittenhouse while it complements the whole. She saw Rittenhouse without parochialism and focused our efforts on the neighborhood's relationship to the larger city, the region, and our nation's history. She wrote of the book, "One of the most important benefits of *Historic Rittenhouse* is intangible—the regaining of a communal identity that is, in part, rooted in our past. We must see the streets and buildings of Rittenhouse with new eyes, as a living part of our environment, reminders of our past, and bench marks for our future. We need Rittenhouse so that we may understand who we are and what will become of us." I share her hope that all who read this book will have a renewed vision of Rittenhouse.

Finally, my gratitude to my husband, Joseph, is incalculable. When, many years ago, he met his bride-to-be on her first visit to Philadelphia in the great waiting room of Frank Furness's Baltimore and Ohio Passenger Station (Twenty-fourth and Chestnut streets, demolished 1963), he did not anticipate with what fervor she would adopt his native city.

*Bobbye Burke*

What you hold in your hands is a testament to a very successful neighborhood. Indeed, for much of its history, Rittenhouse has been more than a neighborhood; it has been virtually synonymous with Philadelphia's center city. One still occasionally encounters Rittenhouse residents who view Society Hill as a pleasant enough nearby suburb, and it is easy to understand why.

As Bobbye Burke points out in her history of the area, Rittenhouse has had its ups and downs. But there has been continuity. Philadelphians never fully abandoned Rittenhouse. It had a revival, but it did not involve artificial resuscitation. Except for the office district at its northern border, Rittenhouse has never been subjected to urban renewal. Partly for that reason, it is a model to which people throughout the world can look for a high quality of urban life.

The population of Rittenhouse has some Old Philadelphians. But it also includes young people who have just moved to the city, the elderly in apartment buildings, children rubbing the horns of Billy in Rittenhouse Square. Its rowhouse buildings contain both grand homes and warrens. They contain art galleries, and shoe repair shops, corner stores, and good restaurants. On its streets you see evidence of a tremendous diversity of architectural styles, you hear music coming through open windows, and you run into a great many interesting people. It's a small town, after all, but quite an extraordinary one.

Rittenhouse has many assets that are quite rare in this country. Although one cannot instantly create a neighborhood like Rittenhouse, with its amazing cultural and architectural riches, it certainly provides an inspiration and a challenge to other American cities. The many sights, sounds, and diversions that are part of any walk through the neighborhood make it a great treasure. Its sense of connectedness is, unfortunately, very rare. Those who live in Rittenhouse are lucky.

But as has so often been said, Philadelphia's characteristic sin is complacency. When you have something good going, you want to believe that it will continue more or less as you assume it has always gone in the past. This is an illusion. Cities do not remain static. Cities are always changing, and not always uniformly. The changes involve the buildings themselves, the people who live in them, the ways in which they live in them, and the ways that external economic forces bring social and physical change.

Rittenhouse is well located, of course, and it has been fortunate over the years. But for a neighborhood to be as successful as this one has been, it must have a keen sense of the importance of its own survival and some strategies to ensure that change will work in its favor.

That is what this book is about. As you look through it, you will get a sense of the dynamism of the neighborhood and its continuing challenges. It is about preservation, of course, but in the sense of preserving basic values and centuries of investment rather than preserving the neighborhood exactly as it was at some theoretical moment around the beginning of this century. The book is not about living in the past; it is about living with change.

The approach can be seen most dramatically in Hugh McCauley's section on home maintenance. The neighborhood began with local clay being turned to bricks, and he notes that our houses, like ourselves, will all, in the long run, be dust. His account of the forces that work to destroy our buildings, from flood to fire to the No. Forty bus, is probably enough to convince many people to be renters forever. We and all our works will return to the earth, but, as he notes, in the meantime we can patch our roofs, make sure our sills are in good order, complain to the city about those buses. We can refrain from doing things that might seem like good ideas but that are ultimately destructive—such as cleaning by sandblasting, installation of metal replacement windows, and stuccoing a problem-ridden brick wall. If we know about the nature of the physical forces that bring change to our buildings, and behave appropriately, the buildings of Rittenhouse will last a lot longer than those of us who now inhabit them. Rittenhouse is a legacy, and it is certainly a solid one.

This same approach can be taken, by analogy, to the other concerns addressed in this book. Indeed, while nearly everything that affects our buildings works to destroy them, external forces that affect the social, economic, and physical fabric of the neighborhood are not necessarily all negative. The important thing is to have a sense of what we are.

The physical continuity of the neighborhood should be the easiest part. Perhaps only Boston's Back Bay area equals the Rittenhouse neighborhood's success in accommodating wildly varying architectural styles and individual tastes in an environment that is ultimately harmonious. Americans visiting Philadelphia often say that the physical character of the streets is somehow European, but a street like Spruce could only have happened in America. American places, from city streets to shopping strips, have long been a hodgepodge of historical references, outpourings of ego, and expressions of technology. As Otto Sperr demonstrates in his discussion of architecture, almost any visual idea or design style you can think of has been adapted in Rittenhouse. Each building in Rittenhouse can be appreciated in its own right, and there are some that nearly knock our eyes out.

But most of the time, the architectural extravagances are perceived as variations within a greater unity. There is a fundamental order to the neighborhood that has generally been preserved quite successfully. It involves the order of the street, and the way in which it is divided into rowhouse lots. The rowhouse architecture makes each building part of a larger building, which is the street. And although an Italianate building might nestle against something that looks rather Dutch, both share the characteristic of masonry construction. Their windows and doorways form a rhythm on the block. Openings in the walls are not made casually but with care, and often, ornament. We have front steps, and railings, and foot scrapers, and need them as much as ever. A few of the area's high-rise buildings have violated this fundamental order, destructively, and there have been some recent rowhouses that have ignored it and ended up looking rather silly. The violations stand out, however, because the basic order remains. Today Rittenhouse has quite a few vacant sites that are ripe for new buildings. This richly eclectic neighborhood is capable of embracing architectural styles that haven't been invented yet. Rittenhouse is strong enough to welcome any kind of expression, as long as it respects the continuity of the street, the disciplines of masonry, the rhythms of windows and doors, and other evidence of human habitation. Physically, Rittenhouse is joyously impure. But we do have our standards.

The question of social change is far more complicated. Ms. Burke's history takes us to the time when the neighborhood's residents organized not as an elite but primarily as a band of former outsiders who wanted to preserve a place they loved. Since that time, the land values in the neighborhood have skyrocketed, and it is clear that although the neighborhood has remained diverse, it is not nearly so democratic as it was only a decade ago. While the neighborhood's tinge of seediness has not been eradicated completely—there are still some heavy concentrations along Walnut Street particularly—the physical and economic upgrading of the neighborhood threatens to narrow the range of age, occupation, and income that has long enlivened the area. In the back of this book, you will see that there are tax breaks and other aids to help landlords afford to operate rental properties, and to keep them physically sound. These should help to preserve some of the neighborhood's rental housing stock. But the market will prevail. While some landlords like their tenants and don't charge as much as they could, most will choose to maximize the return on their investments. Rittenhouse is not the easygoing place it once was. But the answer is not to keep it seedy. Perhaps the best we can do is to keep in mind that diversity is one of the neighborhood's charms.

I should add, incidentally, that not all the reinvestment that is being made in the neighborhood is preserving it. Recently, while trying to help an out-of-town friend find an apartment in the neighborhood, I saw too many instances of well-intentioned people spending a lot of money to do things that utterly destroy the integrity of their interiors. It would have been better to allow many of the buildings to continue crumbling for a year or two until some sensitivity could have been brought to bear. That doesn't mean that Rittenhouse needs to be a neighborhood of restored Victorian parlors. But owners should know the value of what they have, and not throw it away.

This foreword reflects the situation at a particular moment in May 1984. The book is looking for a longer life, because it is meant to be a part of the process of change. It is not the sort of book you can't put down. But the hope is that you will pick it up again and again as you need it. It helps provide a context for the many challenges we face as homeowners, tenants, residents, citizens. I am confident that decades from now, the great values of the Rittenhouse neighborhood will still be apparent and this book will have played a role in their preservation.

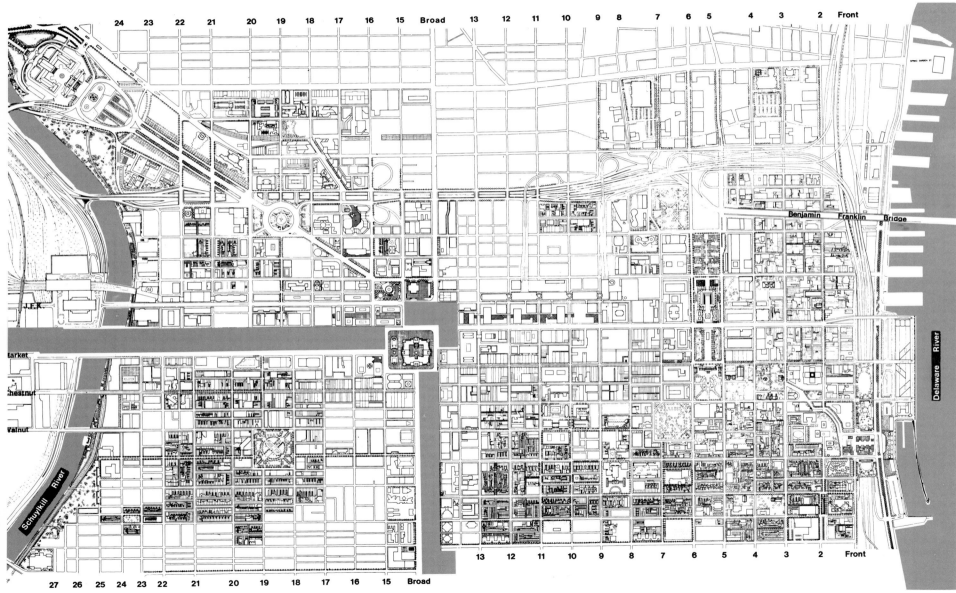

*1. Center City Philadelphia, showing Rittenhouse neighborhood (City Planning Commission)*

The Rittenhouse neighborhood of Philadelphia is the southwest quadrant of William Penn's original city. It is centered at Rittenhouse Square, one of five squares laid out for public use by William Penn's surveyor in 1682. To the north and east of the square are many of Philadelphia's commercial, retail, cultural, and business institutions. South and west of the square is a cohesive and almost intact residential neighborhood which reflects the architectural and social history of Philadelphia from the 1840s to the twentieth century. The residential area is listed in the National Register of Historic Places. Because it has been adjacent to Philadelphia's central business district for more than one hundred years, its growth, decline, and renewal are an integral part of the city's history. Its buildings and streetscapes provide a tangible record of the dynamic processes that have shaped the city's urban core.

Philadelphia's experiences are not unique. They can be duplicated in hundreds of American towns and cities where the future of older downtown residential areas is uncertain. Similar neighborhoods in other cities have been lost in the business and commercial expansion of downtown districts. Only recently have we come to realize how much of our urban heritage has been sacrificed to keep our commercial centers ever-new. The coal baron's mansion, the Art Deco movie "Palace," the Beaux-Arts railroad station, and the modest houses that sheltered the workers in the mills and factories of yesterday's America are gone in many cities, and with them has gone the diversity of use, respect for the past, and visual excitement that make European cities so lively and satisfying. We forget that all cities were once places where people lived; and that the separation of work and dwelling space is a recent—and typically American—phenomenon in the history of cities. Pleasant residential areas exist a block away from Harrod's in London, and condominiums in the Theater of Marcellus (built by Augustus) overlook the Roman Forum today.

Americans, unlike Europeans, have been busy tearing down and building new since Jamestown. (America was not called the New World for nothing.) Until recently we have had no tradition of preserving the past. In fact, Vincent Scully believes that our cities are as they are partly because "we have had less of the old to hold off the new."

This may no longer be true—at least in Philadelphia, which celebrated its tricentennial in 1982. Three centuries of development may seem insignificant when compared with London or Rome, but Philadelphia does have more of the old to hold off the new than most cities. Its built environment is one of the city's most important urban resources. From the master builders who formed the Carpenters' Company through Benjamin Latrobe, Thomas Ustick Walter, and Frank Furness, to George Howe and Louis Kahn, Philadelphia has nurtured greatness in its builders and architects. But its architectural heritage must be seen whole. It is more than the colonial charm of Society Hill or the clean lines of the PSFS building. It is a continuum of creativity that reflects the city's past and defines its future. One of the purposes of this book is to restore Philadelphia's nineteenth-century architectural environment—of which Rittenhouse is the prime example—to its proper place in that continuum.

This book has been planned since 1976 (when Philadelphia's celebration of the national bicentennial seemed to focus exclusively on the city's colonial heritage). Bobbye Burke and Otto Sperr had recently served consecutive terms as president of the Center City Residents' Association, the first art historian and the first architect to head that group. A major accomplishment of their administrations was the 1975 rezoning of the neighborhood after almost ten years of community efforts. By that time they knew its streets and buildings well. Why not publish a booklet about Rittenhouse, the link between colonial and contemporary Philadelphia? They planned to describe the buildings, cite the important architects who worked there, and include a section on building mainte-nance. They were soon joined by Hugh McCauley and Trina Vaux, participants in the publication of the 1977 *Cape May Handbook*, a book similar to what they had in mind. Its success made *Historic Rittenhouse* a real possibility.

It soon became apparent that the description of Rittenhouse buildings and the identification of architects would be little more than a vocabulary of building types and a dictionary of names unless the information was placed within a historical context. The history and devel-opment section was written to fill that need.

Almost every style of building found in nineteenth-century America can also be found in Rittenhouse. To identify each one, its subgroups, and the vernacular buildings that existed simultaneously is a perilous task. Architectural historians have yet to agree on a precise no-menclature for the various forms of nineteenth-century architecture. The section on architectural styles in Ritten-house, with its lists of characteristics typifying each one, photographs of pertinent examples, and a glossary of terms, is designed to help us recognize and respect the diversity of buildings in the community. The discussion of each style's genesis within the social, political, and eco-nomic history of the nineteenth and early twentieth cen-turies will remind the reader that style is more than an accumulation of cornices and mansards; it has social im-plications as well.

To help owners maintain the integrity of a building's architectural style, a section on maintenance was in-cluded. The problems faced by owners are not solely aes-thetic; they concern the very survival of their buildings. The acceleration of building renovation and remodeling in the community—even mutilation and demolition—strengthened the authors' commitment to include a "nuts and bolts" section that would help owners keep their buildings intact. In many cases, owners have been forced to tolerate the mediocre, to destroy their heritage and

their environment, because information on better alter-natives has not been available. We hope this section will provide the information they need to maintain and pre-serve their buildings. We also hope it will encourage ma-sons, carpenters, and other mechanics to respect the original fabric of buildings when making repairs and al-terations, and discourage unsightly renovations and fa-cade alterations. The section on the streetscape empha-sizes how important the various components of the built environment are, and how what we do—or don't do—to our buildings affects our neighbors.

The recent proliferation of preservation regulations and mechanisms made inclusion of the sections on meth-ods and procedures imperative. It is designed to be a layperson's introduction to public and private programs and a guide to the governmental and institutional bu-reaucracies that have grown up around historic preserva-tion. This information, particularly on tax incentives and facade easements, should be especially helpful to owners of buildings within the Rittenhouse National Historic District.

Finally, it is our hope that the publication of this book will encourage donations of pertinent materials to re-search institutions so that others can continue what we have begun. In writing this book we found that historical records concerning Philadelphia in the nineteenth and early twentieth centuries are meager compared with those for the eighteenth century. The illustration of Rittenhouse Square about 1918 (fig. 26) was discovered in a neigh-bor's trash! It is critical that records of the city's architec-tural history be preserved. Fragile photographs and ar-chitectural drawings that may be the only record of a lost building must be cared for properly. The Athenaeum of Philadelphia maintains an archive of architectural draw-ings. The Library Company of Philadelphia and the His-torical Society of Pennsylvania also maintain collections of photographs, newspapers, pamphlets, and manuscripts concerning Philadelphia architects and buildings. These institutions welcome inquiries about the donation, and proper care and storage of such materials.

In the time it has taken to complete *Historic Rittenhouse* there has been much change in the neighborhood and in Philadelphia as a whole. Some historic buildings have come down, but many have been preserved. In the meantime, interest in and concern for preservation of our architectural heritage has been growing among individuals, private organizations, and public agencies. Because Philadelphia is entering a period of great change and development, its future must be charted with care. Change is not to be condemned outright; Rittenhouse came to be because of change and development in the past. Cities are marked by the ways they accommodate change. The greatest preserve a sense of continuity between the past and the present; old and new are richly interwoven, forming the warp and woof of the urban fabric. Too much of one creates a museum frozen in time; too much of the other gives us a city in vogue for a generation only. Philadelphia, as one of the world's great cities, can achieve a delicate balance between the two.

We hope that all who read this book will see Philadelphia with new eyes, that the buildings and streetscapes of Rittenhouse will continue to inspire and delight all who know them.

*Bobbye Burke*
*Otto Sperr*
*Hugh McCauley*
*Trina Vaux*

# HISTORY AND DEVELOPMENT

## BOBBYE BURKE

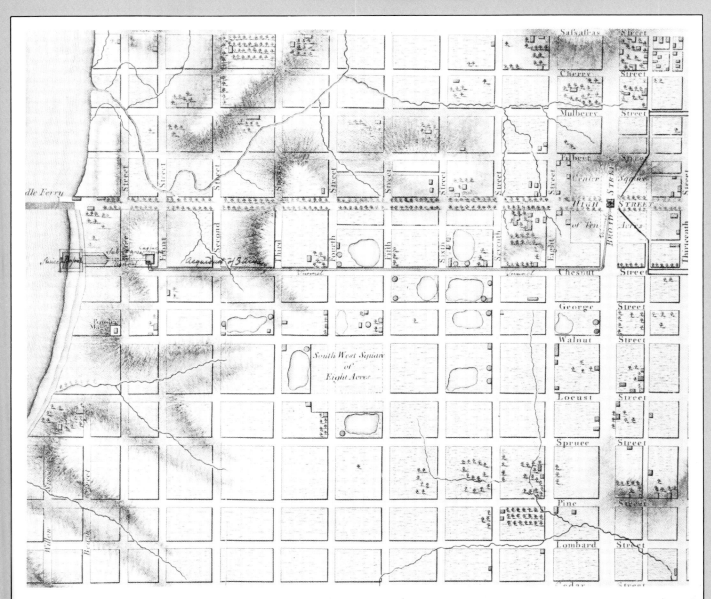

*Plan of the City of Philadelphia and Its Environs (Historical Society of Pennsylvania)*

# Introduction

This is the story of the evolution of an urban community. Its development was determined by its natural resources, its physical plan, and the economic climate of Philadelphia at critical points in its history. It is not simply a tale of the trials of coalheavers and mill workers who lived there, nor is it merely a recounting of the mores of the rich and famous. It is the story of both. True, for a short period, from about 1860 to 1910, Philadelphia's "Victorian Aristocracy"[1] lived in Rittenhouse. But the neighborhood's two-hundred-year history encompasses more than whether the Van Rensselaer livery had solid silver buttons, how many presidents of the Pennsylvania Railroad lived there, or who attended Mrs. Alexander Cassatt's balls.

Settlement began in Rittenhouse shortly after the Revolution. Early land warrants are recorded for Schuylkill lots during the colonial period, but few owners lived there. Rittenhouse's early development along the Schuylkill waterfront and High (Market) Street was a direct response to the area's natural resources and the prevalent transportation patterns. The clay soil was ideal for brickmaking, and the first residents were itinerant workers in the claypits and brickyards that dotted the area.

Only gradually did Philadelphians move west of Broad Street. Not until the late 1820s and early 1830s were rows of brick houses built for middle-class families, and these were clustered close to Broad Street. Thereafter, nineteenth-century residential development can be traced chronologically by the erection of churches: first, Baptist, Methodist, and Roman Catholic for the working class; later, Presbyterian and Episcopalian churches for the middle and upper class. And always, the residential settlement was adjacent to carpenter shops, marble yards, breweries, brickyards, and later trolley "turn-arounds" and repair shops.

The developer played an important role in shaping the physical environment of Rittenhouse. In addition to subdividing and building upon his property, he laid out the numerous secondary streets. Because the location, width, and number of secondary streets varied with the developer's building plans, a hierarchy of urban spaces was created within the persistent gridiron pattern of Penn's original plan.

Many developers in the nineteenth century, like their counterparts today, were reluctant to adopt the latest architectural styles. Many blocks in Rittenhouse contain houses that are commodious and comfortable—even considered grand today—which were *retardataire* when built. On the other hand, when the "Victorian aristocracy" arrived after the Civil War they hired architects who were in the mainstream of current architectural theory and practice. America's foremost designers worked in Rittenhouse, John Notman, Samuel Sloan, Thomas U. Walter, and Napoleon LeBrun before the Civil War, John McArthur, Frank Furness, Theophilus P. Chandler, Wilson Eyre, Jr., Frank Miles Day, Horace Trumbauer, and Cope and Stewardson thereafter.

In the early twentieth century Rittenhouse reflected major shifts in social patterns and land uses when the commuter railroad and the private automobile made it easy for Philadelphians to live ten or fifteen miles from their place of work. As the central business district stretched west of City Hall along Chestnut and Walnut streets, more and more families gave up their homes in town for year-round living in the suburbs. Many of the remaining large houses were made into doctor's offices, rooming houses, and apartments. Some were replaced by apartment and office buildings. Houses on the secondary streets remained, but were run-down and neglected.

After World War II, many saw Rittenhouse, particularly its southern and western edges, as an urban frontier. Among them were Mayor Richardson Dilworth, one of the architects of Philadelphia's municipal reform movement after the war, and Edmund Bacon, the executive director of the City Planning Commission. These urban pioneers repaired and rehabilitated the housing stock, planted trees, and succeeded in establishing the first public school there since 1930. The establishment of the Center City Residents' Association (CCRA) in 1946 was a major step in stabilizing the neighborhood and re-creating a sense of community. Throughout its history, it has been an integral part of community efforts to improve the quality of life in Rittenhouse. Among its accomplishments was initiation of the first comprehensive zoning ordinance for the neighborhood in forty years. The programs and activities of Historic Rittenhouse, Inc. (formerly the Center City Foundation), grew out of CCRA's concern for the preservation of the neighborhood's physical environment.

Much evidence of the history of Rittenhouse remains today. Many buildings by Philadelphia's major architects are still intact, along with block after block of builders' rows and modest workers' houses. It is fortuitous that Rittenhouse has not been "redeveloped" or experienced urban renewal as have similar neighborhoods in Philadelphia and other American cities. No ceremonial boulevard or interstate highway has been cut through its midst, and no expanding hospital, university, or cultural institution has disrupted its street pattern or prevailing land use. It remains a physically cohesive yet socially diverse neighborhood comfortably accommodating business, commerce, and cultural institutions, as well as residents.

# Rittenhouse Before 1800—A Resort for Towns People
Philadelphia's Rittenhouse neighborhood is the southwest quadrant of William Penn's original city, bounded on the north by Market Street, on the east by Broad Street, on the south by South Street, and on the west by the Schuylkill River. Its history would be considerably different had Penn's original plan for the settlement of the city been carried out. His vision of simultaneous development along both the Delaware and Schuylkill rivers is evident in the first city plan prepared in 1682 by his surveyor, Thomas Holme (fig. 2). The ma-

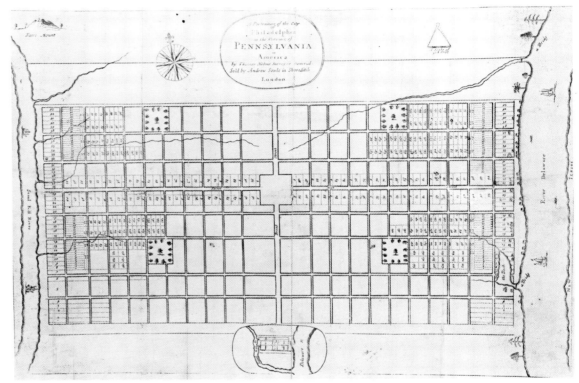

2. *A Portraiture of the City of Philadelphia, Thomas Holme, 1683 (Historical Society of Pennsylvania)*

jor east—west streets are laid out river to river in the plan. All terminate in a principal street parallel to the river, Delaware Front Street on the east and Schuylkill Front Street (now Twenty-Second) on the west, making the street plan west of Broad almost a mirror image of that east of Broad.

Penn's plan for development of the Schuylkill waterfront, so tidy on paper, was thwarted almost immediately. Sandbars downriver impeded navigation on the Schuylkill and the riverbanks proved too marshy for convenient

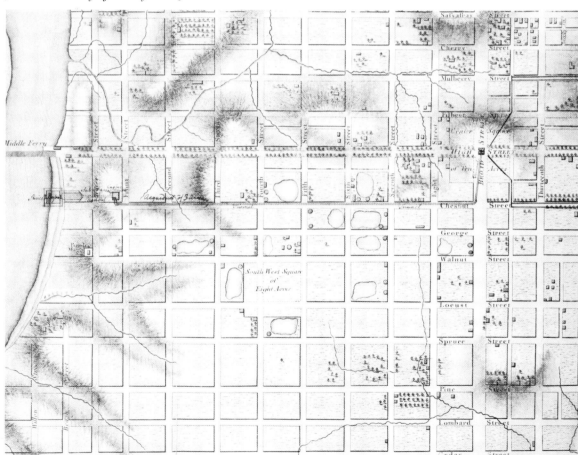

docking of vessels. Philadelphia's commercial and residential growth during the eighteenth century was destined to expand north and south along the wide, easily navigable Delaware River. Both Southwark and the Northern Liberties were developed before Rittenhouse.

The southwest quadrant remained sparsely settled throughout the eighteenth century—a section one traveled through to reach Gray's Ferry or the Middle Ferry at High (Market) Street. The few references found in histories of early Philadelphia confirm the area's remoteness from the bustling city along the Delaware.

In a 1749 letter Benjamin Franklin described a proposed party "on the Banks of the Schuyl-Kill (where Spirits are at the same Time to be fired by a Spark sent from Side to Side thro' the River). A Turky is to be killed for our Dinners by the Electrical Shock; and roasted by the electrical Jack, before a Fire kindled by the Electrified Bottle."[2] An engraving of 1770 shows baptisms and outdoor preaching on the Schuylkill riverbank at Spruce Street. Morgan Edwards, Baptist minister, describes the site as "not only convenient for the celebration of baptism but most delightful for rural sceneries. Hither the towns people in summer resort for recreation and entertainment. . . . Round said spot are large oak, affording fine shade. Underfoot, is a green, variegated with wild flowers and aromatic herbs."[3]

The first known improvements to Rittenhouse were typical of the colonial period: a road, a ferry, and a tavern. The northern boundary, High (Market) Street, was a major Philadelphia thoroughfare throughout the eighteenth century. At its junction with the Schuylkill the busy Middle Ferry served settlers and merchandise moving inland on the way upstate and west from the port of Philadelphia. A tavern was located near the ferry from the 1690s, and increased traffic throughout the next century required a permanent bridge across the Schuylkill by 1804.

The pastoral scene through which travelers went west was inevitably disrupted toward the end of the eighteenth century.

## Early Development—Industry
The marshy terrain of Rittenhouse, unsuitable for extensive farming, proved to be perfect for the manufacture of bricks. The abundance of loamy clay, the ease of constructing kilns, and the proximity of a ready building market in the new

city to the east made brickmaking the earliest and most important industry in the southwest quadrant.

In John Hills's map of 1796 (one of the first maps of Philadelphia that gives details of settlement west of Broad Street), eleven sites for clay excavation are shown between High (Market) and Spruce streets, each with an adjacent ring pit for tempering the clay (fig. 3).[4] Southwest Square, not laid out or named Rittenhouse until 1825, was surrounded on three sides by brickmaking facilities. (Although each brickmaking site on the map is positioned neatly within a square, it is doubtful that the map's orderly gridiron accurately reflects the meanderings of the unpaved streets west of Broad Street.[5])

The rural character of the southwest quadrant of the city made it a good choice for an undesirable industry. It was removed from residential areas but close enough to the city on the Delaware that bricks could easily be delivered to builders. The first anonymous residents of Rittenhouse were probably brickmakers clustered near the claypits and brick kilns.

In the early years of the nineteenth century the area's natural resources were put to use in more refined products. Two earthenware factories were established in the area, John Mullowney's Washington Pottery on High (Market) Street near Schuylkill Sixth,[6] and the Tucker Porcelain Company, founded by Benjamin Tucker. The latter factory, near the river at Chestnut Street, produced the first fine porcelain in America, called Queensware. Scharf and Westcott located a glass factory further south on the river near the present South Street Bridge by 1806. It first made green glass and flint glass, but by 1820 it was manufacturing window glass under the name of Schuylkill Window Glass Manufactory.

South of the claypits, Spruce Street acted as a boundary between settled and unsettled land. The land between Pine and Cedar (South) streets had been reserved by the Penn family for its own use, and title to the strip between Spruce and Pine was held by the Free Society of Traders. Both grants ran river to river. Only after the Divesting Act of 1779, which expropriated the Penn family property, did land south of Spruce Street become available for purchase. After that date the city lots once owned by the Penn family and departed British sympathizers, as well as lots that had never been owned, were sold at a series of public auctions. Some city lots remained unsold up to the mid-1820s when the last auction of city lots was held to raise funds to build John Haviland's Eastern State Penitentiary.

By 1813 Mordecai Lewis had established his white lead plant on Pine Street near Fifteenth, and by 1819 there was a manufacturer of chemicals at Nineteenth and Pine. Some years before, in 1799, an inlet basin had been dug at the foot of Chestnut Street and a steam engine installed to pump Schuylkill River water through pipes along Chestnut Street to the reservoir of Benjamin Latrobe's new waterworks at Center Square.

The types of industries that existed in Rittenhouse during its early history—brickyards, kilns, chemical plants, glass and earthenware factories—are those which one customarily finds on the outskirts of an eighteenth-century American city. They required natural resources, a supply of unskilled labor, a site removed from middle-class residential development, and open space surrounding the operation because of its heat, dirt, smells and/or waste.

## 1800–1820—Absentee Landowners of the "Western Commons"
In the early nineteenth century most of the land in Rittenhouse was owned by persons who did not live there. In 1805, for instance, forty-three persons owned all the land within Locust Ward west of Broad Street, only five of whom lived on the land they owned.[7] Of the five, one was John Mullowney, the pottery maker, who lived in a brick house on one of his properties near the Schuylkill. The others were a carter, who owned

several buildings and twelve horses, a shopkeeper, a cordwainer, and a laborer. By 1820 the number of Locust Ward property owners had increased to ninety-three, but the owner-residents had increased only to eight.

The most prominent names among Locust Ward absentee landowners were those of city officials. The prothonotary, the city recorder, the widow of a city commissioner, the sheriff, and the mayor all owned properties in the ward. Whether they purchased undeveloped city lots as a civic duty or as pure speculation, it was a gesture of faith in the future of the southwest quadrant of the city.

The largest property owner in Locust Ward was William Bingham. Although not a city official, he was a member of the Pennsylvania General Assembly from 1790 to 1795 and U.S. senator from 1795 to 1801. Bingham, whose ancestors had acquired one of Penn's earliest land grants, was considered one of the wealthiest men in America when he married Anne Willing, daughter of banker-merchant Thomas Willing, in 1780. To add to his inherited wealth, he made a fortune while still in his twenties as a Continental agent in the West Indies during the Revolution. The Binghams are remembered for their Anglophilia, their palatial mansion on south Third Street above Spruce, and Mrs. Bingham's salons. Whether entertaining in her mirrored "palace" in town, lavishly furnished in the latest European styles, or at Lansdowne, the Bingham summer home along the Schuylkill, Anne Willing Bingham was the reigning hostess of the "federal court" in Philadelphia. After her death in 1801, Bingham moved to England with his two daughters, who had married Englishmen, Alexander and Henry Baring of the international banking house Baring and Company. Bingham died a few years later, and his estate was administered by his heirs in England. The Rittenhouse property—only a small part of his land holdings in America—was held undeveloped by his heirs until mid-century and after.

From 1805 to 1820 the property assessments in Locust Ward reflect a significant appreciation of land value. As-

sessments in 1805 ranged from $20 for a lot twenty-by-ninety feet on Noodle (Sydenham) Street to $1,000 for an unimproved square between Locust and Spruce, Seventeenth and Eighteenth. By 1820 the original 59 parcels of land in the ward had increased to 101, and an improved square containing a brickyard between Walnut and Locust, Fifteenth and Sixteenth, was assessed at $7,000. The increase in parcels, property owners, and assessments indicates growing real estate interest in the southwest quadrant during the first two decades of the nineteenth century.

Rising real estate values and absentee landowners, however notable, do not make a neighborhood. It is the people who live there and their circumstances that give it character. To learn more about early Rittenhouse, we can turn to the State Tax Assessment ledgers. Although they are not complete, some of the ledgers are available from 1805, 1813, and 1820 for the four wards south of High (Market) Street: Middle, South, Locust, and Cedar wards.[8] The Tax Assessment ledgers give us a picture of this area in the early nineteenth century that population figures cannot.

The tax assessor actually walked the cartways of Rittenhouse, and he confirms the sparse settlement of the "Western Commons" described by Watson in his *Annals*: "Before houses were built [the fields in Rittenhouse] were open commons, clothed with short grass for cows and swine. 35 years ago [1809] so few owners enclosed their lots towards Schuylkill that the street roads of Walnut, Spruce, and Pine could not be traced by the eye beyond Broad Street. . . . Roads traversed the commons at the convenience of the traveler, and brick kilns and their ponds were the chief enclosures or settlements that you saw."[9]

The assessor provided eyewitness information about the people who lived there, their occupations, possessions, and the buildings they occupied. Cows were assessed at $8, and horses, important as a power source before industrialization, were assessed a minimum of $25.

The head tax for males ranged from $.25 for a laborer to $1.00 for a "gentleman." Ninety percent of Locust Ward residents paid the minimum tax, a few tradesmen paid $.37, and a handful of gentlemen paid $1.00. Adult females and blacks were excluded from the head tax although their property was taxed. In Locust Ward west of Broad the assessor found only a few craftsmen, a shopkeeper, some carpenters, a tailor, and a brickmaker. A carver-gilder was located near Broad Street. Most of the listed occupations are semiskilled or unskilled—hostler, cord-wainer, carter, laborer, and one mop and thrum maker who lived near Nineteenth and Spruce.[10]

For the twenty-nine males listed in 1805 there were only twenty-seven houses (nineteen of which were of wood-frame construction.) Even if some households contained two men and no households were headed by women, which is unlikely in an age of early widowhood, the population would barely fit the available housing. By 1813, 104 men were enumerated, but almost half were not identified as living at a specific address. By 1820, the male population had declined to fifty-five, and the previous group of location-less men had disappeared. One can only speculate why, but it seems likely that many of these men were "drifters" employed in the brickyards. Presumably they lived together in workers' housing provided in the only section of Locust Ward west of Broad that was fully developed, the square bounded by Walnut and Locust, Fifteenth and Sixteenth. We know that this square, bisected by Noodle (Sydenham) Street, was the site of a large brickyard and that its $7,000 tax assessment was the second highest in the ward, next to William Bingham's. By 1820 its claypits may have been exhausted or a portion of its brickmaking process mechanized and the drifters had moved on.

The picture of Locust Ward west of Broad that emerges in this period indicates clusters of frame buildings scattered throughout the area, many large unimproved properties, and a group of residents of generally low status. As Meredith Savery observes, "The ward was barely urban."[11]

Some additional information concerning Rittenhouse in the 1820s can be gleaned from local newspapers or existing buildings. In 1815 the immediate residents—probably brickyard owners—of what was to become Rittenhouse Square loaned the City Council $800 toward construction of a fence around the square. Before that there are reports of public meetings complaining about the deplorable condition of the streets and the use of Southwest Square as a depository for night soil. The Schuylkill Hose Company was formed in 1820, although its location is uncertain. In 1825 the neighborhood petitioned the City Council to rename Southwest Square Rittenhouse Square. It may have been at this time that south Nineteenth Street was rerouted around the square. Also in 1825 the handsome building on the west side of Broad Street at Pine (now Philadelphia College of Art), designed by John Haviland, was erected to house the deaf and dumb. Undoubtedly the site was chosen because it was situated in a remote part of the city removed from the busy street activity at the institution's former home on Market Street.

The creation by 1820 of early amusement parks, called "pleasure gardens," at the outskirts of town, Vauxhall Gardens on the east side of Broad Street at Walnut, and Columbian Gardens east of Center Square on Market, testifies to the continuing rural character of the western end of the city.

## Coal Trade in Rittenhouse—The Irish
For a short period in Rittenhouse's history the coal trade brought jobs and development to the western edge of the community. Canals connecting Philadelphia with the Susquehanna River were completed between 1823 and 1827. Thereafter thousands of tons of anthracite were shipped from upstate Pennsylvania to the wharves and warehouses that were built at city expense on the Schuylkill riverbanks from Fairmount to Gray's Ferry.

The workmen who manned the wharves and heaved the coal into wagons and carts were Irish; some were former brickyard workers, but most were newly arrived immigrants. In May of 1835 the Schuylkill coalheavers, three hundred strong, struck the wharves in support of a ten-hour day. The strikers were condemned by the press as "chiefly freshly imported foreigners—who despise and defy the law,"[12] but by June 10 twenty Philadelphia trades were on strike and mass meetings in support of the coalheavers were held in the State House Yard by various trades. Within a year inflation and the Panic of 1836–37 had devastating effects upon American industry and its workers. Nevertheless, historians of American labor credit the coalheavers' strike of 1835 with providing the impetus needed to admit unskilled workers into union membership and to secure the ten-hour day for the laboring man, skilled or unskilled.

The Irish laborers along the river formed the first cohesive Irish presence in Rittenhouse. They, along with a group of Irish living in an area near Nineteenth and Spruce streets called the "Village," caused the establishment of St. Patrick's Roman Catholic Church in 1839. Services were held for two years in a rented frame building on the east side of Nineteenth Street between Manning and Spruce in the center of the Village. But efforts to establish a stable Irish community around the new church were hampered by the uncertain economic climate of the late 1830s. Many of the coalheavers lost their jobs when coal shipments were diverted from the Schuylkill to the Reading Railroad's Port Richmond terminus. In the early 1840s some of St. Patrick's parishioners walked to Port Richmond to follow the coal trade; many families were forced to move there. Nevertheless, by 1841 the congregation was stable enough to move out of its rented quarters into a permanent structure at Twentieth and Murray (Rittenhouse) streets, a modest, stucco-faced brick building, designed by Napoleon LeBrun.

The Village has disappeared and St. Patrick's first church is no longer standing, but physical evidence of this early era can still be found. A few small "court" houses on Manning Street east of Nineteenth remain from the early Irish settlement, as do three small houses on Bonsall (formerly Cope) Street. The latter are all that remain of a larger court of houses, evidently built for workers at the New York and Schuylkill Coal Company immediately adjacent to the wharves. They may be the oldest remaining houses in Rittenhouse.[13]

## Settlement Quickens in 1830s and 1840s

Middle-class residential development began west of Broad Street in the 1830s as a direct result of Philadelphia's business expansion east of Broad. As financial, commercial, and mercantile establishments replaced homes on Market, Chestnut, Sansom, and Walnut streets in the old city, the area around Center Square and along South Broad Street became an attractive residential alternative for the merchants and businessmen whose shops and offices remained in the business district. It was close enough for easy access, but far enough away to offer peace and tranquillity.

Clinton Row, a series of thirteen large houses, was built on the southeast corner of Broad and Chestnut in 1827. Commodious double houses soon lined South Penn Square a block away. The most imposing residence west of Broad Street was a Greek Revival double house at Sixteenth and Chestnut streets. Built in 1828 by Charles and George Blight, wealthy China traders, it had an eighty-foot marble facade designed by John Haviland. Two years later, in 1830, the Blights filled out their block on the south side of Chestnut to Fifteenth with Colonnade Row (fig. 4). Haviland was again the architect, designing ten elegant rowhouses patterned on John Nash's terrace houses in London.

At first the new residents maintained their church affiliations as well as their businesses east of Broad Street. St. Patrick's, built by Irish coalheavers and brickyard

workers, and the Western Bricklayers' Church (Methodist) on Twentieth Street below Walnut, served the working-class residents in the 1830s and 1840s, but the established Episcopal and Presbyterian churches, solidly middle class in the nineteenth century, hesitated to cross Broad Street. In fact, the first Presbyterian congregation to move ventured only to the east side of Broad at Sansom. It was formed in 1826 when a large group, discontented over the rejection by the presbytery of the Reverend John Chambers as their minister, declared itself independent of the Ninth Presbyterian Church on Thirteenth above Market. In 1831 they built their own 1,500-seat building, naming it the Chambers Presbyterian Church.

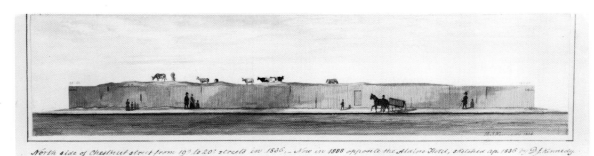

*North side of Chestnut street from 19ᵗʰ to 20ᵗʰ streets in 1836, - Now in 1888 opposite the Aldine Hotel, sketched ap. 1836 by D J Kennedy*

5. *North side of Chestnut from 19th to 20th sts., 1836. Watercolor by D. J. Kennedy*
*(Historical Society of Pennsylvania)*

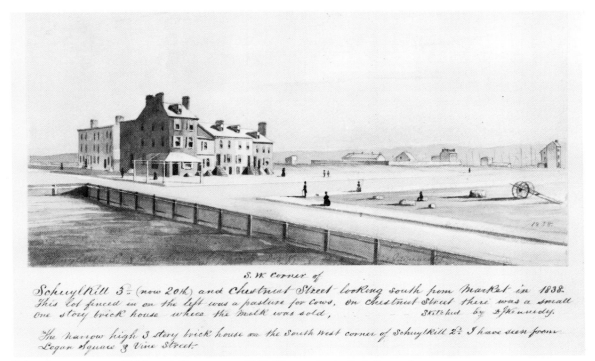

*S. W. corner of*
*Schuylkill 3ᵈ (now 20ᵗʰ) and Chestnut Street looking south from Market in 1838.*
*This lot fenced in on the left was a pasture for cows, on Chestnut Street there was a small*
*one story brick house where the milk was sold, — sketched by D J Kennedy.*

*The narrow high 3 story brick house on the south west corner of Schuylkill 2ᵈ I have seen from*
*Logan Square & Vine Street.*

6. *Southwest corner of 20th and Chestnut sts., 1838. Watercolor by D. J. Kennedy*
*(Historical Society of Pennsylvania)*

A decade later, in 1841, the mother church itself moved west to Sixteenth and Sansom streets. Within ten years this church, the Ninth Presbyterian, had the largest congregation of that faith in the city, and both Ninth and Chambers were serving sizable numbers of parishioners who lived both east and west of Broad Street. The westward move in residential development brought such an abundance of Presbyterians—or discontented splinter groups—that three more Presbyterian churches were built in Rittenhouse by 1857.

The first Episcopal Church west of Broad was across the street from Colonnade Row, Epiphany Episcopal, designed by Thomas U. Walter in 1834. By that date there were signs that the Chestnut Street-South Penn Square area had the makings of an upper middle-class enclave. When Epiphany's new pastor, Stephen Tyng, was recruited from old St. Paul's, affluent Episcopalians west of Broad could point to the fashionable residential development that had already taken place around the church.

By the 1840s, "West of Broad," at least as far as Seventeenth, had become an acceptable address for upper- and middle-class Philadelphians. But west of Eighteenth Street, settlement was still spotty. In 1836, in an area called Goosetown around Twentieth and Spruce streets, there were few houses, according to David Kennedy, "except on the small streets or courts running between" [14] where workers at the brewery at Twenty-First and Spruce lived. Kennedy's visual records document his observations—open fields, pastures, or claypits in close proximity to clustered housing. An 1836 watercolor, for instance, shows cows grazing on elevated ground within a fenced pasture between Market and Chestnut streets, Nineteenth and Twentieth (fig. 5). The milk was sold nearby (fig. 6).

The presence of bucolic open spaces within the city may add a romantic aspect to our perceptions of the urbanization process: As the city absorbed the countryside, pockets of its rural past remained. What does not seem so romantic is the proximity of factories to the homes of rich and poor alike. Haphazard or disorderly as it may appear in the light of current zoning and land use practice, this checkerboard pattern of development was inevitable in an era without public transportation. The juxtaposition of pasturage, garden patches, industry, and a variety of housing was natural for the period.

Upper- and middle-class residents, clustered around Epiphany or Ninth Presbyterian, may have considered themselves part of an elite residential enclave, from which they could commute in private carriages to their counting houses and dry goods establishments in the old city, but the workers at the Morris Iron Works at Sixteenth and Market must have lived around the corner from the factory as well as from the fashionable congregations. And a few blocks west, the Market Street Mission (Episcopal) was ministering to the "destitute and those estranged from Christ's fold"[15] in rented rooms near Twenty-First and Market. After congressman and brick manufacturer James Harper built his fine house on the square in 1839–40, he rode to St. Stephen's Church on South Tenth Street in his carriage. But the laborers in his brickyard on George (Sansom) Street, located directly behind his house, needed to live within walking distance of their work.

James Harper's story is similar to those of hundreds who found opportunity and economic success in nineteenth-century Philadelphia. The Harper family, descended from the seventeenth-century Scottish and English colonizers of Ireland, arrived in Philadelphia in 1791 when James was eight or ten. By 1821 he was one of the city's leading citizens, the owner of a successful brickmaking business, a member of the Common Council, the Board of Prison Inspectors, and the Board of the Guardians of the Poor. A member of the Ancient Order of Hibernians, he was also an active Mason and presided at the special welcome tendered Lafayette (also a Mason) by the Grand Lodge of Pennsylvania during Lafayette's 1824 visit to Philadelphia. From 1833 to 1837 James Harper

served in the United States Congress with Horace Binney and Joseph R. Ingersoll. An anti-Jacksonian, Harper entertained Henry Clay in his Walnut Street home and hired John Neagle, who had painted Clay's portrait, to paint his. By then he was no longer listed in the city directories as a brick manufacturer but as "gentleman."

Harper was active in the Franklin Institute, where he did not fail to notice the latest inventions to improve the brickmaking process: steam-driven pugmills, continuous kilns, and brick molding and pressing machines, "products of American industry," which were regularly exhibited there from 1824 to 1858. He had an opportunity to compare America's industrial progress with that of Europe when he represented Pennsylvania at the Exhibition of the Industry, Genius and Skill of All Nations in London in 1851.

Harper moved to West Walnut Street with confidence that the western section of the city was ripe for development. He boldly purchased almost the entire Walnut Street block facing Rittenhouse Square and subdivided the frontage into large building lots, which he sold with the understanding that bricks from his "backyard" brickyard would be used in constructing large houses there. He reserved 1811 Walnut Street for his own home, and 1821 Walnut for his daughter Annie (Mrs. George Peabody).

The commercial and business expansion of the city has now absorbed the residential community, middle class and otherwise, around Epiphany and Ninth Presbyterian. And James Harper's properties on Rittenhouse Square have given way to a private club and a skyscraper office building. There is little evidence today of workers' housing north of Walnut Street. What evidence we have of any early workers' community can be found mostly along the southern edge of the neighborhood, south of Pine Street, where row after row of narrow houses line the secondary streets (Addison, Waverly, Naudain). Once even smaller court houses dotted this high density area.

7. *The square bounded by 18th, 19th, Lombard, and South sts. in 1858 (Redrawn by Kathleen Coelos from Hexamer and Locher Atlas)*

**FIRE RESISTANCE**

Second Class Masonry Building

Fourth Class Masonry Building

Frame Building

Specially Hazardous Building

LOMBARD STREET

Cotton and Wool Factory

NINETEENTH STREET

EIGHTEENTH STREET

Evans Place

WILLIAM STREET

Hills Court

SOUTH STREET

SCALE: 0 10 20 30 40 50 Feet

Few of the courts remain, but they were common throughout the city in the eighteenth and nineteenth centuries (there were over thirty of them between Sixteenth and Twenty-First streets south of Pine). The courts and their inhabitants provide a dramatic contrast to their middle-class neighbors. To maximize land use, four, six, or eight houses were built facing each other, or in some cases facing a blank wall. Only twelve or fourteen feet wide, these "bandbox" dwellings contained one room per floor. The owner was able to build to the property line, there were no rear yards, and residents shared an outdoor privy and pump in the center of the court or in an alley nearby (fig. 7).

Philadelphians sometimes view these modest "Trinity" houses with romanticism. In fact, few of them were single-family dwellings in the nineteenth century, and lack of sanitation and privacy were realities of daily life for the occupants. It is worth noting, too, that in the 1840s when residents south of Pine were crowded into hundreds of tiny substandard rental houses, many of which lacked essential municipal services—sewerage or running water—entire squares to the north were open fields held by absentee owners for future development.

Many of the persons living in the courts and alleys were employed in one of the half-dozen textile mills south of Pine, although such employment was neither lucrative nor dependable in the 1840s.[16] A weaver's wage was about $4.00 for a six-day week, twelve hours a day. This compares with $7.50 a week for the Schuylkill coal-heavers when they struck in 1835. Moreover, secure employment as a weaver was not guaranteed; it was possible only when cotton was plentiful and cheap, there were no strikes or lockouts, and if newly arrived immigrants did not "scab" and work for less.

The area south of Pine was part of the old Cedar Ward—Spruce to Cedar (South), Seventh Street to the Schuylkill. It was one of the most densely populated sections of the city in 1840, with a population of 11,932.[17] West Cedar Ward was heavily Irish, with perhaps forty or fifty black families living side by side with the white residents. Of the 4,428 persons who lived west of Broad Street in the ward, 220 were black.

Approximately 64 percent of the workers in Cedar West were unskilled or semiskilled, laborers, carters, carpenters, weavers, blacksmiths, and shoemakers.[18] Twelve percent of the employed were engaged in trade as brickmakers, grocers, and small merchants; seventeen tavernkeepers were included in this group. Less than 4 percent were classified as proprietary or official, and twenty-seven of the forty members of this high status group lived within one block of Broad Street, including several teachers, engineers, and "gentlemen." An auctioneer, a lawyer, and one minister, William H. Furness, in this group lived on Pine Street across from the Deaf and Dumb Asylum.

The picture of blacks in west Cedar Ward is bleaker than that of whites. Only fifty-five blacks were employed; the men as laborers, porters, and waiters; the women as washers, cooks, and domestics. Only one black person, a teacher, was listed in the proprietary category.[19]

As we approach the mid-1800s the myth that the history of Rittenhouse is one of upper class capitalists and industrial tycoons becomes less and less credible. Although we will find that many well-to-do Philadelphians did in fact live in Rittenhouse, they did not settle there in any numbers before the 1850s, and they did not live south of Pine Street. For many years they lived in close proximity to breweries, carriage makers, carpenter shops, wallpaper factories, and textile mills, and to Irish mill-workers and blacks, many of whom were impoverished or destitute.

## Rittenhouse at Mid-Century
A "Panoramic View of Philadelphia" looking east from West Philadelphia in 1855 confirms the random pattern of development in Rittenhouse (fig. 8). At the bottom of the view we see the gas works, built in 1836 near the covered Market Street Bridge. Wharves lined a portion of the bank of the Schuylkill, interspersed with several large factory buildings near Locust, Spruce, and Pine. The residential area was concentrated east of Twentieth Street, and Walnut, Locust, and Spruce streets were undeveloped at their western edges. The commercial activity along the river's edge could explain the lack of residential development in the western part of Rittenhouse, but the juxtaposition of densely populated blocks next to large open spaces seems to be a distinctive characteristic of the area in the 1850s.

Another document we can turn to in tracing the development of Rittenhouse is the first atlas of the Seventh

and Eighth wards, published by Hexamer and Locher in 1858.[20] In comparing the Panoramic View with the atlas, a comprehensive picture of the physical development of the neighborhood at mid-century emerges.

Livery stables, small carpenter shops, and lumber and coal yards were scattered throughout the area. After the mid-century demise of the brickmaking industry, Rittenhouse never had a predominant industrial or commercial activity that would distinguish the area, as Kensington was characterized by its mills or Spring Garden by the Baldwin Locomotive Works. The industries

*8. Panoramic View of Philadelphia, lithograph by Asselineau after a watercolor by John Bachman, published by John Caspar Wild, c. 1855 (Historical Society of Pennsylvania)*

that existed were marked by their diversity, and the largest seem always to have been located at the edges of the neighborhood, along High Street, the riverfront, and south of Pine Street. Before city-county consolidation in 1854, the southern and western edges of Rittenhouse were the city limits of Philadelphia. As such they were where the least desirable businesses were often located and many of the poorest and neediest citizens lived.

One of the edges, High (Market) Street, had been a major transportation artery since the eighteenth century. By the 1850s railroad terminals and freight yards were located on Market with tracks in the middle of this wide street. Here omnibus and carriage makers (Murphy and Allison), stove factories (Morris Iron Works), and marble yards (Keystone Marble Works) found an ideal location. From the 1830s street markets served housewives within walking distance below and above Market. The first and largest were the covered sheds in the center of the street from Fifteenth to Seventeenth. Two others followed, one at Nineteenth, another at Twenty-First.

Industrial development along the river had begun early in the nineteenth century with earthenware and glass factories. The busiest river commerce occurred in conjunction with the coal trade of the 1830s, but the wharves were used throughout the nineteenth and early twentieth centuries by stone and marble yards, ice houses, and lumber and coal companies. For many years granite from Maine was cut into Philadelphia curbstones at yards near the Locust and Spruce Street wharves. At one time ice from New England was stored in ice houses along the Schuylkill.

Lombard Street west of Twenty-Fifth was the site of an iron foundry until the 1860s, and some of the textile mills mentioned earlier operated until the end of the century. Twenty-Fifth and South streets was the site of a rubber vulcanizing works as well as a carbarn and repair shop for the Lombard and South Street trolleys.

It should be no surprise that the builder or developer seeking sites for construction of upper- and middle-class housing at mid-century concentrated his search north of Pine Street. There were some obstacles: The Howell Wallpaper Factory occupied the entire north side of the 1900 block of Howell (Delancey) Street; and Perott's Malt House (the brewery mentioned earlier) was on the northeast corner of Twenty-First and Spruce. Nevertheless, by the 1850s a second wave of upper- and middle-class residents sought homes west of Broad Street, this time along Locust and Pine.

Residents were being pushed toward the southwestern part of the city by the encroachment of institutional and commercial uses along Broad and Market streets. Market Street was Philadelphia's busiest commercial-industrial artery. The choice of Broad Street for the site of the Academy of Natural Sciences in 1840 and of the American Academy of Music in 1857 set an institutional tone for that wide thoroughfare. When the Pennsylvania Railroad took over the Central High School site on Juniper Street at South Penn Square for its freight yards in 1853 and the La Pierre Hotel was erected at Broad and Chestnut the same year, the area further west and south became more desirable for residential development. Progress was sparked, as it had been earlier on Chestnut and Sansom streets, by the construction of two Protestant churches, St. Mark's Episcopal and Calvary Presbyterian.

The building of St. Mark's in 1849–50 was an instance where the church preceded its congregation. Representatives of six established Episcopal congregations met in the mid-1840s to plan a church that would "restore Catholic worship" in the Episcopalian rite. The result was St. Mark's, which is regarded as "one of the first American churches to show the influence of the religious revival identified in England with the Camden Society and the Oxford Movement."[21] Designed by John Notman, it is one of the best examples of Gothic Revival architecture in America.

The building of St. Mark's—and Calvary Presbyterian

Church (1851–53) a block east on Locust, also by Not-man[22]—stimulated a mini-boom in architectural historicizing in the immediate area. In 1849 Thomas U. Walter introduced the Italianate style west of Broad when he designed a row of fashionable brownstones on the south side of Pine between Fifteenth and Sixteenth for Mordecai Lewis and his sons on the former site of their white lead factory (fig. 9). In the early 1850s more Italianate houses were erected on Locust Street across from St. Mark's. "Lewis's Row" still stands at 1504–38 Pine Street, as do several of the Locust Street houses: 1604, 1606, 1612, 1618, 1620, and 1622. Similar houses once lined Walnut near Broad Street.

When in 1855 Joseph Harrison, Jr., recently returned from Russia with a fortune made in railroad construction for Czar Nicholas I, chose the east side of Rittenhouse Square at Locust as the site of his new baronial home, po-

*9. Lewis's Row, Thomas Ustick Walter, 1849*
*(Photo by Bernie Cleff)*

tential homebuyers were persuaded that Rittenhouse was the "proper" address—despite the presence of the "destitute and estranged" near Twenty-Second Street, the factories along the river, and the working-class settlement south of Pine Street. The real estate developers were ready.

## Real Estate Development at Mid-Century

Real estate was the road to wealth for many Philadelphians in the nineteenth century, and money made in other endeavors was often invested in land development. An anonymous 1845 writer, in discussing the wealth of the richest Philadelphians, noted that four of the six millionaires in Philadelphia made or inherited their fortunes from real estate.[23] Certainly the case of William Bingham, one of the first large landowners in Rittenhouse, who used his shipping wealth to invest in land, confirms this. The Blight brothers likewise invested their profits from shipping in real estate (Colonnade Row), as did John McCrea.

John McCrea's wealth was made in trade with Europe, China, and South America during the 1820s and 1830s. His thirteen vessels must have formed one of the largest fleets in the port of Philadelphia after Stephen Girard's death in 1831. After suffering bankruptcy several times during the economic uncertainties of the late 1830s, McCrea turned in 1845 from shipping to building. "This time he played a winning hand, and won a fortune."[24] He became one of the largest developers of Rittenhouse real estate and it was he who at mid-century purchased part of the Bingham properties south of Pine Street.

The Blights and the Lewises commissioned architects to design their stylish pacesetting developments—John Haviland for Colonnade Row, Thomas U. Walter for Lewis's Row. John McCrea never used an architect as far as we know but relied on builders or master carpenters. He himself is listed in the city directories as "builder" at 1832 Spruce, and finally in the early 1860s as "gentleman" at

2000–02 Delancey Place. His use of master carpenters rather than architects explains why many McCrea houses in the 1700 and 1800 blocks of Pine, and the 1800 blocks of Spruce and Delancey exhibit a somewhat out-of-date architectural style. The houses at 1700–38 Pine, for instance, built by McCrea in the early 1850s, are in the Greek Revival style popular east of Broad Street twenty years earlier. In fact, when this row was built, more fashionable houses were under construction or had recently been erected in the 1500 block of Pine and the 1600 block of Locust. By the early 1860s McCrea's real estate interests had moved westward to the 2000 block of Delancey and the 2100 block of Pine, where he was still using builders rather than architects.

John McCrea, like James Harper, was Scots-Irish. Son of an importer of Irish linen on Norris Alley (Sansom Street) near Front Street, he took over the family business in 1814. After he gave up his shipping ventures he purchased "extensive tracts . . . in what is now the western end of the Seventh Ward," where he "proceeded to erect a large number of well-equipped brick residences, which he placed on the market with remarkable success."[25] A deed search of almost any block of Spruce, Delancey, or Pine west of Seventeenth Street will indicate a McCrea ownership of some portion of the block between 1845 and 1865 when he died. His wife, Mary, his sons James, Franklin, and Charles, and his son-in-law Charles Wirgman also appear in the records.

In order to understand how real estate developers shaped Rittenhouse, we can return to the 1858 atlas and recall the juxtaposition of densely populated squares next to land upon which no development had occurred. The development of each square depended upon the attitudes of the early owners of large tracts. If an owner like Congressman James Harper on the north side of Rittenhouse Square lived on the block, he subdivided the block into 22-, 25-, and 26-foot lots to encourage other middle-class residents to live there. If, by contrast, the owner did not live on the block, he saw the land as an investment and opportunity for profit-making.[26] John McCrea, who purchased the entire square between Seventeenth, Eighteenth, Pine, and Lombard streets, originally owned by William Bingham, is a typical example. When this square—396 by 286 feet—was first purchased at public auction in 1782, it was laid out as six lots 66 feet wide running from Pine to Lombard. After McCrea established the secondary streets and subdivided the square, the original six lots became *eighty-three* building lots of varying widths: 20 feet on Pine Street, 16 feet on Addison, and 17 feet on Lombard. McCrea left hardly an inch of land within the square undeveloped: three small houses 13 feet, 4 inches wide were neatly wedged in on Eighteenth Street at the end of the Addison Street row.

Arbitrary lot size subdivision by a developer and proliferation of secondary streets was not unique to Rittenhouse, nor to the nineteenth century. The precedent had been set early in Penn's proprietorship when it became apparent that Holme's original street plan had created "superblocks" so large that subdivision seemed reasonable and appropriate from the start. It was common practice east of Broad and continued in Rittenhouse throughout the nineteenth century so that few squares are without two or three secondary streets. (Incidentally, McCrea's Pine-Lombard square is not the largest in Rittenhouse. The square bounded by Twentieth, Twenty-First, Spruce, and Pine streets is 495 by 470 feet; the square bounded by Twentieth, Twenty-First, Walnut, and Locust streets is 495 by 364 feet.)

The lot size set by a developer may seem insignificant on a city plan or map. In fact, it determines the floor plan of the house to be built and in turn the socio-economic status of its resident. In houses 18, 20, or 22 feet wide (Spruce, Walnut, etc.), one finds vestibules, foyers, and spacious stairwells and landings. Depending upon the design, the second and third floor middle rooms can receive light and air by means of an L-shaped plan with a narrow rear wing. However, a 14- or 16-foot-wide house (Waverly, Panama, etc.) on a shallow lot must be built as a rectangle, two rooms deep with light and air from front and rear only. The area given to vestibules or entryways, if any, must be taken from the main living space. Many stairwells in these houses are centrally located spirals that hug the party wall in order that light and air can reach the front and rear rooms.

The Walnut and Spruce Street houses contained parlors, formal dining rooms, upstairs sitting rooms, and libraries. Many of the fourth floors in these large houses were where the "living in" servants were quartered, especially cooks, whose duties began early and ended late, and nursemaids who supervised the children. Coachmen, laundresses, and other servants most often lived "out" on the secondary streets south of Pine.

Residents still refer to portions of the neighborhood as the "big" streets or the "little" streets. In a paradoxical turn of events, the houses on the "big" streets are seldom occupied by single families today but have become multifamily apartment buildings, and the houses on the "little" streets are much in demand for single-family living.

Residents and visitors alike enjoy Rittenhouse's "little" streets. A stroll down any of them can yield glimpses of well-kept shops, galleries, clubs, bookstores, and attractive homes in what were once stables, auxiliary buildings, and vernacular workers' houses. To drive through the neighborhood using the "little" streets is another matter; almost all of them are dead ends or jog when they meet the north–south numbered streets. This is because each square was subdivided by an individual developer and each developer's decision as to the number, size, and placement of secondary streets within his square was independent of the developer one or two blocks away. The street names we know—Delancey, Addison, Chancellor, Latimer, Waverly, and Manning—are twentieth-century identifications, imposing a cartographer's order on the area. They once had names that changed from block to

10. 2200 block Rittenhouse St. (formerly "F" St.). A row of vernacular workers' houses (Photo by Bernie Cleff)

block: Helmuth, Carver, Burton, Heberton, Howell, Factory, Asylum, Ashburton, Ringgold, and Compromise, each given by a developer who laid out a street in the midst of his subdivision. The history of each is unique; some were the sites of rows of workers' houses, others had middle-class homes, still others were simply service alleys. The developer of the subdivision determined the fate of the "little" street.

Sometimes the houses on the secondary streets which were built for mechanics or workers preceded the houses on the large streets: Houses on the 2000 and 2200 block of Rittenhouse (fig. 10) and the 2300 block of Manning were constructed before the Spruce Street houses in the same blocks.

11. *English Village, 22nd St. below Walnut. Spencer Roberts, architect, c. 1925 (Photo by Bernie Cleff)*

12. *Interior of former stable on site of present Acorn Garage, 22nd and Pine sts. (Private collection)*

There are a few squares in Rittenhouse where developers' plans were set aside, and housing developed spontaneously on the "little" streets. The small houses on the 2100 block of Cypress resulted when owners of some of the residences on Spruce Street to the north sold off portions of their back lots. The houses on the east side of the 200 block of Van Pelt have similar histories, but the west side of the block was used for stables and carriage houses. The 2000 block of Chancellor was also the site of carriage houses and stables, in this instance for the large mansions on Walnut Street.

In other cases a large parcel became available for development and a unique design integrity resulted when an entire block was planned and constructed at one time. For instance, the demise of the Spruce and Pine Street trolley barn west of Twenty-Second Street south of Spruce gave William Weightman an opportunity in 1877 to construct an impressive row of French Second Empire houses on what was Trinity Place (2200 Delancey Place). When the Children's Hospital moved from Twenty-Second Street south of Walnut in 1923, English Village was constructed on the site in a stylish Cotswold cottage mode (fig. 11). In the twentieth century, Panama Mall was built on the site of an abandoned coal yard and Croskey Mews where a public school once was. It is intriguing that these inward-facing developments, now called "Mews," "Mall," or "Village," recall the design of the workers' courts that once dotted the area.

Another interesting aspect of development has been the use of former livery stable sites for auto parking, such as the Acorn Garage at Twenty-Second and Pine streets and the Rittenhouse garages in the 2000 block of Rittenhouse Street (fig. 12).

The development of the 2000 block of Walnut and Chancellor streets illustrates the way a typical square in the western section of Rittenhouse evolved. Between 1844 and 1853, William Kirk, a local brickmaker (his brickyard was at Twenty-Third and Spruce), purchased a succession of parcels within the square from Federal Judge John Kane, shipping merchant Robert Taylor, and the estate of Thomas Morris. The deeds note that the land was part of a 1683 land warrant to Alexander Beardsley. In fact, a portion of the land between the present St. James Place and Chancellor Street was still owned by its first purchasers when Kirk bought it in 1850.

The square was crisscrossed by alleys and cartways and dotted with workers' housing. Kirk laid out Heberton (Chancellor) Street in 1855 and began to subdivide his 205-foot-deep Walnut Street lots into various frontages. The first two lots to be developed were 2006–08 Walnut, when on April 12, 1855, Kirk entered into an agreement with William Maule,[27] builder and lumberyard owner, who agreed to use Kirk's bricks in erecting two "four-story brick dwelling houses with rich brownstone fronts."[28]

The south side of the 2000 block of Walnut was developed westward, house by house, over the next decade. The erection of a double house at 2000–02 for noted publisher, scholar, and civic reformer Henry C. Lea in 1867, and the building of the Second Presbyterian Church in 1869 at Twenty-First Street, marked both ends of the block with substantial buildings. When James Scott hired Theophilus P. Chandler to design his Jacobean mansion at 2032–34 in 1882, this block was one of the most fashionable in Rittenhouse (fig. 13). Its residents included banker and lawyer Jonathan D. Sergeant, dry goods manufacturers Caleb J. Milne and Herman P. Kremer, publishers Craige Lippincott and James Elverson, and merchant John Wanamaker, who purchased the Scott house in 1894. By that time the workers' houses on the back alleys had come down so that carriage houses for the Walnut Street residents could be built, the workers who occupied them had moved on, and William Kirk's listing in the city directories had been changed from brickmaker to "gentleman."

13. 2000 block Walnut St., south side, 1932. First Presbyterian Church at right (Philadelphia City Archives)

14. *Northeast corner of 18th and Locust sts., c. 1920. Harrison mansion to the left on 18th; Harrison Row to the far right on Locust St. (Historical Society of Pennsylvania)*

## West of Rittenhouse Square—Post–Civil War Development

By the end of the Civil War Rittenhouse Square was completely surrounded by private homes. The last lots to be developed were on the west side where the Academy of Notre Dame and the Joshua B. Lippincott house were built in the 1860s, south of John Notman's recently completed Holy Trinity Episcopal Church (1857–59).

The Harrison mansion on Eighteenth Street on the east side of the square was the most opulent residence in the city, with one wing reserved as a picture gallery (fig. 14).[29] Joseph and Sarah Harrison often invited their

fellow board members from the Pennsylvania Academy of the Fine Arts to visit their painting collection. It included several paintings now considered masterpieces of American art: *William Penn's Treaty with the Indians* by Benjamin West, *The Artist in His Museum* by Charles Willson Peale, John Vanderlyn's *Ariadne Asleep on the Island of Naxos*, and one of Gilbert Stuart's portraits of George Washington. Forty canvases of American Indians, "painted from life" by Pennsylvanian George Catlin, added a touch of exoticism to the galleries.

The Harrison garden stretched east to Seventeenth. The design recalled European landscape practice for "garden fronts" of great houses Harrison knew from his travels, and its geometric arrangement of formal walkways and plantings surpassed Rittenhouse Square in horticultural riches. The garden was planned as a communal area from its inception and was shared with the residents of Harrison Row, ten grand houses built by Harrison along Locust Street and rented to families "of the right sort."

Some of the original houses on the square were beginning to seem plain and old-fashioned compared with the Harrison mansion, and they would soon be remodeled and updated by their owners. Others would be demolished, to be replaced by more stylish edifices to suit the new families who would be drawn to Rittenhouse over the next thirty years.[30] With no more building lots directly on the square, families who wanted to live in Rittenhouse had to look west along Walnut and Spruce streets where intense residential development was beginning. Walnut, Delancey, Locust, and Spruce streets west of Twentieth, and the 2200 block of St. James Place are among the blocks that were developed in the 1870s, 1880s, and 1890s. Even Twenty-Second Street—the old Schuylkill Front—would become a fashionable address by the end of the century.[31]

A special set of circumstances set the stage for the new residential development west of the square. Blocks that had been held undeveloped by their owners were quickly subdivided for housing when residential use became more profitable than the storage of lumber, stone, and marble. At the same time, the river industry along the Schuylkill was diminishing, making the western edge of the community more attractive for middle-class housing. The city's access to water transportation, so vital to its survival in the eighteenth and early nineteenth centuries, was no longer necessary to its economic growth. In the second half of the century Philadelphia turned away from its rivers and looked to its railroad rights-of-way as paths to prosperity. "If there were to be any single symbol of Philadelphia during this period it would be a steam locomotive; an idol whose temple was, eventually, Broad Street Station; whose priests, wreathed in the incense of steam and soot, ranged from the workers . . . to those almost sacred beings, the directors and presidents, particularly those of *The Railroad*, the Pennsylvania Railroad."[32]

The availability of land so near the homes of Philadelphia's first families on the square brought a new kind of developer to the area, one who was willing to invest in distinctively designed rows of houses instead of the ubiquitous "Quaker boxes" Philadelphia's carpenters and bricklayers had been turning out for over a hundred years. The late-century developers were a different lot from the brickmakers Kirk and Harper and the failed shipping merchant McCrea. They were men of established wealth and prominence like Thomas H. Powers and William Weightman, partners in the largest chemical manufacturing concern in America (predecessor of Merck and Company), Henry C. Gibson, liquor importer and distiller, Joseph B. Altemus and Lemuel Coffin, wholesale drygoods merchants, and Ebeneezer Burgess Warren.

Moses King, in his vanity publication of 1902, *Philadelphia and Notable Philadelphians*, lists Warren's occupation as "capitalist." Although King does not give the source of his capital, Warren is listed in the city directories as a roofer and paver, with offices at 226 Walnut Street and at Schuylkill's Locust Street wharf, so it is likely

that his firm profited when streets were opened and rows of houses were built west of Rittenhouse Square. He is described by King as "an eminent man of affairs and art connoisseur, who did much to develop this aristocratic locality (west of Rittenhouse Square)."[33]

Henry C. Gibson purchased land on Walnut Street west of Twenty-First Street shortly after Kennedy's 1862 watercolor of it was done (fig. 15). In the illustration only two houses, at least one of which is wood-frame construction, occupy the north side of the block between Twenty-First and the present Van Pelt Street. They are set back in a quasi-rural setting, with wooden fences marking the rear yards of houses on George (Sansom) Street and the House of the Good Shepherd on Twenty-Second Street. Gibson purchased the site, "in front or breadth on Walnut Street 164 foot and extending in depth 120.6 foot," in

*15. Northwest corner of Walnut and 21st sts., 1862. Watercolor by D. J. Kennedy (Historical Society of Pennsylvania)*

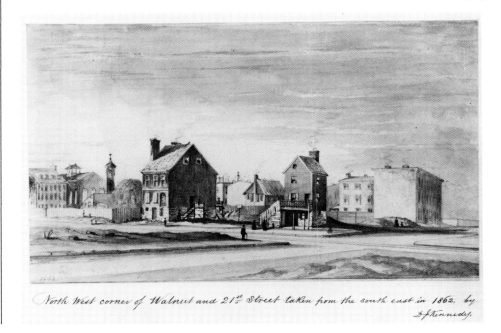

North West corner of Walnut and 21st Street taken from the south east in 1862. by
D. J. Kennedy.

1869, laid out Albion (Van Pelt) Street, and sold the parcel to Ebeneezer Warren two years later. By 1873 substantial residences with 26- and 38-foot frontages on Walnut Street were erected.

Gibson also owned the south side of the block, which he subdivided into similar wide frontages. The 48-foot double lot at the corner of Twenty-Second Street, running 136 feet south to a "new street opened by Henry C. Gibson" was sold in 1869 to George W. Childs, publisher of the *Public Ledger*, for the erection of a marble mansion that rivaled the Harrison's on the square. Many of the families who were drawn to Rittenhouse after the Civil War were ready to display their wealth and eager to live near the city's richest and most powerful families on the square (the Harrisons, Drexels, Browns, Rosengartens, and Lennigs, and later the Scotts, Fraziers, and Cassatts). If the newcomers could not live *on* the square, some were determined that their houses west of the square would be as grand.

Others chose handsome and commodious homes on the 2200 block of St. James Place, developed by Gibson in 1874; the 2200 block of Trinity (Delancey) Place (fig. 16), developed by William Weightman in 1877; or the 2000 block of Spruce Street (fig. 17), developed by Ebeneezer Warren, Joseph Altemus, and Lemuel Coffin in the 1870s. The houses were tasteful and solid, like their occupants. Many of the newcomers were descendants of—or had married into—old Philadelphia families. Whether they were or sought to be proper Philadelphians, a tinge of conservatism marked the clientele for the developers' rows, as well as for all but a few of the architect-designed houses in Rittenhouse.

In the section west of the square the architect-designed buildings reflect the coming of age of America's architectural profession after the Civil War. Between 1870 and 1905 many of the city's important designers began their practice or reached their artistic maturity on Rittenhouse buildings. John McArthur, Frank Furness, Theophilus P. Chandler, G. W. and W. D. Hewitt, Horace Trumbauer, Wilson Eyre, Jr., Frank Miles Day, Addison Hutton, Joseph Huston, Willis Hale, Edgar V. Seeler, Charles Barton Keen, Hazelhurst and Huckel, and Cope and Stewardson all worked in the area. Nowhere else can one find such a concentration of the work of Philadelphia's most important nineteenth-century architects.

Much like the earlier residential boom near Sixteenth and Locust in the 1850s, the upper-class development west of Rittenhouse Square was sparked by the erection of two Protestant churches on West Walnut Street, St. James's Episcopal Church at Twenty-Second (Fraser, Furness, and Hewitt, 1869–70), and Second (now First) Presbyterian Church at Twenty-First (Henry Sims, 1869–72). In a simi-

lar fashion major architects were attracted to the area around the churches. The intersection of Twenty-Second and Walnut contained the Childs mansion, designed by John McArthur in 1869, the brick Venetian palazzo by Addison Hutton and John Ord at the southwest corner (1877), Frank Furness's Victorian Gothic house for George B. Preston on the northeast corner (1884), and St. James's Church with its imposing tower anchoring the intersection. East and west on Walnut Street rows of big, handsome houses soon stretched from the square to the Schuylkill (figs. 18 and 19).

Around the corner and behind the high-style residences on the "big" streets, clerks, servants, and unskilled workers continued to live in the tiny courts and alleys. The residents of the modest houses on the "little" streets were never far away from their rich neighbors. Six families are enumerated in the 1880 census in the court houses at George (Sansom) and Albion (Van Pelt) streets directly behind the newly built houses on Walnut Street.

*FAR LEFT: 18. 2200 block Walnut St., south side, 1888. Frank Furness designed 2202; Furness and Hewitt designed 2204–06–08. Only vestiges of these buildings remain behind the twentieth-century alterations to the block. The four houses at the western end of the block have been replaced by a ten-story apartment house. (Philadelphia City Archives)*

*LEFT: 19. 2200 block Walnut St., north side, 1923. A portion of St. James's Episcopal Church is at the right. (Philadelphia City Archives)*

The families were headed by William Gorman and John Morton, laborers, Patrick McCall, a coachman, Daniel Leonard, grocery clerk, Patrick Kane, gardener, and Michael Scanlon, an employee in a Turkish bath. They, their wives, and the thirteen children in the court must have watched with interest the demolition of the House of the Good Shepherd on Twenty-Second Street and the construction of the fashionable houses that replaced it in the 1880s.

The row of houses built on the site of the Good Shepherd home and chapel, 123–33 South Twenty-Second Street, is among the most important still standing in Rittenhouse (fig. 20). Within this one row are the best examples surviving in the neighborhood of the work of

Chandler, Furness, and the Hewitt Brothers. The first was 133 South Twenty-Second, designed by Theophilus P. Chandler for physician James H. Hutchinson in 1882. Its polychrome brick and brownstone facade is a typical Chandler scheme for what has come to be called "High Victorian." A picturesque asymmetry has been created within what is actually a balanced and ordered facade. An off-center balcony and peaked gable, with round-headed windows at some openings, rectangular at others (some in pairs, others tripled), create a visual delight. As one's eye reaches the 1882 carved in the highest gable, a series of clustered Tudor chimneypots reminds the viewer of its medieval English antecedents.

George W. and William D. Hewitt in 1886 were respon-

*20. 123–33 S. 22nd St. (Drawn by Kathleen Coelos and Richard Tatara)*

123          125          127          129–31          133

sible for two of the houses, 129–31 for Travis Cochran, and 125 for lawyer and civic reformer John Christian Bullitt. The Cochran house seems subdued beside the Hutchinson house, but closer examination reveals virtuoso brick and stone work. The Hewitts emphasized the 44-foot width of the house, the widest on the block, with a series of brownstone stringcourses but also included a series of brick pilasters as vertical accents. Like 133, this house also has a balcony, from which its owners once looked out over St. James's Church.

The Bullitt house at 125 is one of the Hewitt brothers' most inventive schemes for a city house. Perhaps the competition of Chandler nearby, or the fact that George Hewitt's former partner, Frank Furness, was building the Robert Lewis house next door at the same time, encouraged their best efforts. They also may have had in mind Wilson Eyre, Jr.'s, admiration for ancient crafts in their use of pink sandstone and naturalistic carved ornament over the doorway. And again, a balcony is included, this time with an iron basketweave railing through which iron vines and flowers are entwined.

Frank Furness's house for Robert Lewis at 123 terminates the row with a flourish. His emphatic three-story building butts aggressively against the row of four-story houses, and its muscle-flexing bays, gables, and turrets seem to surge upward toward the other houses. On a narrow lot, the house's cantilevered bays over the Sansom Street sidewalk gain space, and invite light on three sides with oversized windows. When one remembers that before one-way streets this row of houses would have been viewed from both north and south on Twenty-Second Street, and that Furness's Preston house once stood at the end of the row at Walnut Street, one realizes how dramatically Frank Furness's corner houses once framed this remarkable row.

The last building in the row to be completed was designed in 1890 by Constable Brothers and T. Mellon Rogers. While less notable than its neighbors, it does not detract from the architectural tone of the streetscape.

Twenty-Second Street was further confirmed as an upper-class enclave with the building of the Church of the New Jerusalem by Theophilus P. Chandler in 1882, and the First Unitarian Church by Frank Furness in 1885–86. Wilson Eyre, Jr., added his picturesque style to the area with the Tudor Revival Bradsbury Bedell house at 101 South Twenty-Second Street (1888), and St. Anthony's Clubhouse at 32 South Twenty-Second (1889). The year before, academician Edmund Darch Lewis's Queen Anne Revival double house had been designed by Hazelhurst and Huckel next door at 28–30.

Chandler was the acknowledged leader of the architectural profession in Philadelphia in the 1880s and served as president of the local chapter of the American Institute of Architects from 1888 to 1899. A member of a prominent Boston family, his maternal grandfather (William Schlatter) was the principal founder of the Church of the New Jerusalem in America and the Chandlers had been early financial backers of E. I. du Pont's gunpowder business. After study at Harvard's Lawrence Technical Institute and extensive travel in Europe, Chandler settled in Philadelphia in 1872, where he married Sophie Madeline du Pont. Urbane and well connected socially, Chandler lived in Rittenhouse and received many commissions from his neighbors. In addition to the Church of the New Jerusalem and the Hutchinson house on Twenty-Second Street, he designed the Scott-Wanamaker House at 2032–34 Walnut in 1882, the chapel of the First Presbyterian Church in 1884, the Frank C. Wyeth house at 1912 Rittenhouse Square in 1886, and the Sartain house at 2006 Walnut Street in 1888. Later, in 1903–04, he designed the Bishop Mackay-Smith house at 251 South Twenty-Second Street, now Chandler Place.

The 1876 Centennial, in which America's colonial past was glorified, had a somewhat belated effect on local architectural styles. As the century wore on, however, it became increasingly apparent that interest in the nation's past met a deep need in American society, stimulating an interest in genealogy, eighteenth-century antiques, and tales of the "olden days" by contemporary writers. This backward look had a major impact on American architects and their critics; it legitimized their quest for an indigenous American architecture. Philadelphia's eighteenth-century Georgian architecture offered more than nostalgia to local architects. The buildings were seen as native examples of order, geometric simplicity, and logical planning, basic concepts of current training at the Ecole des Beaux-Arts in Paris. Chandler, ever the taste-maker, put the stamp of approval on the Colonial Revival in Rittenhouse when, in 1899, he chose a Neo-Georgian mode for iron merchant Frank Samuel's house at 2136 Locust Street.

Chandler was an obvious choice to head the University of Pennsylvania's first School of Architecture when it was established in 1890. His emphasis on "correctness" as a basic principle of design characterized the school's course of study well into the twentieth century. When twenty-seven-year-old Paul Philippe Cret, a graduate of the Ecole des Beaux-Arts, was chosen to head the school a few years later, he did so at the request of students and alumni whose taste had been formed by Chandler. Under Cret's leadership from 1903 to 1940, the School of Fine Arts at the university became the center of Beaux-Arts training in America.[34]

By the end of the century, west of Rittenhouse Square had become the most sought-after residential section in the city, so much so that some of the earlier Italianate houses on Walnut Street were torn down and replaced by buildings in the new Beaux-Arts or English Revival style. Cope and Stewardson, a firm whose partners were trained at Harvard, the Ecole des Beaux-Arts in Paris, and with Theophilus P. Chandler, helped set the standards for architectural correctness in Rittenhouse.[35] The Thomas McKean, Jr., houses at 1921–23 Walnut of 1897 are prime examples of the firm's work.[36]

Joseph Huston, who had trained in Frank Furness's office, designed two houses in the block, 1913 Walnut for merchant William Wanamaker, and 1917 Walnut for iron and steel manufacturer Francis Potts. Huston, the architect for the Pennsylvania State Capitol, turned away from Furness's Victorian eclecticism in favor of historical revivalism: Renaissance for the Potts house and Jacobean for Wanamaker. Clients now valued archaeological correctness, coupled with the newest inventions. Newspaper accounts describe the Potts house as containing "all the latest modern improvements," including "steam heating, electric and gas lighting, electric bells, annunciators, speaking tubes, . . . wardrobes."[37]

A period of renovation and stylish refurbishing also occurred on Locust Street west of the square at the turn of the century. Many of the houses in the 2000 and 2100 blocks were built or updated in the new Beaux-Arts, Queen Anne, Neo-Georgian, or English Revival styles. Young Horace Trumbauer (b. 1869) followed the "chaste and simple" Regency Revival mode for the house at 2145 Locust (229 South Twenty-Second Street). Edgar V. Seeler, a graduate of the Massachusetts Institute of Technology and the Ecole des Beaux-Arts in Paris, altered 2042 Locust, and Willis Hale (the architect of the P.A.B. Widener mansion at Broad and Girard streets, now demolished) designed 2024 Locust Street. Wilson Eyre, Jr., designed the two houses at 2101 and 2103 Locust in a Queen Anne Revival style with his customary respect for the brick craftsmanship thought to be present in medieval vernacular buildings. R. G. Kennedy, a major architect in the English Revival style, designed 2100–02 for the Henry family, and Baker and Dallett, formerly in Frank Furness's office, designed the Neo-Georgian houses at 2122–26 Locust for the Catherwood and Cresswell families.

In 1905 Jay Cooke, Jr., son of the Civil War financier, hired Kennedy, Hays, and Kelsey to design his splendid city house at 2128 Locust Street. The Cooke mansion, together with Chandler's Samuel house at the corner of

Twenty-Second Street, so upstaged the plain brick houses then on the north side of this block that they were shortly replaced with a group of houses meant to please the Anglophile taste of the time. Charles Barton Keen designed six of them—2125, 2131, 2137, 2139, 2141, 2143—in a textbook demonstration of Georgian, Regency, and Tudor Revival styles.

The area west of Rittenhouse Square along Walnut, Locust, Spruce, and Delancey reflects the distinctive residential development patterns of middle- and upper-class Philadelphians after the Civil War. Many of the houses are of stone rather than the ever-present brick of pre–Civil War Philadelphia, and many pay sophisticated tribute to nineteenth-century architectural theorists: Ruskin's love of ornament and polychrome surfaces, and Viollet-le-Duc's search for an organic structural system based on forms of the past. One finds the heavy sculptural details and mansard roofs of the French Second Empire, the intimate scale and cozy interiors of late-century Queen Anne, and the idiosyncratic craftsmanship of the Arts and Crafts movement. There are even a few buildings displaying "Stick Style" dormers. The area is also graced with some of the finest examples of Neo-Georgian and Beaux-Arts classicism in the city.

Many of its streetscapes are much as they were at the turn of the century and most of its buildings are still intact. To walk the streets west of Rittenhouse Square is to understand the tastes and aspirations of a generation of Philadelphians. One is tempted to imagine that their search for "what a building wants to be" often engaged the thoughts of Philadelphia's most important twentieth-century architect, Louis I. Kahn, as he walked these same streets for almost thirty years before his death in 1974.[38]

## The Twentieth Century
In the late nineteenth and early twentieth centuries Philadelphians began to refer to the area of town between the Delaware and Schuylkill rivers as "Center City." The term was adopted to differenti-

ate the old city from the boroughs and townships that had been absorbed within the city limits through city-county consolidation in 1854. By that act, Penn's seventeenth-century utopia of 2.27 square miles became an urban metropolis of 127 square miles.

By 1900 almost every Center-City street was traversed by a trolley line, and for eight cents (round trip, fifteen cents) Philadelphians from Chestnut Hill, Frankford, Strawberry Mansion, and South and West Philadelphia rode the trolleys to Center City for shopping, dining, business, or entertainment. The trolleys, along with the Market Street Subway–Elevated system, completed to Fifteenth Street in 1907, and the suburban commuter lines of the Pennsylvania and Reading railroads, constituted the most comprehensive public transportation system of any American city. And all lines led to Center City.

The focal point of this new Center City was City Hall, the flamboyant French Second Empire building at the intersection of Broad and Market streets. Described by Richard Webster as "a marble masterpiece of High Victorian Eclecticism,"[39] its construction took thirty years (1871–1901) and changed the development pattern of Philadelphia from a linear one, street by street west from the Delaware, to a centrifugal one where development occurred in waves from the center.

The central business district, concentrated east of Broad Street in the nineteenth century, followed the city's boosters toward Broad and Market streets in the thirty years that City Hall was under construction and immediately after it was completed. Banks, trust companies, hotels, office "skyscrapers," department stores, and cultural institutions vied for space in the shadow of the "Public Buildings."

The building of City Hall was a public works project on a grand scale. Its erection at the intersection of the city's two major thoroughfares, its lavish ornament, and its use of the most expensive and lasting materials, proclaimed to all who saw it that Philadelphia's municipal

at the Bellevue-Stratford or a concert at the Academy of Music, their first view of Philadelphia's downtown was the sparkling granite and marble pile directly ahead, topped with its statue of William Penn.

A glance to the right upon leaving the station's Market Street exit revealed the eleven-story Harrison Building at Fifteenth and Market streets, recently built by Cope and Stewardson for the Harrison Trust. It faced the Arcade Building on West Penn Square designed by Furness, Evans, and Company for the Pennsylvania Railroad with amenities that were new and exotic for Philadelphia—arcaded sidewalks on all four sides and a covered pedestrian bridge above the traffic of Market Street which connected the building to the Broad Street Station (fig. 21).

On South Broad Street at South Penn Square, pedestrians stopped and crowds gathered to gaze up at the bronze busts of presidents on the fourteen-story Betz Building on the southeast corner of the intersection, or the Chicago-style bay windows of Furness's West End Trust on the southwest corner. At Broad and Chestnut Addison Hutton's turreted fourteen-story Girard Trust Building on the northeast corner faced the seventeen-story Real Estate Trust on the southeast corner. Directly south, the North American Building on the east side of Broad Street pushed to twenty stories in 1902. That same year the southern tower of the Land Title Building across the street reached an unbelievable twenty-two stories. An anonymous writer described Broad and Walnut streets a few years later in 1923: "Here is the new financial centre of the city . . . the strength and stability of Philadelphia enterprise and finance, industry and trade. . . . Here is the sign of the accumulation of old Philadelphia, the activities of the present, the promise of the continually expanding future."[40]

By that time, the Bellevue-Stratford and Ritz Carlton hotels on the southwest and southeast corner of Broad and Walnut, and the Walton Hotel on the southeast corner of Broad and Locust streets had been built in the midst of

*21. City Hall Tower at Night, 1919. Lithograph by Herbert Pullinger (Free Library of Philadelphia)*

government was powerful—and rich. And so were the city's business and commercial institutions that clustered nearby.

In the early decades of the twentieth century, most out-of-town visitors arrived in Center City by train at Frank Furness's Broad Street Station of the Pennsylvania Railroad on West Penn Square. Whether they planned to shop at John Wanamaker's new dry goods department store, visit a lawyer in the Land Title Building, lunch at the Union League or the Art Club, or attend a debutante ball what had become a cultural oasis. The Union League, the Art Club, the Academy of Music, the Broad Street Theatre, Horticulture Hall, Beth Eden Baptist Church, and the School of Industrial Design (now Philadelphia College of Art) all lined South Broad Street from Sansom to Pine streets (fig. 22).[41] But few homes were found there or on Chestnut and Walnut streets nearby. One of the last big mansions, the Dundas-Lippincott house on the northeast corner of Broad and Walnut streets, built in 1839, was torn down in 1905.

The attitude of Rittenhouse residents was doubtless ambiguous toward the business and commercial encroachments at the edges of the community. While they applauded the city's progress and its economic expansion in the years before the First World War, they probably wondered where it would end. It had taken 150 years from Penn's arrival for settlement to reach Broad Street. In less than three decades after 1880, Broad and Market streets had become the commercial and financial hub of a five-county metropolitan area, attempting within a few squares to absorb the physical changes made necessary by a new age of merchandising, banking, and finance. Rittenhouse, no longer at the pastoral edge of the city, was forced to confront urban change so rapid that the neighborhood was in comparative disarray for the next fifty years.

Even though many families had built summer homes in the western and northern suburbs as early as the 1880s, it seems certain that Rittenhouse residents did not abandon their beloved community lightly. It was not easy to leave the churches where they and their children had married, or the familiar streets where friends and relatives had lived for so long. The proximity of clubs (The Rittenhouse, Philadelphia, Union League, Manufacturers', Racquet, Acorn, Contemporary, New Century, the Browning Society, and the new Art Club) and the devotion of residents to a variety of philanthropic and charitable institutions persuaded some residents to remain in town.

The Emergency Aid, the Children's Aid Society, the Civic Club, the Red Cross, the Eighth Ward Settlement House, the Women's Suffrage Society, and the mission activities of the local churches were worthy and important causes supported by local ladies and gentlemen.

Many doctors and university professors had found Rittenhouse a convenient and pleasant place to live. Philadelphia had been an important medical center since colonial times. With six hospitals located nearby (Jefferson, Hahnemann, Children's, Graduate, Pennsylvania Hospital, and the Hospital of the University of Pennsylvania), it is easy to understand why physicians continued to reside in Rittenhouse. Spruce Street west of Broad became known as "doctors' row," and many doctors who maintained their offices there also lived in the commodious brownstones. The University of Pennsylvania, relocated to West Philadelphia in the 1870s, was in the midst of its biggest expansion in the early twentieth century under Provost

*22. South Broad St., anonymous postcard, c. 1908*

*23. Rittenhouse Square. Drawing by Jessie Wilcox Smith. From the Philadelphia Art Alliance Post Card Series, c. 1923*

Charles Custis Harrison. Many members of the faculty followed the lead of Harrison, who lived at 1618 Locust Street, and made their home in Rittenhouse.

The redesign of Rittenhouse Square by Paul Cret in 1913–14, promoted by Mrs. J. Willis Martin and Dr. J. William White, helped to steady the community temporarily. Its shady tree-lined paths, inviting greensward, and comfortable benches created a focus for families who remained in Rittenhouse. Generations of toddlers with their nurses considered the square their playground. Older children from Notre Dame Academy, Episcopal Academy at Juniper and Locust streets, William Penn Charter School on Twelfth Street below Market, and Miss Irwin's School on Delancey Place met in the square after school (fig. 23). It was customary for churchgoers to stroll through the square after Sunday morning services before returning home for the midday meal.

The Rittenhouse Square Improvement Association was formed in 1913 to fund Paul Cret's redesign of the square and $30,000 was quickly subscribed by local residents for this purpose. Early in 1914, when it became apparent that more funds would be needed to complete Cret's plan and maintain the square in the future, Mrs. Martin and Mrs. George Gordon Meade organized a sale of flowers in the square to raise the necessary funds. On May 20, 1914, the first Rittenhouse Square Flower Market was held inside the central balustrade. The Flower Market, considerably expanded in size and scope, has been held each spring since then.

The Improvement Association took full responsibility for all plantings, landscaping, maintenance, and improvements in the square for many years. It employed and supervised several gardeners until 1927 when the Fairmount Park Commission, under the leadership of E. T. Stotesbury and Eli Kirk Price, took over responsibility for the square. The Improvement Association continued to work cooperatively with the commission thereafter until the formation of Friends of Rittenhouse Square in 1976.

By the 1920s, however, shifting social patterns and market forces that encouraged tall building construction were having an effect on the residential community. West Walnut Street is described by an anonymous newspaper writer in 1923 as "in a troublesome state of flux. A look through the street directory of five years ago reveals how many of the old families along Walnut Street have sold their stately town houses to their tailors and retired to the Main Line."[42]

The largest houses were the most difficult to maintain as single-family residences. The substantial numbers of servants necessary to keep them up were no longer available. Built in the nineteenth century, most were by this time in need of major repairs to heating and electrical systems, plumbing, and roofs. With high ceilings, dozens of large windows requiring hundreds of yards of curtain and drapery material, not to mention storm windows or new sash, and 3,000 to 5,000 square feet of floor space to carpet, wax, and clean, these buildings were viewed by some owners as white elephants (fig. 24). Others saw that demolition and new construction on the sites offered greater investment opportunities, and many of the great houses came down to be replaced by apartment and office buildings.

The corner properties went first: The Thomas Alexander Scott house was torn down for 1830 Rittenhouse Square, followed by the John Hare Powel-John H. McFadden house for the Wellington Apartments. The William West Frazier house was replaced by the 250 South Eighteenth Apartments; the Physick-Roberts house was demolished to build the Rittenhouse Plaza Apartments. The Repplier-Gibson-Brock house came down for the Chateau Crillon; the Thomas M. McKean house for the Chatham Apartments; the Henry C. Lea house for a funeral establishment; and the David Jayne mansion at Nineteenth and Chestnut streets for a movie theater.

Some old houses were saved when cultural or philanthropic groups took them over. Samuel Wetherill's house at 251 South Eighteenth became the home of the Art Alliance in 1926. The mansion at 1923 Walnut, designed for the McKean family by Cope and Stewardson, and the home of Eva and E. T. Stotesbury after 1910, became the clubhouse of the Philopatrian Society in 1926. The Red Cross was first headquartered in the Joseph Harrison mansion at 225 South Eighteenth, then in the Charlton Yarnall house at Seventeenth and Locust streets. The

*24. Northwest corner, 20th and Walnut sts., 1927*
*(Philadelphia City Archives)*

Emergency Aid, also housed in the Harrison mansion, later moved to 1629 Locust Street, the former home of E. C. Knight, Jr. Mary Louise Curtis Bok established the Curtis Institute of Music in 1924 in the George W. Childs Drexel mansion on the square, and the church offices of the Episcopal diocese were housed in the Fairman Rogers-Alexander Cassatt house next to Holy Trinity Church until 1975. The handsome marble house of George W. Childs at the southeast corner of Twenty-Second and Walnut streets was first a dancing school, then a swimming club, a little theater, and finally a nightclub before it was torn down after a fire in 1970 for a parking lot.

The demolition of the Thomas Alexander Scott mansion in 1913 for the erection of the first apartment house on Rittenhouse Square was a turning point in the history of the neighborhood. The writer of a contemporary newspaper account (fig. 25) dramatically described the demolition: "The contractors . . . are under agreement to wipe the old house off the map in a hurry. . . . The pickaxes ate into the $20,000 mahogany ceiling and paneled walls of the library. . . . Just inside . . . was a lofty open hall with a ten-foot high fireplace . . . [which] . . . cost $1,200 and anyone who wants it can now have it for $30." With derision for the Victorian style of the 1870s, he bewails "that utterly impossible, over-ornate, wholly inartistic period."[43] Seventy years after the local newspaperman covered his story—an old house on the square torn down for a new and better use—we read his comments with fresh eyes. We mourn the loss of so many artifacts of another age, and the craftsmanship that went into their creation. In retrospect, there is some sadness when one reads about a way of life "rapidly melting away" because of social and economic forces beyond anyone's control.

The year the Scott mansion came down, 1913, was also the year the Income Tax Amendment to the Constitution was ratified, bringing about some of the greatest social changes in modern America. The redistribution of incomes that followed the amendment brought an end to

*25. Newspaper clipping, Philadelphia Telegraph, February 24, 1913 (Historical Society of Pennsylvania)*

26. *Rittenhouse Square, c. 1918 (Private collection)*

on the square in 1913–14. Hereafter, syndicates, developers, real estate trusts, and corporations would build tall buildings on the square for families who found it more convenient to live in apartments than in homes of their own. The choice of Rittenhouse Square as the site for the finest apartments in the city continued the square's pre-eminence as a residential address, although in one sense "living on the square" today can be seen as egalitarian rather than exclusive. Where in the past the parlor windows of only a few families overlooked the beauty of the square, now hundreds of families can share the view when they live one above another in apartments.

Soon after 1830 Rittenhouse Square was built, the apartment house at 135 South Eighteenth Street and the Wellington at Nineteenth and Walnut streets went up. Tall buildings continued to be built in Rittenhouse throughout the twenties. This was the decade when the term "skyscraper" was coined for buildings that were changing America's skyline: the Chicago Tribune Tower of 1922–25, the Chrysler Building of 1928, and the Waldorf-Astoria Hotel and Empire State Building, both built in 1930. It was also the time when major apartment house construction occurred on Manhattan's Central Park West and Fifth Avenue.

In the six years between 1923 and 1929, 1900 Rittenhouse Square, the Rittenhouse Plaza (1901 Walnut Street), the Barclay Hotel (East Rittenhouse Square), the Warwick Hotel (Seventeenth and Locust streets), the Chateau Crillon (222 West Rittenhouse Square), 250 South Eighteenth Street Apartments, the Penn Athletic Club (now Rittenhouse Regency, 225 South Eighteenth Street), and the Drake Apartment Hotel (1512 Spruce Street) were all built.

It is ironic that a New York firm, Sugarman, Hess, and Berger, was hired to design an apartment building on the same site where another New York firm, McKim, Mead, and White, had built a Renaissance palazzo in brownstone for Thomas Wanamaker little more than two dec-

what Wayne Andrews called "the age of elegance"[44] in America and changed the types of buildings constructed, the practice of leading architects, and the characteristics of their patrons. The erection of 1830 Rittenhouse Square in 1914 was only the beginning of what has become a living document of twentieth-century "tall building" design in Rittenhouse (fig. 26).

When Samuel Wetherill purchased the Scott property, he was "representing a Syndicate." Not even a Wetherill could independently build a high-rise apartment house ades before. When 1900 Rittenhouse Square was built in 1924, it was a sophisticated design response to its Beaux-Arts neighbor across Nineteenth Street, similar to it in height and volume, choice of limestone base, and with a comparable elegance in lobby and apartment spaces. These two apartment towers were to form a visual gateway to South Nineteenth Street for the next quarter of a century.

Also in 1924, the Rittenhouse Plaza was designed by McLanahan and Bencker. A year later, in 1925, the Seventeenth Street portion of the Warwick Hotel was built by Frank Hahn and S. Brian Baylinson. The first section reached west one hundred feet on Locust Street and replaced several houses in Harrison Row. When the hotel was extended an additional hundred feet in 1928, the remaining houses in the row came down. The Harrison mansion at 225 South Eighteenth Street was demolished in 1926 and the cornerstone for Zantzinger, Borie, and Medary's Penn Athletic Club was laid. When it opened in 1928, 11,427 persons held membership cards entitling them to use the club's facilities. By the depression year of 1931, club membership had fallen to 4,000. Prices were reduced in the club's restaurants and athletic fees were lowered to encourage the remaining members to use the facilities. But the club failed to survive at this location. In 1942 the building was sold to the United States government, an auction was held to dispose of its furnishings and equipment, and the club moved to 1801 Walnut Street, Alexander Van Rensselaer's former home. The lively decorative finials, balconies, and other facade embellishments were removed from the building by the government.

The apartment house at 250 South Eighteenth Street, designed by McIlvain and Roberts, opened in 1928 on the site of the Frank Furness-designed house of William West Frazier. Horace Trumbauer's twenty-seven-story Chateau Crillon was built in 1927. After a full career designing Neo-Baroque suburban palaces, Neo-Georgian city houses, and Neo-Renaissance hotels, Trumbauer ended as inventively as he had begun—with a Neo-Lombardic Romanesque skyscraper that recalls the campanile and towers of North Italian medieval cities. The same year, Versus T. Ritter and Howell Lewis Shay, architects of the Packard Building (1924) and later the Market Street National Bank (1930) and the United States Custom House (1933), were designing the Drake Apartment Hotel. Although the Drake is pure Art Deco in its dramatic setbacks, polychrome ornament, and emphatic skyline profile, its lavish Spanish Baroque decoration is unique.

No major construction occurred during the 1930s and 1940s, years of depression and war. The building halt was so precipitous that the southeast corner of Eighteenth and Walnut streets, where the mansions of William Weightman and John Richardson had been razed in the summer of 1929, remained a parking lot for twenty years.

During the war many large homes were converted to rooming houses and apartments. Some doctors continued to maintain their offices and homes along Spruce Street, but parts of Addison, Panama, and Waverly streets were run-down and neglected. There were so few children in Rittenhouse that there was no need for a public school. The last, the Anna Hallowell Elementary School at Twenty-Third and Lombard streets, closed in 1930.

By 1946 Philadelphia's commercial and business expansion had moved so far west on Chestnut and Walnut streets that the city fathers saw Rittenhouse Square as an appropriate site for an underground garage. It was to be located conveniently at the southwestern edge of Center City's office, theater, and shopping district where the resident population seemed to be diffuse and indifferent. The local renters, property owners, and shopkeepers, at first lethargic, began to grumble privately, shared their concern with neighbors and friends, and held a public meeting. It was to be the first of hundreds held during the next four decades to discuss the development and improvement of the community.

The Center City Residents' Association (CCRA) grew out of that first public meeting. Its first president, E. Walter Hudson, was not a resident of one of the old nineteenth-century Victorian mansions but the manager of a twentieth-century apartment house, and the CCRA's first office was in the basement of that building, The Embassy at 2100 Walnut Street. Among the organization's founders were W. Clark Hanna, Philip Klein, George Gordon Meade, and Furey Ellis. After succeeding in its immediate task of preventing the building of a garage under Rittenhouse Square, and with only a few hundred members, the CCRA hired legal counsel to represent the association before the Zoning Board of Adjustment. If the community was to survive, the common practice of "spot" zoning and the indiscriminate granting of zoning variances had to be addressed.

By the mid-1960s it became apparent that a new zoning ordinance reflecting the private investment that had taken place in Rittenhouse since the war was necessary. In May 1975, after eight years of consultation with the City Planning Commission and many meetings with local property owners, developers, and institutions, arranged by the residents' association, the City Council passed the first comprehensive zoning ordinance for Rittenhouse since 1931. The ordinance recognized the demise of heavy industrial uses along the river so that Schuylkill River Park, a dream of planners and residents since 1926, could go forward. It maintained the mix of residential and light commercial uses so that the corner "mom and pop" stores would continue. It confirmed the residential uses south of Walnut Street with R–10 and R–10A designations, and R–15 for multifamily uses on the "big" streets east of Twentieth Street.[45]

The CCRA's newsletters and the minutes of its board and membership meetings since 1946 are now deposited with Temple University's Urban Archives. The files tell a story of a community affirming itself. Commitment to Rittenhouse Square brought neighbors together after World War II, as it had in 1815 when local residents loaned funds to the City Council to fence the square. The sense of community grew. Families with children returned; schools were relocated there. Trees were replanted on its streets, and playgrounds and parks were refurbished or re-created. Annual house tours, holiday tree lightings in the square, and community suppers consolidated the community's sense of itself as a "real" neighborhood, not a nostalgic re-creation of Victorian America but a diverse twentieth-century urban community.

Diversity is the strength of Rittenhouse, as it has always been. In the nineteenth century mansions were built next to claypits; millworkers and servants lived nearby. Cotton mills, trolley barns, and livery stables were around the corner from the fashionable brownstones. Today office buildings and shops bring workers and clients and customers to Rittenhouse. Hotels, restaurants, art galleries, and cultural institutions bring visitors to the neighborhood. Rittenhouse residents live in walk-up apartments, renovated stables on back alleys, mansions on Spruce and Delancey, sleek high-rise condominiums, and in modest retirement hotels. It is not a somnolent residential neighborhood with a mythical past of Victorian greatness, nor is it an area whose future will be shaped by market forces alone.

Philadelphia's downtown is little more than two square miles, within which its business, commercial, cultural, entertainment, and residential needs must be accommodated. It is a tribute to the city's civic, business, and political leaders that each of these urban constituencies regards diversity of land use in Center City as one of Philadelphia's major strengths. To balance the city's need for economic growth and a fair return for investors with its citizens' desire for a city of human scale and meaning has not been easy, and it has not occurred in a vacuum.

The persons who live and work in Rittenhouse have become increasingly involved in planning the community's future. Historic Rittenhouse, Inc., the Friends of

Rittenhouse Square, and the Center City Association of Proprietors were formed in the 1970s and they, like the CCRA, are responding to the changing needs of Rittenhouse.

When the CCRA first established a Planning Committee in 1960, there were questions about what the committee's objective should be and doubts about whether ordinary citizens could participate effectively in the urban planning process. Out of that initial committee came the 1975 zoning ordinance and Schuylkill River Park in 1979. Beyond these tangible results, the greatest benefit has been that the concept of planning, so foreign to Ritten-house residents in the 1940s and 1950s (or the 1840s and 1850s), has become a part of the community's *modus operandi*.

The first residents of the "Western Commons" had no need for planning. In a simpler age the brick kiln was located next to the claypit, and the well-worn cartways easily accommodated all who wished to reach a ferry. In today's complex urban society, the responsibility for planning the future of the Rittenhouse community rests with all who live, work, visit, or invest there. The future of the southwest quadrant of William Penn's utopian city depends on all of us.

# ARCHITECTURAL STYLES

## OTTO SPERR

*Rittenhouse streetscape (Photo by Bernie Cleff)*

*27. 2031 Locust St. and 2023–25 Locust St., T. B. Lippincott House*
*(Photo by George E. Thomas)*

## Introduction

This section is intended as a guide to the major styles of buildings found in Rittenhouse. It is an invitation to the pleasure of knowing what one is looking at—or of knowing what one has hurried past for many years. It will focus on the particular configuration of buildings great and small, prominent and secondary. All contribute to the ever-changing environment of this lively neighborhood.

The word "style" has many popular meanings. Here it is defined as a pattern of choices made by groups of people living in a specific time and circumstance. In architecture and building, these choices have both conscious and subconscious aspects. At an objective level, they are usually based on money. A fanlight or arched transom above a door costs more than a horizontal wood lintel. At the roofline a cornice with a complex profile and many supporting brackets costs much more than today's strip of aluminum or yesterday's flat barge board.

In addition to being based on financial means, a choice of building style reflects the values of the owner—or the buyer whom the developer hopes to attract. Therein lies the subjective, emotional content of style. It can provide a profound clue to the beliefs and feelings of people of another time. In this sense, style can indicate to us what our predecessors held to be important and what they hoped to become. In the streets and buildings of Rittenhouse it forms a social document mirroring the long-ago choices of none of us and the recent choices of some of us.

## The Row Tradition and High-Rise Construction

One of the unifying aspects of the buildings in Rittenhouse, whether vernacular or high style, rowhouse or high-rise, is the practice of building attached structures that line up at the sidewalk. This common agreement, a civilized and mutually respectful gesture of alignment within the larger blockfront, results in the physical order of most of the streets of the neighborhood.

In Philadelphia no building tradition is more pervasive than that of row construction. But nowhere in the city are row buildings more varied in scale and character than in Rittenhouse. North, South, and West Philadelphia have many more rows that have survived, but generally these reflect later, larger developments with entire blocks of nearly identical construction intended for economically similar occupants. The physical variety of Rittenhouse is the result of several factors: the social and economic diversity of its residential and working population, the rapid changes of taste and technology in the nineteenth and twentieth centuries, and the development of major and secondary streets lined with low-rise and high-rise structures.

This neighborhood of attached buildings was precisely contrary to William Penn's original vision of a city of detached houses surrounded by large gardens (a dream influenced by the experience of the great London fire of 1666). Penn's clear, lucid plan for his new "towne" gave the colonial city of Philadelphia and subsequently Rittenhouse, its southwest quadrant, a distinct physical form. It was based upon a highly regular and predictable grid of major east-west and north-south streets of uniform widths of fifty to sixty feet, forming "squares." Economic and population pressures for more intensive development soon qualified this simple abstract plan with an intricate system of smaller streets of widths varying from twenty to thirty feet. These lace in and out and stop and start within the larger "squares," adding varied secondary street corridors to the neighborhood.

However, the simultaneously regular and irregular street plan is only one component of the streetscape. The other consists of the row structures themselves, at once defining and animating the streets with their simple or intricate compositions of solids and voids and the advance and recession of their massing. The facades of Rittenhouse, varying in height and width, in simplicity and sophistication, provide, as Vincent Scully has said, "a dialogue across time" (fig. 27). The neighborhood in which this rich and complex dialogue takes place is less than one square mile, yet it contains small one-room-to-a-floor bandbox houses, great mansions of the 1850s to 1920s, and twenty-story apartment and office buildings. The latter take their places as part of the row, often at corners, but on occasion in the middle of blocks.

In Rittenhouse, as elsewhere, the predominant architectural form is vernacular. Buildings in this tradition provide the background for the structures that were intended to manifest style and that contribute most to the pleasure of exploration. The following pages describe the styles that can be found in Rittenhouse. It should be noted, however, that any attempt to define structures by stylistic categories requires exceptions. This is particularly true of nineteenth-century design which was simultaneously influenced by several different historic styles. Since the buildings often combine sources, recognizing various styles of this period needs some skill in visual analysis. The buildings of Rittenhouse invite the effort and reward with the pleasure of looking and knowing.

# Vernacular

28. Vernacular, 2411, 2413 Pine St. (Photo by Bernie Cleff)

NOT all buildings have style. To suggest that they do stretches the meaning of style beyond clarity. It is more useful to observe that the majority of buildings in Rittenhouse (and elsewhere) can be called vernacular. Usually designed by developers and builders, rather than trained architects, they are conservative structures built fairly narrowly within the conventions of preceding decades of construction. The choices revealed by these vernacular buildings are direct and simple. They are traditional solutions. They suggest that financial resources were limited, with few funds available for embellishments. Despite these limits, however (or perhaps because of them), vernacular buildings may be more beautiful than some buildings that are a clear and consistent affirmation of a particular style.

In Rittenhouse most of the surviving vernacular buildings are small structures, generally of a rowhouse or rowhouse-with-ground-floor-shop arrangement. Many of the larger vernacular structures, including stables, factories, and mills that once dotted the neighborhood have been replaced. The brewery that stood on the northeast corner of Twenty-First and Spruce until the 1870s was torn down to make way for elegantly styled houses. Graduate Hospital occupies the former site of a textile mill.

One of the limits of the vernacular tradition as it survives in Rittenhouse is its focus on simple purposes such as the housing of one family, or at most, a few families. The earliest surviving buildings are such houses (fig. 28). Their tradition continues to the present day with some developer-built housing of the late 1970s (as at 1726–44 Lombard Street) built to look like the vernacular rowhouses of two hundred years earlier.

The houses at 2401 Pine and 2401 Spruce are good examples of some of the earliest vernacular housing in the neighborhood. Probably dating from the late 1830s, each house is two stories high with a garrett. They have flat unmodeled brick facades with sandstone or wood sills and lintels and a simple wooden barge board at the cornice. Both houses have gabled roofs of a marked slope interrupted by dormer windows which provide light and air. Each entrance has a brick arch surrounding a glass transom over the door. Such glass transoms were sometimes framed with painted pine fanlights that attempted to recall the leaded-glass fanlights of more expensive Federal style houses of thirty years earlier. Doorways and the shutters flanking the window openings punctuate facades that look almost timeless. Intended as modest mechanics' or laborers' dwellings, most surviving examples of these early vernacular buildings are generally found near the western (Schuylkill River) edge of the neighborhood, although the Kennedy watercolors show that they were once present throughout Rittenhouse (see fig. 6).

Later vernacular buildings are often larger, generally three stories high, with roofs that look flat (fig. 29). Their cornices are either wood with carved brackets or, later, stamped galvanized sheet metal. The latter material gave builders an inexpensive means of providing the intricate ornamental patterns that in more expensive houses were being executed in wood or stone. This is typical of the way in which components of vernacular buildings recall some of the details of high-style structures. These vernacular houses of the late nineteenth century also reflect some of the increased comfort available to families of shopkeepers and craftsmen as a result of the heightened business activity of the Civil War and post–Civil War years.

Few vernacular houses were constructed after World War I because by then the neighborhood was fully built up. The depression of the 1930s did eventually make land available for development as factories failed and local public schools were sold, but it was not until after World War II that construction of vernacular housing by developers resumed. ☐

29. Vernacular, 321 S. Smedley St. (Photo by Bernie Cleff)

## Classical Revival, Late 1830s–1860s

EXAMPLES

*1812, 1814 Delancey Place*

*1815, 1817 Delancey Place*

*2016 Delancey Street*

*1803–23 Pine Street*

DESCRIPTIVE CHARACTERISTICS

*Brick facade, flat, generally unmodeled, undifferentiated, no special bonding effects*

*Flat roof with shallow slope*

*Stone lintel and sills*

*Stone arch at front door, typically with keystone and impost blocks*

*Stone water table*

*Exterior wooden shutters (often later removed)*

*Stone steps*

*Cast-iron cellar grates*

*Double-hung windows, typically four-over-four*

IN Rittenhouse, as elsewhere, in the 1830s, 1840s, and 1850s there were several styles that were popular at the same time: Classical Revival, Greek Revival, and Gothic Revival. (The Egyptian and Lombardic-Romanesque Revivals of the same period are hardly represented in Rittenhouse.[1]) Although their characteristics are varied, they derived from a common point of view, a belief that styles could be "associated" with certain qualities or functions of buildings. Thus, Classical Revival architecture was associated with the purported virtue of the ancient Greeks and Romans. Gothic Revival architecture was associated not with the lusty life of the Middle Ages but with Christian moral authority.

The enthusiasm over the possibilities inherent in a reexamination of the architecture of earlier periods was not new. It is one of the recurring aspects of building in any era in Europe and America. However, in this early nineteenth-century period it was spurred by an acceleration of discoveries of classical sites in Greece and Italy and by the growth of Philadelphia and its economy.

In the 1830s and 1840s the identity and role of architects became more defined; practitioners who had emerged from the master-builder tradition began to call themselves "architects" in the city directories (Samuel Sloan, John Notman, Thomas U. Walter). Yet the evidence from this period in Rittenhouse clearly shows that the use of builders' handbooks or pattern books in revival styles continued to be the prevailing practice. Such books contained engravings illustrating details of particular styles and methods for the fabrication of their components. They met the need of new clients and developers eager for appropriate models. As enthusiasm for a style waned, subsequent editions of these handbooks replaced the illustrations of the style in decline with updated ones showing newer styles.

The period of Classical, Greek, Italianate, and Gothic Revival styles as illustrated in pattern books coincided with the first large-scale development of Rittenhouse.

30. *Classical Revival, 1815, 1817 Delancey Pl. (Photo by Bernie Cleff)*

These early decades witnessed the initial dramatic transformation of the area from a patchwork of brickyards and kilns, farms, and woods into a new and expanding edge of the city. The 1830s and 1840s were years of change and dislocation of earlier values. They were years of populist Jacksonian America in Rittenhouse.

made its houses more desirable in the twentieth century. As a result, they have been more subject to changes of taste. Some of the most elegant of these once Classical Revival rowhouses are now "Recreated Georgian" and are pleasing anomalies as examples of a style that historically never existed in the area.

The houses at 1812, 1814, 1815, 1817, and 2016 Delancey (figs. 30 and 31) show the characteristics of relatively unaltered Classical Revival style. Their (loosely) classical origin is evident in the clear formal organization of the facades into zones. At the base there is a marble water table pierced by cellar windows with handsome cast-iron grates. This water table appears to support a flat brick facade with butter-thin mortar joints. The window openings are largest at the first level—sometimes floor to ceiling. Together with the arched, stone-framed entrance, they denote the major floor. The second-, third-, and fourth-floor windows become progressively smaller. A broad wooden cornice supported by curved consoles or brackets completes an orderly arrangement.

This period favored white or pale colors for trim and cornice. The wooden details are often broader and more simplified than the thin, delicate profiles that were the choice during the preceding Federal period. Such flattened profiles can be seen in the shutters at 2015 Delancey and in the doors and mantels of the period. Although executed in wood, the shapes of many components of Classical Revival and Greek Revival reflect the stone-cutter's tradition.

*31. Classical Revival, 2016 Delancey Pl. (Photo by Bernie Cleff)*

The examples of Classical Revival that survive are found most often on what in the nineteenth century were secondary streets, such as Delancey (although Classical Revival houses once lined Walnut and Chestnut near Broad Street, and South Penn Square). The fact that Delancey now has less vehicular traffic than other streets has

## Greek Revival, 1840s–Late 1850s

EXAMPLES

*1704–28, 1725, 1727, 1729, 1731, 1734 Pine Street*

*1800–06, 1812–36 Pine Street*

DESCRIPTIVE CHARACTERISTICS

*Facade brick or stucco on brick; flat, undifferentiated, little or no variation within the plane of the facade from water table to cornice. Sometimes stucco is scored to suggest stone.*

*Flat roof with shallow slope*

*Stone lintels and sills at windows*

*Stone triangular pediments above front doors*

*Stone water table*

*Stone steps*

*Cast-iron cellar grates*

*Double-hung windows, typically one-over-one*

*32. Greek Revival, 1725, 1727 Pine St. (Photo by Bernie Cleff)*

GREEK REVIVAL style buildings share many of the attributes of Classical Revival structures built at the same time. Like those of the Classical Revival, these houses show an ordered progression from stone water table at the base of the facade up to small "attic" windows at the fourth floor level. There are, however, differences that identify the style as separate.

Asher Benjamin wrote in the second edition of his popular handbook *The Practical House Carpenter* of 1830, "Since my last publication the Roman [Classical] school of architecture has been entirely changed for the Grecian. The Roman orders are composed of small and ungraceful parts. . . . Grecian mouldings . . . consist of large bold parts . . . so strongly marked that each member of the profile is plainly seen . . . and can be executed at less expense."[2]

These Greek Revival houses show a particular severity of form, with unadorned brick, stone, or stucco walls. The facades have significantly more wall surface than openings, and the details are larger and simpler.

Some of the best examples of the style are at 1725, 1727 (fig. 32), 1729, and 1731 Pine Street. Here the gray-beige marble base forms the exterior wall surface up to the second floor, with deep incisions of the marble to emphasize its horizontal coursing and its quality as a material. This stonework is capped by a continuous molding. The stucco face of the second, third, and fourth floors is scored to look like dressed stone, further demonstrating the preference of the Greek Revival style builder and buyer for stone—had budget permitted. These houses further indicate their style by the projecting dentils in the cornices. They are difficult to see because of the current dark color of trim and cornice that is inappropriate to the period. Greek key motifs appear in the cellar window grates and railings on this block.

The houses in the 1800 block of Pine on the south side have paired doors below a single shared triangular pediment which recalls in much simplified form the shape of a Greek temple front. The Greek Revival houses of the 1700 (fig. 33) and 1800 blocks of Pine present a characteristic restraint in which the individual house is clearly secondary to the unity of the block. No exposed downspout divides house from house. The result is an urban setting of great dignity with continuity from facade to facade. Their regular rhythms of walls punctuated by uniform window openings mark this rowhouse Greek Revival as the resolution of an idealized and balanced style. □

*33. Greek Revival, 1724 Pine St. (Photo by Bernie Cleff)*

## Gothic Revival, 1840s and 1850s

EXAMPLES

1625 Locust Street (St. Mark's Church, 1849–50, John Notman)

1710 Spruce Street

DESCRIPTIVE CHARACTERISTICS

Brownstone or brownstone and brick facade

Steeply pitched, gabled roof or in rowhouses a flat roof

Sometimes a crenelated eave

Carved and often hooded stone lintels with pendants

Often paired windows with diamond-shaped leaded panes or lancets with tracery

Cast-iron cellar grates

34. Gothic Revival—1850s, 1710 Spruce St. (Photo by Bernie Cleff)

GOTHIC REVIVAL styles can be divided into several phases. By the mid-1840s Gothic had emerged as a serious challenge to Greek and Classical Revival styles in American residential and church design. This was in large measure a consequence of the popularity of the publications of Andrew Jackson Downing in which he recommended picturesque Gothic designs for "castles" and cottages. He wrote in 1846, "The Greek temple disease has passed its crises."[3] The early phase of Gothic Revival emphasized various associated values such as its moral superiority to Greek and Roman sources. It also evoked the mystery and romance of the settings of the Gothic novels of the period. Architecturally, it favored eccentric rooflines, clustered chimneys, bays with lancet windows, circular towers, and inside, nooks for reading and meditation. It is unlikely that Rittenhouse ever had a significant number of early Gothic Revival buildings. The irregular and asymmetrical preferences of the style did not lend themselves to row lots but were better suited to country properties or to detached buildings such as John Notman's St. Mark's Church of 1849–50. Downing recommended for those "who could not gaze out their windows onto crags and torrents," a milder and more domesticated version of Gothic, the Tudor style.

The building at 1710 Spruce Street (fig. 34) which is of the 1850s shows this Tudor effort to adapt Gothic style to the relatively flat planar nature of rowhouse construction. The result is a brownstone and brick facade in dark earth colors, an obvious rejection of the whitened palette of the Classical and Greek Revival. Tudor arch openings enframe the windows and doors. The spandrel panels below the first floor windows have quatrefoil patterns. Trefoils occur at the spring of the window and door arches.

The fourth floor shows six windows that are narrow enough to serve as the lancet windows of Gothic architecture. The cornice is wood carved in a series of pointed arches. However, it is the combined two-story and four-

*35. Gothic Revival—1860s, 2216, 2218 St. James Pl.*
*(Photo by Bernie Cleff)*

story alignment of the facade that is particularly arresting. A building with this variation in height at the front would have been unthinkable within the canons of Classical and Greek Revival design. Its irregularity suited Gothic Revival taste exactly and is an appropriate transition to John McArthur's Tenth Presbyterian Church of Lombardic-Romanesque design next door.

Gothic Revival never lost its association with moral values. Through the influence of the French theoretician and architect Viollet-le-Duc, however, a belief in the rational character of Gothic construction and its ability to span large spaces free of columns encouraged its broader use. The forms of Gothic masonry architecture soon appeared in cast-iron columns, beams, and prefabricated building fronts. They were used for commercial buildings as well as churches. The exterior of Trinity Memorial Church at 2200 Spruce Street shows this inventive use of a new material in "Gothic" flying buttresses which permitted the interior to be both wide and free of columns.

Gothic Revival architecture also tended to become increasingly archaeologically correct. St Mark's was a faithful copy of an English medieval church. It was executed in a manner fully acceptable to the English architect A. W. Pugin and the English ecclesiologists who promoted Gothic as the only appropriate Christian style. (Eighteenth-century churches in England and America had been designed in Renaissance-derived styles; at that time the term "Gothick" was synonymous with barbaric.)

The houses at 2216 and 2218 St. James Place (fig. 35) are High Victorian Gothic within the constraints of rowhouse design. They recall the wide influence of the prolific English critic and social theorist John Ruskin, who in 1851 published the first of three volumes called *The Stones of Venice* in which he celebrated the particular Gothic and Byzantine buildings of that city.

These houses and others on St. James Place emphasize color through the use of stone and brick of varying hues and finishes. The rhythm of their pointed brick arches is made even more insistent by contrasting stone trim that springs from impost blocks carved in the shape of leaves. This use of a natural ornamental detail is entirely consistent with Ruskin's recommendations, as is the use of stringcourses, lintels, and finials at the combined stone and brick cornice. The stone finials that break the roofline are "what points and flashes of light are in the color of a painting or of nature."[4] □

## Gothic Revival, 1860s and 1870s

*EXAMPLES*

*2216 and 2218 St. James Place*

*DESCRIPTIVE CHARACTERISTICS*

*Flat brick facade with flush brick joints*

*Flat roof with roofline punctuated by stone finials at the cornice*

*Stone lintels with pointed brick arches at window, stone hoods with carved stone imposts*

*Stone water table*

*Stone front steps*

*Paired entrance doors*

*Double-hung windows, one-over-one*

*Stone cornice combined with corbeled brick*

## Italianate, 1840s–1870s

### EXAMPLES

*1508–28, 1534–36 Pine Street (Lewis's Row, 1849, Thomas Ustick Walter)*

*1602–04 Locust Street (1604, c. 1852, John Notman)*

*1714–20, 1728–30 Spruce Street*

*2008–18 Walnut Street*

### DESCRIPTIVE CHARACTERISTICS

*Brick or brownstone facade marked by horizontal stringcourses*

*Flat roof with shallow slope*

*Bold double-curve consoles or brackets*

*Lintels above windows and doors project vigorously and dramatically*

*Sometimes stone arches form a full surround of the window*

*Sills below windows may be supported by stone brackets*

*Water table projects forward with course lines deeply incised*

*Windows are double-hung, four-over-four (1500 block of Pine) or, later, one-over-one (1800 block of Spruce or 2000 block of Walnut)*

*Windows are differentiated by floor level, with nearly square windows at attic level and floor-to-ceiling windows at the first floor level*

*36. Italianate, 1524, 1526 Pine St., Lewis's Row (Photo by Bernie Cleff)*

THE Italianate style was nationally the most popular style of the 1850s for urban row construction. The facades of Italian Renaissance palazzi offered a prototype for John Notman's Athenaeum on Washington Square of 1845–47 and for Thomas U. Walter's Lewis's Row of 1849 (fig. 36). Walter (who later designed the dome of the United States Capitol) adopted the characteristics of a Renaissance facade using native brownstone instead of brick, with lintels, sills, and vigorous cornices in bold relief. Notman, Walter, and their generation of mid-nineteenth-century master-builder architects served middle-class residents who welcomed associations of permanence and European civilization.

The houses at 1618 and 1620 Locust by Notman and others are excellent examples of Italianate style. The Isaac Lea House at 1622 of 1851 is prototypical, with bracketed cornice, stringcourse at the second-floor sill line, and floor-to-ceiling windows on the main floor. (Its painted facade of brownstone color with sand admixture is an excellent approach to the problems of brownstone spalling.) However, the later Italianate rowhouses in the 2000 block of Walnut, especially numbers 2008 to 2018 (fig. 37), constitute what is probably the finest surviving group of Italianate structures in Philadelphia. Although buildings of this type abound in New York, Philadelphia has very few examples of what was an excellent adaptive response to increasingly trafficked streets, namely the high front stoop above a full English basement with full or partial cellar below grade. □

*37. Italianate, 2008, 2010 Walnut St. (Photo by Bernie Cleff)*

*Doors are paneled with deep reveals, often strongly recessed within a highly modeled surround*

*Front steps may number five or six (as in Lewis's Row) or may rise almost a full basement story above the street (2010–18 Walnut Street)*

## Second Empire Revival, 1860s and 1870s

*EXAMPLES*

*2202 St. James Place*

*2202–08, 2212–26, 2201–25 Delancey Place*

*2002–12 and 2011–21 Spruce Street*

*DESCRIPTIVE CHARACTERISTICS*

*Two- and three-story brownstone, limestone, or brick front*

*Slate mansard roof with dormers capped by segmental or triangular pediments*

*Sometimes ironwork at roofline*

*Wood cornice with metopes, triglyphs, and dentils, built-in gutters*

*Surround at windows and front door is always stone*

*Sometimes bay windows, but at first floor only*

*All windows treated similarly within any single floor*

*Stone steps numbering at least seven or more*

*Cast-iron cellar window grates*

THE period of building generally known in the United States as Second Empire coincides with perhaps the largest-scale expansion of Rittenhouse. The result was extensive blockfronts of stone or brick with mansard roofs which characterize the neighborhood, particularly west of Nineteenth Street and north of Pine.

This was an era in which French leadership in art, architecture, and city planning was without challenge. Many Americans traveled to France to see the great International Expositions of 1855 and 1867. They returned deeply impressed with the transformation of Paris under Napoleon III into a modern city of expansive boulevards and parks, the world center of achievement in the arts and industry. It was also at this time that the beginnings of the formal European training of Americans as architects began. Earlier "architects" such as Notman, Sloan, and others had acquired skills through an apprenticeship within the building trades, and were partially dependent upon pattern books, which showed both architect/builder and carpenter what to copy. In the 1860s and 1870s, however, newly sophisticated clients sought trained architects who were directly familiar with European practice and could develop designs of increasing uniqueness and originality. The founding of the American Institute of Architects in 1857 and the initiation of courses in architecture at MIT, Columbia, and the University of Pennsylvania later in the century were in response to the need for a professionally defined manner of practice.

The popular use of the term "Second Empire" has, according to David Van Zanten, obscured the fact that there are at least two fundamentally different approaches in the architecture of the period, both in France and the United States.[5] These two approaches can be termed Revival and Neo-Grec.

Second Empire Revival is best exemplified locally by Philadelphia City Hall (1871–1901), designed by John McArthur. In rowhouse construction it is evident at 2002 to 2012 and 2011 to 2021 Spruce Street (fig. 39) of the late

*38. Second Empire Revival, 2202 St. James Pl. (Photo by Bernie Cleff)*

1860s. The rowhouse examples do not have the successive levels of classical orders superimposed on each other that characterize Second Empire Revival public buildings, but they do generally follow the formula of three floors with slate mansard roof of the French prototypes. Facades are often brownstone, limestone, or brick with limestone trim. Ornamental details usually reflect sixteenth- and seventeenth-century French Renaissance sources. Window and door openings are parts of a balanced, repetitive, resolved composition. The choice of this style was meant to signify the sophistication of the occupants and their good (i.e., French) taste. □

*39. Second Empire Revival, 2011–21 Spruce St.*
*(Photo by Bernie Cleff)*

## Neo-Grec Second Empire, Late 1860s and 1870s

*EXAMPLES*

*2036, 2038 Spruce Street*

*235 South Twenty-First Street (Thomas Hockley House, 1875, Frank Furness)*

*2023–45 Spruce Street*

*2102–06 Spruce Street*

*2113 Spruce Street*

*2300–22 and 2301–23 Delancey Place*

*DESCRIPTIVE CHARACTERISTICS*

*Two- and three-story brownstone, limestone, or variegated brick front*

*Slate mansard roof with hooded dormers or gable*

*Bay windows (almost always)*

*Stone or brick cornice with built-in gutter and often concealed downspouts*

*Chamfered corners or engaged columns at sides of door and window openings*

*Stone water table with deeply incised joints*

*Incised, stylized ornamental detail, either naturalistic or geometric in origin*

40. *Neo-Grec, 2036, 2038 Spruce St. (Photo by Bernie Cleff)*

ALTHOUGH the number of Neo-Grec rowhouses in Rittenhouse is far fewer than the number of Second Empire Revival houses, their importance in the development of what has been called "the first truly mature, independent American architecture"[6] warrants their separate discussion. The salient difference between Second Empire Revival and Neo-Grec Second Empire is that the former is relatively canonical in its forms, proportions, and ornamental details. Cornices generally look like Renaissance-derived cornices complete with metope and dentil. Arches have keystones and impost blocks. The overall composition is such that all of the parts could be predicted from any one part.

Neo-Grec Second Empire, by contrast, involves the willful exaggeration or distortion of architectural elements in an effort to achieve buildings of unique character. The houses at 2036 and 2038 Spruce Street (fig. 40) of 1872 show an awesomely exaggerated entrance at 2038 opposed by a one story bay at 2036. The anthemion or Greek palmette, not seen widely since the Greek Revival of thirty years earlier, is played against highly naturalistic bands of ivy leaves above the entry. Other ornamentation consists of repeated, deeply incised geometric lines and pointed bosses. The houses have an intense, vigorous, almost battlemented aspect as they assert their presence on the street. Discreet taste has been set aside.

In the houses opposite, 2023 (fig. 41) to 2045 Spruce Street, the ornamentation is pure Neo-Grec with sharply incised, flowing, linear foliage played against mechanically repetitive diamond-shaped cuts at lintels complete with Greek acroteria. The dormers of these houses of the late 1870s have blunted, flat hoods similar to the projecting bay of the nearby Hockley House of 1875 by Frank Furness (fig. 42). Like 2036 and 2038 Spruce Street, this house shows the Neo-Grec style expressive of the acts of support, of entrance, and of opening. Neo-Grec architecture demands an active response. □

*41. Neo-Grec, 2023, 2025 Spruce St. (Photo by Bernie Cleff)*

*42. Neo-Grec, 235 S. 21st St., Thomas Hockley House (Photo by Bernie Cleff)*

*Variation of both the shape of window openings and the grouping of openings within any one facade*

*Double-hung windows, usually one-over-one*

*Cast-iron cellar window grates*

## Queen Anne Revival, 1880s and Early 1890s

*EXAMPLES*

*2400–20, 2424–28 Spruce Street*

*1920–30 Pine Street (1889, Frank Miles Day)*

*248–54 South Twenty-Third Street*

*2013–21 Locust Street*

*323 South Eighteenth Street*

*321–25 South Twentieth Street*

*1828, 1911, 1923 Spruce Street*

*335 South Twenty-First Street*

*DESCRIPTIVE CHARACTERISTICS*

*Variation of materials of the facade; generally brick with brownstone or limestone trim; or brick or stucco, sometimes with decoratively shaped shingles*

*Extensive use of various kinds of brick and brick bonds, often molded brick, tinted mortar joints; belt courses of stone or brick*

*Generally clustered, prominent chimneys*

*Bay windows are common, sometimes wide and sometimes of the narrow, triangulated, two-window type; also round windows*

43. Queen Anne Revival, 321–25 S. 20th St.
(Photo by Bernie Cleff)

THE abrupt collapse of France in the Franco-Prussian War of 1870 and the subsequent brutal conflict among the French in the Communard riots dealt a severe blow to the authority of the French Second Empire style. In the United States the financial panic of 1873–74, which was triggered by the Credit Mobilier scandal, gravely embarrassed the Grant administration, whose official public building style had been Second Empire Revival. While the importance of national union had been reaffirmed by the Civil War, the assassination of Lincoln and the near impeachment of President Johnson encouraged a national mood of safe return to the values of our founders, of rediscovering our colonial and, for some, English origins.

The style that prefigured our own national Colonial Revival (which has never entirely subsided either in the suburbs or in the 1950s resurrection of Society Hill) was Queen Anne Revival. This style became extremely popular both for development housing and for the houses of private clients in the 1880s. It was chiefly influenced by the residential work of two Englishmen, Norman Shaw and Philip Webb, whose buildings of the 1870s were widely published in the professional magazines that were circulated in America beginning in the 1880s. Their work was loosely based on seventeenth-century English country manor houses where medieval, Renaissance, and Dutch elements were combined. Hence, the Queen Anne style reflects a variety of sources. Because it emphasizes dramatic and variegated form, it often succeeds best in the city at corners.

Queen Anne houses in Rittenhouse may include Renaissance-derived Palladian windows, an arched center window with rectangular side lights (1911 Spruce Street, 335 South Twenty-First), Jacobean-looking clustered chimneys, windows with stained or colored glass in small panes, gables turned toward the street, and turrets at corners. A gable end may be Dutch stepped (1923 Spruce Street), gambrel- or barn-shaped (323 South Eighteenth Street), an equilateral triangle (335 South Twenty-

First Street), or a broken double scroll shape (2021 Locust Street, fig. 44).

In the Queen Anne style texture and contrasts of color and materials are all-important. The interest in a fully three-dimensional relief within a rowhouse facade is pursued by means of bays, both broad and large (1828 Spruce Street) and narrow and vertical (2404, 2406 Spruce Street). Sharp contrasts of types and sizes of window openings are often found in this last residential style to have been built on an extensive scale in Rittenhouse. □

*Often arched windows on first floors; sometimes arched windows at third floors*

*Variation in the shapes and groupings of windows; sometimes Palladian windows in gables*

*Use of terra-cotta or stamped tin panels*

*Windows often have transom sections of stained glass*

*44. Queen Anne Revival, 2013–21 Locust St. (Photo by Bernie Cleff)*

*45. Queen Anne Revival, 1920–30 Pine St. (Photo by Bernie Cleff)*

## Beaux-Arts, 1890s to 1920s

*DESCRIPTIVE CHARACTERISTICS*

*Distinctive buildings no longer built as one of several similar in a row*

*Symmetrical or balanced organization of facades*

I F the period from 1865 to 1885 was one of freewheeling individualism and new enterprises, 1885 to 1915 was an era of corporate consolidation. Trusts and cartels replaced the single entrepreneur. Some architects formed "corporate" practices with a division of duties among designers, engineers, draftsmen, accountants, and managers. Immigration to the United States swelled, and the formal identification of those deemed to constitute American "society" was confirmed in registers published in many cities. Good taste in architecture was, like the interest in genealogy, evidence of one's place in the social hierarchy.

The Beaux-Arts style suited a need for order, for architectural practice on a large scale, and for an agreed-upon vision for a nation that was now a continental and an international power. Its source, the Napoleonic Ecole des Beaux-Arts offered an ancient pedigree deriving from the seventeenth-century French Academy and determined European training in architecture and the fine arts for succeeding generations. By the 1890s the Ecole dominated American architectural study as well.

Some writers split the Renaissance-derived buildings of the 1890s to 1930s into two styles, Beaux-Arts and "Classical Revival of the Twentieth Century." The latter employed Beaux-Arts principles and methods but with fewer enrichments.[7]

The principles of the Beaux-Arts style included an emphasis on design according to "laws of composition." The observance of these rules sometimes overrode consideration of specific activities within the building. Beaux-Arts architects placed great value on controlled design and on a balance of mass and void. Although Renaissance prototypes had to be adapted and used correctly, there was some latitude in the ornamentation and detailing.

Beaux-Arts buildings of varying sizes and uses again show the mansard roof (last seen locally in the Second Empire style) but with several levels of dormers: the E. C. Knight, Jr., House (fig. 46), the Bellevue-Stratford Hotel

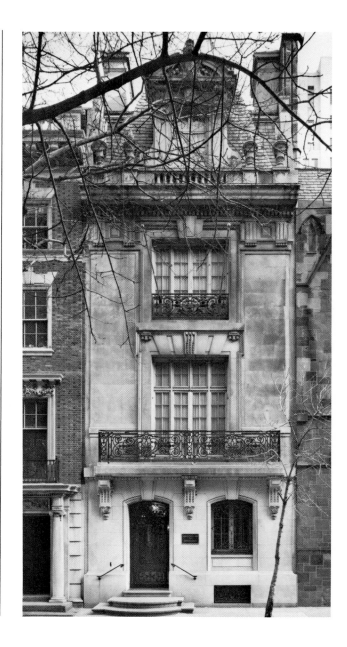

(fig. 47), and the Lippincott House. Some examples have dormers topped by triangular pediments, some by segmental pediments, and some by round pediments. While the facade of the Knight House only appears to be symmetrical, the Bellevue-Stratford and the Lippincott House are absolutely symmetrical with the front door on center. For a city house, such placement was contrary to custom. The house at 133 South Eighteenth Street opposes a wide, arched entry with an arched window. The support of a center bay rises from the spring of the arches.

*46. Beaux-Arts, 1629 Locust St., E. C. Knight, Jr., House (Photo by Bernie Cleff)*

*Detail, Lippincott House (Photo by George E. Thomas)*

*47. Beaux-Arts, southwest corner Broad and Walnut sts., Bellevue-Stratford Hotel (Photo by Bernie Cleff)*

*Limestone, brick with limestone trim, quoins, belt courses and cornices; occasionally granite*

*Copper or slate mansard or low hipped roofs, often hidden by parapets or balustrades*

*Renaissance-derived progression in which the stone of the base is deeply incised and the walls or upper stories are flat*

*Window surrounds similarly hierarchical, with more enrichments for the lower floor and simpler treatment for the upper floor*

*Ornamental detail Renaissance in origin, often with carved wall panels and supports for bays and balconies*

48. *Beaux-Arts, 251 S. 18th St., Samuel P. Wetherill House, now the Art Alliance (Photo by Bernie Cleff)*

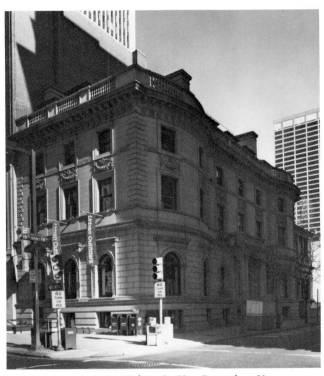

49. *Beaux-Arts, 1801 Walnut St., Van Rensselaer House (Photo by Bernie Cleff)*

The influence of French Renaissance architecture with its abundant enrichment of surfaces by coursing and rustication of lower stories and projection of upper balconies and bays was not the only Beaux-Arts approach in Rittenhouse. Other buildings showed greater restraint, contrasting large areas of smooth ashlar walls with rich detail confined to window surrounds, cornices, and spandrel panels, as in the Cramp House (now Knapp Hall of the Curtis Institute of Music) and the Wetherill House (fig. 48) (now the Art Alliance).

The Van Rensselaer House (fig. 49) and the Rittenhouse Club (fig. 50) show an intermediate level of enrichment. Both buildings have curving bays flanking their entrances. They model the mass of the buildings in the sunlight. The pink Sardizzo granite of the Van Rensselaer House adds glint to its surfaces. Both buildings have roof-

line balustrades. These buildings and the College of Physicians of Philadelphia also shape their setting by stone railings or walls with piers and ironwork or a garden at the sidewalk line. All present a gentle rise of steps, usually leading to an ornate wrought-iron and glass outer door or a gate.

The Beaux-Arts skill in relating buildings to their public spaces and to gardens is clear in the plan for Rittenhouse Square by Paul Philippe Cret, implemented during and after World War I. All the principles are manifest. Two diagonal crosswalks converge on a gentle rise of land in the center forming a court defined by a continuous stone balustrade. Chestnut trees and London Plane trees flank paired walkways, with statuary, fountain, and pool as focuses located only on axes. A secondary circular walkway surrounds the whole, while the edge of the square is separated from the encircling streets by broad sidewalks and edge planting with low retaining walls. The square acts as a forecourt for the buildings surrounding it and, today, is a gateway to the residential neighborhood.

Most of the Beaux-Arts buildings discussed are now public or semipublic. This mirrors national acceptance of the Beaux-Arts as our institutional building style almost up to World War II. So beguiling was this Beaux-Arts vision of the grand plan that it not only led to Philadelphia's great "City Beautiful" creation of the Benjamin Franklin Parkway, but it suggested to some another parkway that would have cut a diagonal swath from Gray's Ferry Avenue through Rittenhouse to Rittenhouse Square.[8] It was a characteristic Beaux-Arts gesture of balancing one axis of movement with another. In this case, however, the laws of composition did not prevail. ☐

*50. Beaux-Arts, 1811–13 Walnut St., Rittenhouse Club (Photo by Bernie Cleff)*

## Georgian Revival, 1895–1941

EXAMPLES

*234 South Twenty-Second Street*

*306 South Nineteenth Street (Edward Brinton Smith House, 1900–1901, Cope and Stewardson)*

*2136 Locust Street (Frank Samuel House, 1899, Theophilus P. Chandler)*

*1630 Locust Street (James Markoe House, 1900, Cope and Stewardson)*

DESCRIPTIVE CHARACTERISTICS

*Brick facade with stone or brick quoins, often Flemish bond*

*Hipped roofs with dormers*

*Stone or terra-cotta cornices with dentils*

*Brick or stone belt courses*

*Palladian windows, eight-over-eight windows, major windows at second floor*

*Stone water table on lower floor*

## Late Nineteenth- and Early Twentieth-Century Period Revivals

THE Period Revival styles that were current before 1929 can be discussed together because they are chronologically coincidental and share moderately accurate historical details and proportions. As the "good taste" of the 1860s and early 1870s was demonstrated by awareness of French sources, near the turn of the century good taste often recalled English historical styles. For social purposes (the importance of which is evident in literature of the period) a correct Georgian or English Medieval Revival house served far better than the mongrel Queen Anne style or willfully experimental Neo-Grec Second Empire. The latter were almost universally derided as inexplicably grotesque follies. It was consistent with their philosophical and social posture of withdrawal that Period Revival houses often responded pragmatically to increasing auto traffic on the streets of Rittenhouse by placing their living rooms on the second floor front (unless the house was on a picturesque court or a quiet street). This had a further advantage of permitting the second-floor living room to develop across the full width of the house. ☐

*51. Georgian Revival, 234 S. 22nd St. (Photo by Bernie Cleff)*

*52. Georgian Revival, 1630 Locust St., James Markoe House
(Photo by Bernie Cleff)*

*53. Georgian Revival, 306 S. 19th St.,
Edward Brinton Smith House (Photo by Bernie Cleff)*

## *Medieval and Tudor Revivals, 1904–1929*

*EXAMPLES*

*2200 Locust Street (Henry C. Butcher House, 1904, Field and Medary)*

*2143 Locust Street (1905, Charles Barton Keen)*

*2009 Pine Street*

*1920 Panama Street*

*DESCRIPTIVE CHARACTERISTICS*

*Brick with stone trim, stucco with or without half-timbering, often Flemish bond with wide mortar joints*

*Gable end toward street*

*Groups of windows, casement type, relatively small, often with transoms above*

*Sometimes leaded-glass window with diamond-shaped panes*

54. *Tudor Revival, 2009 Pine St. (Photo by Bernie Cleff)*

55. *Tudor Revival, 2143 Locust St. (Photo by Bernie Cleff)*

THE Mediterranean Revival style of the 1920s is demonstrated by a few examples. Like the Georgian and Medieval Period Revivals, it refers back in time, in this case to the earliest European architecture introduced into the Americas, namely the Spanish Colonial of the sixteenth century. The revival of Spanish Colonial was an architectural theme for the highly scenographic Panama-Pacific Exposition of 1915 in San Francisco. The facade at 321 South Seventeenth Street (fig. 58) is a romantic Philadelphia rowhouse adaptation, complete with stucco front, projecting vigas, tile work, and terra-cotta roof tile hoods over windows. Behind it to the east is the intricate outline of the Drake Hotel of 1928 which is a mix of Spanish Colonial and Art Deco styles at the scale of a high-rise.

56. *Tudor Revival, 2200 Locust St., Henry C. Butcher House (Photo by Bernie Cleff)*

*57. Medieval Revival, 1920 Panama St.*
*(Photo by George E. Thomas)*

A group of houses built in the 1960s and early 1970s in the 2000 block of Waverly Street suggests that a form of Mediterranean Revival has had an extended popularity. These houses show rough cast stuccoed walls with ironwork and arched forms. There was a renewed interest in the vernacular architecture of the Mediterranean when they were built. ☐

*59. Mediterranean Revival, 313 S. Smedley St. (Photo by Bernie Cleff)*

*58. Mediterranean Revival, 321 S. 17th St. (Photo by Bernie Cleff)*

## *Mediterranean Revival, 1920s–1960s*

*EXAMPLES*

*321 South Seventeenth Street*

*313 South Smedley Street*

*2040 Waverly Street*

*DESCRIPTIVE CHARACTERISTICS*

*Stucco walls, often rough cast; also stone walls*

*Use of clay roof tile in earlier phases of style*

*Ornamental ironwork at windows*

*Balconies*

## Art Deco, 1924–1940

*EXAMPLES*

*2208 Delancey Place*

*1901 Walnut Street (Rittenhouse Plaza Apartments, 1924, McLanahan and Bencker)*

## Twentieth-Century Non-Revival Styles

THE two Twentieth-Century Non-Revival styles known as Art Deco and International Style were both European in origin. Of the two, Art Deco (from the Paris Exposition des Arts Decoratifs et Industrieles Modernes of 1925) was, despite its futurist manifesto, the more evolutionary, since it continued to use French Beaux-Arts principles of symmetrical plan and massing. Art Deco pilasters show base and capital supporting arch or architrave but with stylized floral or geometric detail that recalls Mayan, native American, or Near Eastern sources.

The remodeled rowhouse at 2210 Delancey Street accomplishes a characteristically Art Deco symmetry by matching a front door on the left with a kitchen door on the right. (This was socially unthinkable in nineteenth-century practice, which would have provided for them either as "above and below" or as "front door and back door.")

It is significant that the finest example of residential Art Deco in Rittenhouse is a high-rise apartment house—the Rittenhouse Plaza at 1901 Walnut Street (fig. 60). Not the earliest of the apartment buildings on the square, the Rittenhouse Plaza was a 1924 design by McLanahan and Bencker. (Bencker also did many of the Horn and Hardart Automats.) The building draws the green space and water of Rittenhouse Square into its forecourt and rises to a climax of geometrically patterned, succeeding vertical planes, each setback forming dramatic terraces overlooking the neighborhood skyline. In the 1920s this skyline was becoming punctuated by a few apartment buildings. Today what had started in 1913 with a nineteen-story tower at 1830 Rittenhouse Square, interrupting a prevailing four-story residential skyline, is a developing wall along the northern edge of the neighborhood.

Unlike Art Deco, the International style was revolutionary and polemical. It also had a philosophical base of

*60. Art Deco, 1901 Walnut St., Rittenhouse Plaza Apartments (Photo by Bernie Cleff)*

social and economic reform. It was both antihistorical and futurist, a highly understandable point of view if we consider that it grew out of the European experiences of the Russian Revolution of 1917 and the German Revolution of 1919, as well as the shock of World War I. However, in Rittenhouse, as in most of the United States, the International style does not appear to have been adopted until the depression of the 1930s and therefore is fully represented by only one building, 2005 Delancey Place (fig. 61) of 1932 by George Howe. (His PSFS building, built a year earlier and designed with the Swiss William Lescaze, is the finest building in this style in America.) The Delancey building has a painted gray brick facade which minimizes the texture and reality of its construction. Its dark blue steel casements reduce the window frame in a similarly minimalist way to make of door and window openings pure voids in a visually thin, nonsubstantive wall.

After World War II typically International-style use of large expanses of glass, of minimal detailing, and avoidance of ornament came to be considered a corporate and architectural norm of progressive thinking. This perhaps made it easier for at least the backs of properties in Rittenhouse to develop radical International stylisms in the 1960s and 1970s. Examples of this backdoor International style can be seen from the 1900 block of Naudain Street looking north to the back of the houses on the south side of the 1900 block of Lombard Street. With their white stucco finish, sliding glass doors, terracing, and metal pipe railings, they recall the steamship and industrial metaphors of the French architect Le Corbusier and the German Bauhaus architects of the 1920s. □

61. International Style, 2005 Delancey Pl., Maurice Speiser House (Photo by George E. Thomas)

## International Style, 1930s–Present

### EXAMPLE

*2005 Delancey Place (Maurice Speiser House, 1933, George Howe)*

### DESCRIPTIVE CHARACTERISTICS

*Brick or stucco walls generally flat and unmodeled*

*Steel casement sash*

*No ornamental detail in International Style*

*Stylized natural or geometric ornamental detail in metal or terra-cotta panels in Art Deco*

*Railings of horizontal wrought steel bar stock or stainless steel*

Conclusion  Several criteria were used in deciding which examples of styles to discuss in this book. The examples do not attempt to be complete; many more representatives of each style exist. The chief criterion, however, and one difficult to impose, was that the example chosen be a consistent and relatively unaltered demonstration of the exterior characteristics of the style. For buildings that have withstood a century of continuing use and desirability, this proved to be a challenge. It prevented including many buildings that contribute to the flavor of the area.

As for the choice of styles, each one had to be represented by at least a few buildings in the neighborhood. For instance, a style frequently found in other parts of North America is the rough-hewn, lithic, Richardsonian Romanesque of the 1880s and early 1890s. It was not included because in Rittenhouse it exists in only one good example, the Baptist Church at the southeast corner of Seventeenth and Sansom streets.

The frequency and speed with which styles overlapped and changed in the nineteenth and twentieth centuries because of wider literacy and accelerated graphic and photographic communication has made them difficult to isolate and thus identify. In seventeenth- and eighteenth-century America and at any previous time in Europe, architectural styles developed at a slower pace.

Fewer people made more gradual and exploratory shifts in stylistic choices, and styles progressed from archaic, awkward beginnings, to resolved maturity, to mannered conclusions. In twentieth-century Rittenhouse the earliest buildings of the Beaux-Arts arrived polished and complete.

It would be a mistake to conclude that the appearance of Rittenhouse is now fixed because the area is built-up or because a portion of it forms the largest National Register Historic District in Pennsylvania. As earlier shifts have suggested, style is a vehicle for the expression of changing feeling, beginning in Rittenhouse with our young nation's Classical and Greek Revivals, to the Second Empire with its vision of unified streetscapes, to the individualism of Queen Anne Revival, to the elegant denials of the International style.

There remain some parking lots awaiting new structures. Elsewhere current uses will also shift. A few renovations and additions can now be seen in the current Post-Modern style that again revives elements of classical design, ornament, and color in yet another way. The streets of Rittenhouse form ongoing galleries in which intense and personal communications are offered for the sensitive response of passers-by. There is both the responsibility to maintain this varied place and the need to enact thoughtful change.

# MAINTENANCE AND PRESERVATION

HUGH J. McCAULEY

*62. Decorative detail (Photo by Bernie Cleff)*

# Introduction

Rittenhouse is an important historic neighborhood with a valuable collection of nineteenth-century buildings. The buildings lend the community its charm and create an attractive place to live. Because of its popularity, the entire neighborhood is now under great pressure from overcrowding, overdevelopment, expanding Center-City commercialism, and high real estate values. This book has been written in response to such pressures and the problems now faced by property owners. The intent of the maintenance section of the book is to inform and instruct owners and residents of Rittenhouse in the technical and practical aspects of historic architecture and to encourage them to treat their old buildings with care. It is a guide for all owners of structures in the neighborhood to help them understand how their buildings can be preserved, maintained, and possibly restored. It is a guide that also applies to nineteenth-century urban masonry buildings throughout the country. The "nuts and bolts" information presented here may not be complete and may not answer all of the questions you have about your building, but it covers the most important problems found in the buildings in this historic neighborhood.

The construction methods described are those commonly used in Rittenhouse before 1900. There are, however, many differences in construction between buildings, and use of low-grade materials and faulty workmanship were common in the nineteenth century as now. The architect-designed, built-to-specifications, and thoroughly supervised building is rare.

Decay and dust are the eventual destiny of man and all of his construction. Once built, a building will begin to change very slowly; it will age and wear, finally returning to the basic elements from which it was made. Any methods used in delaying the process of decomposition may fall under the general heading of preservation. The most important first step in preserving a building is to understand the nature of the structure; the second is proper maintenance.

Armed with an understanding of proper physical methods of preservation, one may be able to fight off the ravages of time. All of the information one can gather and use in the repair and maintenance of one's building is like a health insurance plan for the most important of investments. But care must be taken to do what is appropriate for each situation. Too many mistakes have been made by people who did not understand their building, resulting in "well-intentioned" modernizations and improvements by house-proud owners who simply did not have their facts right. The work has often caused damage and defacement of landmark structures. From front stoop to chimney top, each building in Rittenhouse is in need of recognition, understanding, and care. This section is a guide, not a gospel, designed to help avoid mistakes both of omission and commission.

The following information is provided only for the interest of the readers. In publishing this advice the authors imply no guarantee and accept no responsibility for damage caused by others. The information is educational, not to be used as specifications.

# URGENT CONSIDERATIONS

All of our buildings are made of the same elements: earth (minerals), air (oxygen and all other gases), fire (needed to make building materials), and water (moisture that holds them all together). Handled properly, the ancient elements are all of use to us; handled improperly, they can cause harm. The last two are urgent concerns of the owner of a building, no matter what the use.

# Fire

The interior and almost one third of the exterior of every house in Rittenhouse is combustible. Fire hazards abound in most houses and apartment houses. Use the following checklist to examine your property so you can prevent a fire from starting. Begin in the basement and proceed up through the building with an eye to cor-

Earth     Air     Fire     Water

*63. Ancient symbols for the basic elements*

recting hazards. Try to imagine where a fire is most likely to start.

**Electrical Equipment**  All equipment for electrical distribution should be accessible, easily visible, and free from rust and dust. Old wire that may feed new should not have any splices or pigtail junctions (in which the ends of two or more wires are twisted together to make a connection). All junctions must be made in a proper metal box attached to the structure. All insulated wires must also be secured to the structure, not dangling like wet pasta or tucked up between joists like a rat's nest. If you see any suspicious or outright problem areas in the wiring, call a registered electrician to inspect. All switches, receptacles, and light fixtures should be grounded and well anchored to the wall, with secure cover plates. They should be spark-free when used. Check the maximum load allowed on the distribution box against the actual load being used. Air conditioners, toaster ovens, freezers, power tools, and other appliances now in use may not have been present when your system was originally installed; be sure you have sufficient power to run them safely. Beware: Old, weak knob and tube wiring which is ungrounded can be deadly to you and your building.

**Heating System**  Get to know your system like a friend.

Read the tags and ask of those who know (the gas company, a heating contractor) what the system should do. Gas-fired heaters most commonly provide the heat for a water boiler for radiation or by heat exchange to a ducted air system. Both should be carefully examined at the beginning of each heating season. Oil-fired systems can be more problematic than gas because they produce unburned oil soot which clings to the chimney walls. If this material is not removed, it can cause a fire in the flue which will backfire into the heater and the basement or shoot sparks out onto the roof. Many fires each fall are caused by old oil heaters that have not been adjusted or replaced at the proper time. Have your boiler serviced at least every two years. Electric heat pumps are the very newest thing but so expensive to operate that they are generally found only in recent buildings. Their fire hazards are few and relate to electrical equipment. Beware: Kerosene space heaters are designed for cabins in the woods, not for Center City houses.

**Storage Areas**  Heat plants and electrical equipment should not be located in the same places as bulk storage. Be sure that rags, paper, paint, and solvents are kept away from the heating system and domestic water boiler. If you have the space, build a storage room for low-hazard materials. Use fireproof gypsum wall board and a tightly fitting solid core door in a cool, dry area of the basement—but not under the stair. Paints and solvents should be kept totally away from the electrical and heating systems, on open metal shelving, and each container should be kept tightly closed when not in use. Such material should be thrown out when age has rendered it useless because it may be dangerous to keep it stored.

**Cooking Equipment**  The ordinary gas range may become a bomb with age. If it behaves strangely, call the gas company immediately. When lives are at stake do not suffer with quirks that a cranky old stove may develop.

Never try to heat the house with the oven or burners from a stove. Electric ranges are not as hazardous, but old models often have problems. Again, do not use a possibly dangerous appliance. A toaster oven can be very dangerous because it is often installed in a place where the wiring is not adequate to handle the load. Feel the plug and the face plate of the receptacle after the first use. If they are hot to the touch, there is a problem. A new circuit with larger wire may have to be installed. This is true for many modern electrical appliances, including electrical space heaters.

***Fire Suppression and Detection***   Every building occupied for any use must have some system for detection and alarm as well as suppression of fire. It is very inexpensive to install a new smoke detector-alarm system designed to alert all occupants if the agents of combustion are present. It is not always stressed, however, that fire-fighting equipment is also necessary in every building. Have a fire extinguisher of approved type at the entry to the basement and in the kitchen (the city fire department has information to guide your purchase). Both should be in plain view and handy. Never try to fight a fire without first calling the fire department.

***Fire Prevention Training***   Ask the city fire department for information on fire prevention. Have a fire drill at home twice each year, one in spring and another in fall. Be serious about it. There is nothing more frightening than a raging blaze; it causes panic and death.

# Water   Water, like fire, is one of the basic elements we depend upon for life but of which we must also be very careful. Both elements are dangerous if not controlled. Flooding in this neighborhood is rare, but water can be dangerous to buildings in other ways. Use the following checklist to examine your building for water damage.

***Basement Dampness***   Examine the floor and walls of the basement to see if water has eroded or rotted structural material. Some causes of dampness are easily identified and dealt with. A clogged rear yard drain is often the source. A worn-out iron drain pipe or leaking water valve are problems any plumber can solve. Underground water seeping up into a basement slab or absorbed by the foundation walls and eventually into the wood floor framing can lead to real structural damage. If a high water table (underground water) is present and causing the problem, a pit and sump pump may be necessary. This method of eliminating dampness is not foolproof; an expert evaluation may have to be made before it is used.

***Roof and Sill Leaks***   The roof is one of the areas most vulnerable to structural damage. Occasional rains, allowed to enter the structure of the roof over many years, will eventually cause decay and softness of the boards and timbers, which is very expensive damage. During each rainy season in Philadelphia there is a report of house collapse in which people are hurt or crushed. The collapse may be attributed to the age of the building or excess water damage to the structure. Very often the cause is a long-neglected roof leak, missing downspout, and water seeping through basement walls, all combining to erode the delicate threads that hold the structure together. The older the structure, the more careful one must be to keep water out. A roof inspection should be done at least every five years even if no evidence exists of leaking. The area between the ceiling and the underside of the roof is often accessible and can be seen with a light. A topside examination is not always conclusive when looking for a leak, but it may reveal a downspout clogged with leaves or wildlife. A yearly cleaning of the gutter and downspout is necessary in houses surrounded by trees. Other areas vulnerable to water damage are the window sills where old wood is split and worn. Here rain will seep into the sill and eventually into the masonry walls, causing erosion of the mortar that holds the building structure together. If it is not quickly repaired, the structural damage can be dangerous. Some sills can be filled and painted to remedy the problem, but metal coverings or total replacement may be necessary depending on the amount of damage.

## Mistakes

In dealing with old buildings aesthetic considerations are as important as structural ones; often the two are related. Matters of taste can be thorny issues when dealing with a building recognized by some as an example of an important historical style. An owner may not agree with experts and may demand his right to do whatever he wants with his private property. Many building owners with the best of intentions and adequate funds have created problems in the process of rehabilitating a facade.

Distressed buildings have been badly damaged, for example, by sandblasting—the worst mistake. A brick or soft stone facade should never be sandblasted. It will result in immediate damage equal to several hundred years of weather and natural wear. The immediate mechanical wear caused by sand and water blasted on clay bricks, sandstone, limestone, and terra cotta will etch the surface, allowing more weather penetration. The weather will erode the material and expose more surface to gathering dirt. There is no good reason for sandblasting a building. If a facade is thought to be dirty, it can be cleaned by using soft brushes, mild water, and baking soda. The cleaning should be done by hand or low pressure spray. Do not apply acid; it too will harm the brick and mortar. Caustic soda in mild solution is the most stringent method one should use. Testing in a low, easy-to-examine area can help in making the decision to clean or not to clean.

The painting or sealing of a hard brick facade is also unnecessary. The paint or sealant will peel, giving access to water, which will seep between the paint or sealant and the brick. Natural evaporation cannot then take place and the freeze-thaw cycle will cause the moisture in the masonry to split bricks. Too often a painted facade will need to be painted much more frequently than any woodwork just to keep it looking clean. Removing paint from masonry is only safely done by using a good paint remover—not acid—with nonabrasive tools.

There are many examples of modernization on the facades of buildings in Rittenhouse. Doors and frames have been removed and replaced with frames, side lights, transoms, and doors of inappropriate size, scale, and design (fig. 64). The same problems occur with windows and cornices, when very often these elements are only in need of repair and painting. Gross changes to a facade by way of elements removed or altered can create practical problems as well as the disfigurement of an otherwise attractive and possibly historic building. Never reduce window sizes, lower the lintel, or build up the sill if you want to retain the true value (aesthetic and economic) of your building. The reason that property has held high value in this neighborhood is often directly related to the original condition of architectural elements of the exterior. The whole street will suffer if one building is treated in an unsuitable manner. Do not remove and discard original architectural elements even if they are worn or rotted. Always try to restore these parts of the building. Use the principal of same-for-same. New parts can be made from photos or tracings of originals so that the accurate historic appearance can be maintained.

Paint or stucco on masonry, sandblasting, modern alterations, removal of ornamentation all damage the integrity of the architecture and very often damage the structure as well. They also diminish the economic value of the building and the neighborhood. Try to observe the authentic architecture of the area. Read the building facade and allow it to communicate to you all the lessons of style it has to offer. Notice the mistakes others have made and avoid them when planning your own work.

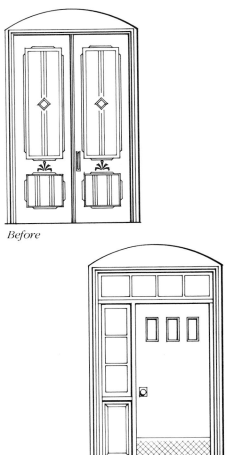

*Before*

*After*

64. *Among the many mistakes made in modernization is a careless disregard for original valuable material.*

65. *Fresh demolition of a very old "Trinity" house (Photo by Hugh McCauley)*

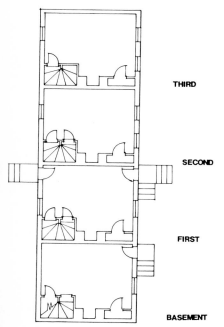

THIRD

SECOND

FIRST

BASEMENT

66. *Typical "Trinity" house plan, 1760s–1840s, for tenant worker. Rear yard additions were built, space permitting.*

# CONSTRUCTION

## Floor Plans

The floor plan of a building reflects the needs and aspirations of the builder and the occupant and is governed by considerations of cost, aesthetics, lot size and configuration, and available technology.

Until the mid-nineteenth century, when there was no central heating, insulation, hot water boiler, or indoor plumbing, floor plans were generally simple and uniform. The builders of the old city east of Broad Street usually designed square houses, one or two rooms deep (figs. 65 and 66). Since the only source of heat was the fireplace, rooms were small and doors separating every room from hall or stair were necessary to contain the warmth, as was the vestibule.

A common adaptation of the square plan is the "L," sometimes referred to as the Girard Plan (for Stephen

Girard, the merchant and developer who may or may not have invented it) (figs. 67 and 68). In the L Plan a long leg was added at the rear of the square in order to afford more interior space. This plan produced the best distribution of structure to lot at ground level. It not only created a useful side areaway, but, more important, allowed light and air to enter almost every room on each floor in a long string of rooms. In this way no "dead" rooms would be created as they were in Europe and old New York City. The practice of adding the leg to existing buildings grew in popularity so that new construction incorporated the L from the outset. Philadelphia city atlas maps show the L Plan as the dominant house plan throughout most neighborhoods, as well as in Rittenhouse.

During the last half of the nineteenth century the gradual availability of mechanical systems for heat and plumbing tended to alter the way some houses were designed. A greater variety of plans was possible, and larger houses and rooms became more practical. Nevertheless, cost remained an important factor, and in nineteenth-century Rittenhouse, while some houses were being built with all the modern devices and in the latest style, others were constructed a few blocks away in the standard method—old-fashioned, perhaps, but reliable and predictable in every way, especially cost.

It is safe to assume that very small houses developed by an institution or landlord for rent to unskilled mill-workers of the 1830s to 1850s would be one room deep, three stories high, and would have a kitchen in the basement and a fireplace in each room, as well as a dry privy in the yard or alley. At the same time, houses being built by industrious mechanics for their own families would have been economical but larger and would have had more conveniences (fig. 69). Nearby, the more expensive homes of managers and aspiring gentlemen would have more space and decoration, larger rooms with higher ceilings, and rooms for servants.

After the Civil War coal-fired central heating, with

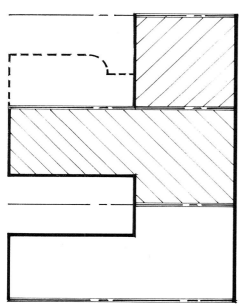

67. *The L Plan, sometimes called the Girard Plan, house, 1840s–90s, for the aspiring manager and family*

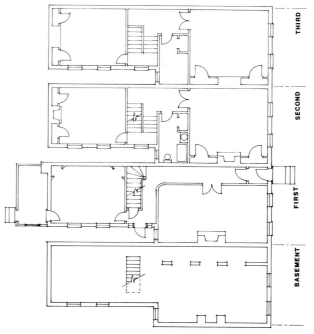

68. *Typical L Plan house. The rear wing is original to the design.*

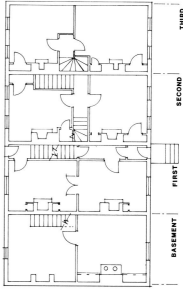

69. *One of the many variations of a two-room-deep house, 1830s–60s, for industrious mechanic and family. Rear yard additions were very common.*

ducts distributing warm air to more than one room at a time, became available to households of modest means. To the poor in their "Trinity" houses on the fringe of Rittenhouse it was not available until the end of World War I. Yet even with early central heating, the major rooms of a house generally had several small coal grates with shallow chimney shafts in addition to hot air registers.

Throughout the 1870s the need for coal grates to augment the central heating was diminishing. Rooms became larger as distribution of ductwork was improved. The coal-fired heaters grew larger with the houses. More grand houses were being built from new patterns of design. Steam replaced hot air; iron pipes circulated heat by radiation; boilers became more complex, and some were

making hot water for bathing as well as heating. Toilets were the last great indoor improvement; bathrooms containing only a tub and washstand had come indoors long before the w.c.

In nineteenth-century Rittenhouse choices were fewer and progress was slower than now. Blocks of houses were often built by the same developer from the same plan, so that everyone in a row lived in the same way. Today variety is available and affordable. The houses in those same uniform blocks differ widely from each other in the way interior space is used. Yet in modified plans of nineteenth-century buildings it is easy to see where spaces have been altered and where modern conveniences have been shoehorned into locations that resent the change.

## Footings and Foundations

Rowhouse construction in Philadelphia has changed very little since the 1750s. In the 1980s the same basic materials and methods are still employed to build the red brick town houses in which Philadelphians have chosen to live for the last nine generations. Modern conveniences and life styles have not seriously diminished the value placed on the security and simple comfort offered by the rowhouse. In order to understand and take care of a rowhouse it is important to know something about the methods used to construct it.

The foundations of most rowhouses stand on footings that transmit all of the weight of the building into the earth below both the street level and the frost line. In the nineteenth century footings consisted of a firm base of flat stones laid two rows high with overlapping staggered joints. During construction these stones were set in a shallow trench all around the perimeter of the future building below the planned basement floor line (fig. 70). Concrete, invented by the ancient Romans and rediscovered by early nineteenth-century Scottish builders, was not much used for footings and foundations in this country until the late nineteenth century. Today concrete is used exclusively for this purpose. In Rittenhouse dur-

ing the first half of the nineteenth century builders used plugwall or slugwall foundations, which very often have no footings at all. These are bound to be weak and will crack and shift sooner than foundations with footings. However, many such walls are still standing today and have been doing their job for over a hundred years with no signs of serious trouble. Good soil conditions under the wall naturally help keep things in order.

Today in Rittenhouse many older buildings are being renovated, restored, and rehabilitated. Basements are being improved and made into living space and old foundations are being affected. Never disturb old footings and foundations without the supervision of an engineer or architect who has the experience necessary to deal with older buildings.

Foundation walls support the structure above the basement and transfer the weight to the footings, which in turn distribute the loads into the earth. Early foundations in Rittenhouse were constructed of rubble, a mixture of broken stone from several kinds of rock, rejected and broken bricks, and often as much as 40 or 50 percent mud mortar (fig. 71). The mortar was made on site from unwashed sand and local red and yellow clay (sometimes called puddle clay). It was mixed in a pit with great quantities of crude lime made from burned oyster shells or limestone waste or dust. When dry, such walls were strong enough to support the building above. The foundation walls were finished off by parging or troweling excess mud-mortar on the face of the wall to make it smooth. When the building was completed the walls were whitewashed with lime and water mixed to the consistency of heavy paint.

Throughout the nineteenth century these old methods of foundation construction were used in most vernacular buildings in Rittenhouse, and money was saved for trimming the visible areas above grade. In the latter part of the century specifications for more costly high-style construction called for mortar made of portland ce-

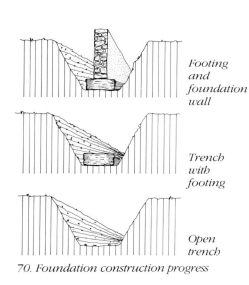

*Footing and foundation wall*

*Trench with footing*

*Open trench*

70. Foundation construction progress

71. Old and new foundation construction

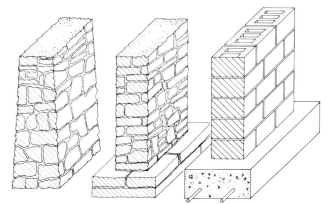

*Early plugwall of rubble stone with no footing*   *Regular stone wall on spread stone footing*   *Modern foundation construction with reinforcing and manufactured modular masonry*

ment, pure lime, and clean bar sand. When laid up with hard brick, this modern mortar, although more expensive, was far stronger and more durable.

Shifting earth under the footings and foundation walls is not a major problem in Rittenhouse, at least not from natural causes. Very little structural damage will result from the natural slow motion of the earth's crust. Cracking from settlement has to be expected. There is real danger, however, from frequent vibrations caused by heavy bus and overloaded truck traffic on some streets in this Center-City neighborhood (fig. 72). Large vehicles speeding over bumpy streets have an effect similar to an earthquake and have caused damage to many buildings. The streets were not designed to sustain great weight; repair of potholes is not a municipal priority. The impact of dynamic loads from traffic has caused and will cause the earth to bounce up and down, shaking the buildings and eventually loosening masonry and framing. Frequency of vibration is an important factor and, unlike natural earthquakes, can and should be controlled. The city streets department, the transit corporation, your insurance company, and neighbors should be notified if structural damage is detected. A city building inspector should examine any building having problems possibly caused by traffic. A "go-slow order" to the transit company can be issued by the city, the city can be asked to repair the uneven street; a local petition issued to the mayor and local newspapers will at least make the problem known. (A test and remedy for damage caused will be discussed in the section on exterior walls.)

Water has already been mentioned as an urgent consideration. In large amounts it is an enemy of both older and newer building foundations. Excess subsurface water or water from a flooded yard, faulty downspout, or leaking plumbing can erode the earth below the footing or foundation wall as well as the binding mortar of the wall, and cause the structure to shift. Examine the foundations of your building; check for a line of sweat or dampness on the basement wall. If investigation reveals no external

or plumbing source of moisture, the problem may be caused by a high water table, an ancient water course below the building, or a neighbor's plumbing or gutter system. If a sweat line is visible, the old foundation wall is acting like a sponge, absorbing the moisture up into the masonry where it evaporates into the atmosphere (fig. 73). A small dehumidifier may be used to relieve any musty smells or mildew and accelerate the evaporation process. This may not cure the problem at the source, in which case a sump pit may have to be installed with a pump to take the water out of the ground before it soaks into the floor or walls. A frequently used method of dealing with damp or wet basement walls is to parge or coat them with a water-proofing cement. In some cases this will drive the moisture and sweat line higher and eventually into the floor framing above, causing damp rot of the wood joists and floor boards. If the sump pump method is used, there is a chance that the underground water will be drawn out too fast, causing the earth around and under the foundations to shrink. This could result in shifting masonry, cracks, and structural damage. The problem and solutions should be evaluated by an engineer or architect who is experienced in dealing with older buildings.

Lack of water can also be a problem. Foundation walls that dry out and lose too much moisture will become unstable. Some moisture is necessary to keep the rubble and mud-mortar together. If the old mortar is powdering and falling away, new cement pointing and stucco casting can be done to restore the structure of the walls, and a small humidifier may have to be installed to replace the necessary moisture.

Sudden changes in either extreme—too much moisture followed by too little—can cause havoc and should be avoided.

Evaluate the problem and the solution so that you may understand it and make the right decision. The basement of your investment must be strong enough to support the rest of the structure.

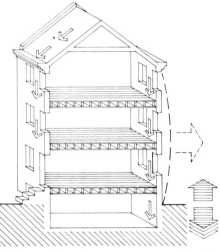

72. *Street vibrations cause stress on facade.*

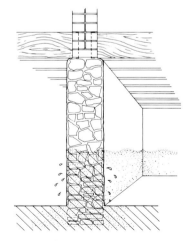

73. *Wet basement wall may act as sponge, soaking up subsurface water.*

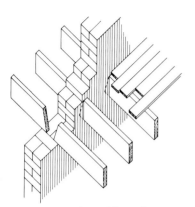

*74. Party wall and floor framing showing fire-cut joists*

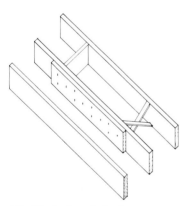

*75. Flitch plate bolted to weak or cracked joist with open bridging and solid bridging*

## Floor Framing

In most Center-City houses the basement offers the best vantage point from which to evaluate the nature of the structure. It also may reveal the most serious defects. Examination of foundation walls and careful inspection of wood floor joists will show how the building was made and how it has been treated by former owners, time, and wear.

When the foundation walls were complete up to the first floor line, the builders installed the first floor joists. The brick walls were then built around the ends of the joists, forming pockets in which the wood sits (fig. 74). The pockets usually allowed at least three inches of bearing for the joists. Usually spanning from side wall to side wall parallel to the street, joists were most often spaced at twelve, sixteen, eighteen, or twenty inches center to center, and were two and a half to three inches thick by eight to twelve inches deep. Most joists were spruce, oak, hemlock, or one of various pine woods. Very expensive grand houses were framed out using oak joists, which are the strongest material but not usual in Rittenhouse. (Old hemlock joists may repel wood-boring insects because of the pitch or resin that is a natural preservative and poison.)

The floor boards were nailed to the top of the wood joists while masons were constructing the exterior and carpenters were constructing the interior walls and partitions. The process was, and still is, done by hand with a crew of craftsmen and laborers constantly getting in one another's way. Built-in defects often were, and are, the result. They don't build them as they used to. They never did.

The first, most important problem to look for in framing is infestation by termites and wood borers. Evidence can easily be seen in the basement at the end of each joist where it rests on the foundation wall. A flashlight and penknife will tell. Push the knife blade into the bottom and side of each joist as close to the wall as possible. If the blade of the knife will not penetrate, there is no problem. If, however, the wood is spongy, there may be wood rot. If dry mud and/or wood powder falls out when the knife is twisted, termites are or have been present. They must be exterminated. If extensive wood eating has taken place and joists are weak, repairs will have to be made to strengthen the structure and restore stability.

There are several ways of doing this, which can be employed either separately or together, depending on circumstances. Application of epoxy or other recently developed wood-reinforcing chemicals may help to solve the problem. In some cases whole beams may have to be replaced. In others, flitching may restore stability. Flitching is done by securing to the old joist with lag or through bolts a new joist or plate of steel or plywood (fig. 75). Wet or dry rot can be detected in the same manner as termites, and repairs made in similar fashion.

Many of the houses of Rittenhouse have been abused by unknowing owners and their mechanics. Excessive loads on unreinforced floors have caused joists to twist, fatigue, and crack. The failure of one joist usually means weakening of several on either side of it. A sag in the floor will usually tell where to look in the basement below. If damage is discovered and correction is necessary, one or more joists may be jacked up to their original position and flitched.

Be careful how you and your mechanics treat the building. Plumbers, heating contractors, and electricians have been known to cut through floor joists to install their materials and equipment without concern for structure. Changing partitions, walls, supports, and columns without making probes into the structure to determine how the change will affect the building could result in damage. The builders of nineteenth-century Rittenhouse buildings used common sense. When reusing these same buildings, common sense, as well as care, must again be employed and stressed.

## Party Walls

Since almost all the private dwellings built in Rittenhouse are rowhouses, special note must be made of the way party walls are constructed, what they do, and how they protect us. Rowhouses are all joined together at common walls or party walls shared on both sides, with an invisible property line running through the wall. The first mission of the party wall is structural. All the floor joists span from party wall to party wall on each floor, carrying the combined loads of self-weight, fixtures, furniture, and people. Some very small early nineteenth-century houses span front to rear. These are rare. The second mission of the party wall is to create a fire barrier between the dwellings in the row. Brick masonry construction is reasonably fireproof and allows a certain amount of time from the start of a fire on one side to its escape on the other. In the nineteenth century fire insurance companies required that a masonry party wall be at least eight inches thick between dwellings, allowing four hours before a fire moved from one house to the next. Temperatures generated by home fires, however, may become so hot that the party wall will split and permit the flames and heat to breach the barrier.

Party walls are constructed of orange (salmon) bricks laid up in mortar, two wyths, or thicknesses, wide, and plastered on both sides (fig. 76). Some courses in the wall are made entirely of headers that bind the two wyths together. The party wall should extend at least twelve inches above the roof surface to ensure that a roof fire will not spread too quickly to adjacent buildings. Many rows of houses in this neighborhood have a common roof covering several buildings with no parapets in between, a potentially dangerous situation about which we can do nothing. Awareness of the condition, however, should inspire us to be particularly careful about fire. As mentioned earlier, installation of fire detectors is advisable.

Wood joists, the timbers that support the floor, rest on the party walls at either side of the house (fig. 77). The timbers are cut to a taper on the long bottom edge that bears on the wall; the top simply supports floor boards.

76. *Party wall with facade removed (Photo by Bernie Cleff)*

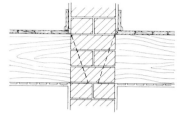

77. *Section through party wall at floor framing*

This taper cut is called the fire cut. In a disastrous fire when the joists burn through and fall out of their pockets, this shape will prevent structural upset of the wall. If a square-cut joist rotated from the pocket in a masonry wall, the action could lift and weaken the party wall, causing damage to adjacent structures.

Faulty construction of party walls is rare even in older, modest rowhouses in Philadelphia, but any weakness will become immediately obvious if an adjacent building is demolished (fig. 78). Rowhouses are structurally interdependent. Remove one house in a row, and all the others are weakened, especially the ones on either side of the demolition. Buildings collapse regularly in Philadelphia and life and property are lost because of adjacent rowhouse demolition. Rehabilitation is always cheaper and far more desirable than such loss.

78. *A rare party wall of wood planks with lath and plaster (no fire barrier) (Photo by Hugh McCauley)*

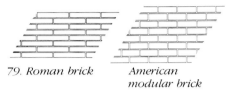

79. *Roman brick*    *American modular brick*

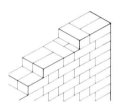

80. *Flemish bond wall*

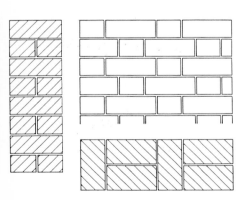

81. *Plan, elevation, and section of Flemish bond wall*

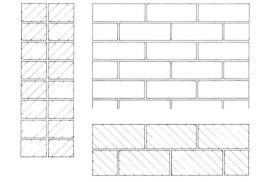

82. *Stretcher, or American, bond wall*

83. *Plan, elevation, and section of Stretcher bond wall*

Exterior Walls    By the time Rittenhouse was being built and settled, no wooden facades were permitted to be constructed in the city, although there are a few isolated examples of clapboard house fronts surviving in this neighborhood. The great London fire of 1666 galvanized the new city planners and urban dwellers of Philadelphia into insisting on fireproof masonry construction in all new buildings (although the rule was not always obeyed). Red brick Philadelphia was as much a reaction to this fear of fire as it was a response to the availability of good, cheap, local red clay.

Most of the dwellings in Rittenhouse are two-, three-, and four-story rowhouses with red brick and white marble or painted wood trim. Many billions of bricks were made in this neighborhood, dug from its pits, fired in its kilns, and laid up by its masons in the walls we see today (fig. 79). Bricks are made from red, loamy, impure clay which is pressed or molded into shape by hand or by ma-

chine, and fired in an oven or kiln to desired hardness. Most face bricks, used on the weathering side, are red, hard, and smooth, and have a life expectancy of many hundreds of years. The backup, so-called salmon brick is orange, soft, and coarse, and will decompose much faster, especially when not protected from the elements. In places where a century ago a careless mason picked soft, porous orange bricks and laid them up with hard bricks, we can now see the odd ones melting and decomposing.

The front wall or facade of a building was built by expert masons who laid the bricks in a wet, sticky mortar. The masons desired the mortar to be ductile and softer than the bricks when dry; they knew by experience that a hard mortar will crack before it gives, or cause the bricks to crack if stress builds up in the wall. A mortar mix of water, cement, and sand, heavy in lime, and sometimes tinted with color, was used in the nineteenth century almost to the exclusion of cement. Portland cement, which is hard and brittle when cured, was not used extensively in the nineteenth century as it is in modern mortar. Laid up in two vertical layers, or wyths, the brick facades, front and rear, were constructed on top of the foundation wall from the first floor line to the cornice, where the facade meets the roof. Even though the facade never carried the loads that the party wall did, it had to be strong enough to resist wind, weather, vibrations, roof loads, and time.

The bond pattern of the brickwork in early Rittenhouse buildings was as functional as it was ornamental. Of the many available styles of brickwork, Flemish bond (figs. 80 and 81) was very popular in colonial Philadelphia and through the 1840s in this neighborhood. After the early 1850s American, or stretcher, bond (figs. 82 and 83), with very thin mortar joints, was thought to be more attractive in its neat, streamlined effect. This trend away from Flemish bond has left us with problems. Because the two wyths are not tied together with headers in American bond, they act separately and are less stable. Pointing of the brickwork was usually done as the wall was going

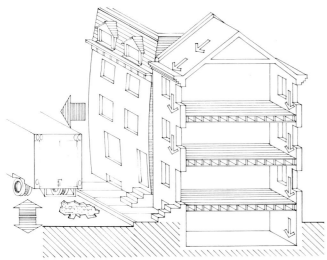

84. *Heavy vehicles on broken streets cause earth tremors and facade damage.*

up, in one of many styles, both functional and attractive.

In the early twentieth century some brick facades were cast over with art stucco work. Using plaster molding shapers, the artists worked the wet stucco, producing brownstone appearance for very little money. Often this treatment served two purposes: to hide old scars or flaws in masonry and to enhance or update a simple building. If the basic wall was sound, this stucco (usually colored dark brown) survives now in good condition.

As mentioned earlier, heavy truck and bus traffic over uneven or broken paving in the street produces shock waves that can actually rattle brickwork loose and cause sheer cracks (vertical and diagonal splits of the brick) at the connection of the front and side walls (fig. 84). This kind of constant shaking will damage any brick facade, no matter how well built. It is especially damaging to a wall of stretcher (American) bond where the two wyths are not a structural unit. The two-wyth wall will separate and each wyth will move independently.

Street excavations left open and allowed to fill with water cause other problems. The water can undermine building foundations, resulting in unnatural and accelerated settling and cracking.

Another cause of cracking is differential settlement. Some buildings in a row were built separately from their neighbors, either earlier or later. In such cases foundation walls and facades may be independent, with cold joints at the corners so there is no connection between transverse and longitudinal walls. Ideally, all walls should act as one unit, sharing the loads from footing to cornice. Cracks may occur when different parts of the building move in different directions. A rowhouse may be called a machine for living, but in fact it is a building, not a mechanism. Mechanisms are designed and built to move. Rowhouses can stand only a limited amount of slow motion.

Examine the exterior walls of your building for diagonal cracks which will appear to step up, following horizontal and vertical brick joints (fig. 85). Look carefully at the bricks around the window frames. A bow in the wall can sometimes be seen better there. Look up the face of the wall from the street. Humps or ripples in the brickwork will tell what is happening. Test for plumb down the face by a weighted string suspended from the top of the wall under the cornice (fig. 86). The basic rule is that if the space between the plumb line and the outside face of the wall at the pavement is equal to or greater than the thickness of the wall (eight to twelve inches), the wall is seriously out of plumb. Action may have to be taken to halt the motion of the wall but full correction can only be made by taking down the wall and rebuilding.

On the interior examine the plaster cracks at the corners where the side and front walls meet. Some cracks may be from old settlement that occurred early in the life of the building; they may be natural to the structure and cause no problem to its useful life and stability. More recent motion in the earth, construction flaws, street vibra-

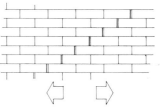

85. *Facade bow may stretch brick, opening vertical mortar joints.*

*Foundation settlement may cause bricks to slip, opening horizontal mortar joints.*

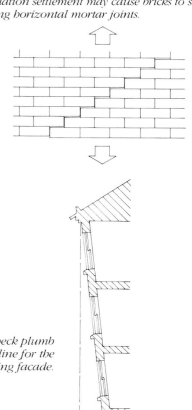

86. *Check plumb line for the leaning facade.*

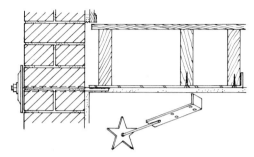

*Weld iron strap to long bolt*

*87. Star bolt methods*

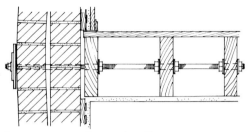

*Do not correct distorted wall,
stop motion and distortion*

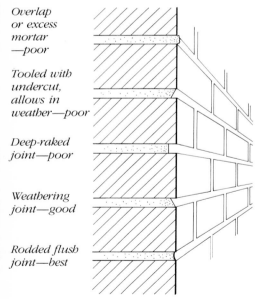

*Overlap
or excess
mortar
—poor*

*Tooled with
undercut,
allows in
weather—poor*

*Deep-raked
joint—poor*

*Weathering
joint—good*

*Rodded flush
joint—best*

*88. Types of mortar joints in brickwork*

tions, or other current sources will continue to work on the walls and cause increasing damage. If there is any doubt about continuing motion in the structural walls, have paper tape telltales placed on the cracks in protected areas. Date them and watch them over a period of weeks to see whether they move or break, indicating movement of the structure.

Call a structural engineer or an architect if there is any doubt of the stability of the facade. Never have structural work done by a contractor until an analysis has been made by a professional. If the damage is so bad that a new wall must be constructed, be sure the new brick and mortar match the old in appearance, and that the wall is bound to the building and to itself in a structurally proper manner. Modern metal wall ties can be used to help bond the masonry together. In some cases, the less radical method of installing star bolts that tie the wall to the joists may be the way to slow down any damage (fig. 87). Check city regulations at the department of Licenses and Inspections before star bolts are used.

**Pointing** When repointing is necessary because of wear and erosion, get a testing laboratory to analyze the existing mortar. Try to match the original appearance and mix of the ingredients as well as the thickness of the joints (fig. 88). Improper pointing with a mixture that is too hard or too soft could result in damage to an otherwise sound brick wall. Very often repointing is not necessary at all, but may be recommended by a contractor in need of work. Minor patch pointing may be all that is needed to give the wall a neat restored appearance.

**Cleaning** Face brick is vulnerable to harm in the cleaning process if abrasive, acidic, or caustic means are used. Never sandblast a brick facade. It is like washing one's face with sandpaper and steel wool instead of soap and water. Sandblasting removes the protective face of the brick causing damage that will age the building by one hundred to two hundred years. Acid and caustic cleaning chemicals can also be very dangerous. Acid will remove the smooth hard face of the brick and attack the mortar, dissolving the cement and lime. Damage from these inappropriate methods of cleaning may not be visible for a few years but will result in permanent injury and shorten the life of the building. Beware of contractors' recommendations to use such methods to clean an older building. Cleaning old masonry should be done with brushes and a mild solution of detergent, without the aid of power tools. The best way to evaluate how to do any cleaning project is to have a test area cleaned and left to dry for ten days before commissioning the whole project. The test area will give all the indications of how your wall will look when entirely cleaned.

**Efflorescence** White salt stains on face brick are called efflorescence, usually the result of water vapor migrating through the wall from an internal source (fig. 89). The most common sources of efflorescence are overflowing roof gutters or internal roof drains, rotted or split downspouts, and heavy rain wind-driven into a freshly cleaned or sandblasted brick wall. Often the bricks just below a window sill show white stains, indicating that the rain water has leaked into the wall through a rotted wood sill or broken stone. Once the evidence begins to appear, corrective measures can be taken. First the source and cause of the leaking water must be found and repaired to stop further damage. New roofing, sheet metal patching, simple carpentry and painting, or a dab of caulking may solve the problem. The exterior stains must dry for a season and then be observed for a period to be certain that no further leakage is taking place. Finally, the efflorescent white powder may be scrubbed off the surface of the brick with dry brushes, then wiped with damp sponges.

*89. Efflorescence stains on brick facade at 22nd and Sansom sts. (Photo by Trina Vaux)*

### Masonry Coatings—Sealers and Paints

Exterior paint and sealers applied over masonry are generally unnecessary. Recent experiments have shown that they prevent moisture in the wall from escaping through normal evaporation. Compound problems may occur if moisture enters an unsealed area high on the wall and migrates to a lower sealed area where it is trapped between the brick and the coating. In such events the weather cycle will freeze the water trapped in the brick, causing the brick to crack, split, and decompose. Once a sealing compound is applied to a masonry wall it is almost impossible to remove it properly without damaging the masonry.

Painting a brick facade in the middle of a block of row houses is also not recommended because it detracts from the intended design. It breaks up the harmony of the street facade in a way never intended by the designers and builders. Once a brick facade is painted, the vicious cycle begins with the flaking, peeling, and repainting or well-intended but damaging sand or caustic chemical cleaning processes.

If you have a once-painted facade that is not original and want to restore the brickwork by removing the paint, do not allow a contractor to use blasting or caustic acids. Paint remover compounds are available that are guaranteed not to damage the brick if specifications and recommended methods are followed by the contractor. Always ask questions, examine the proposed materials, and weigh the advantages and disadvantages before permitting work to be done. Always ask for a free test and allow time to observe the results before having all the work done.

Some buildings were originally meant to have painted facades for protection of soft bricks and for design color. If, through old photographs or records, it is discovered that paint was original to the facade, do not sandblast or remove the paint. Restore it.

### Stucco

Never stucco an older brick facade. It will not enhance the building or solve any structural problems,

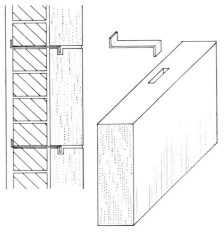

90. *Regular-cut face stone secured with metal cramp*

and the scoring necessary to make the stucco adhere to the brick causes irreversible damage. In addition, wire mesh nailed to bricks may cause or hide damage under the stucco. Do not conceal structural problems that should be corrected. From the 1880s to 1920 art stucco was applied to ordinary brick facades to give an air of taste and wealth. Many were superb designs that can be easily restored as necessary but only by an expert stucco contractor.

**Stone Facades**   Cut stone masonry facades are various and numerous in Rittenhouse. Stone used as the outer skin of a masonry wall is similar to face brick and installed in much the same way, with soft backup brick used for the wall behind the stone face. The skin of stone is usually four inches thick and cut into panels several feet on a side. Metal wall ties called cramps are employed to lock the brick to the face stone (fig. 90). These ties or cramps were needed since there was no opportunity to bond the thicknesses of brick (inside) to the stone (outside) by header courses.

The choice of stone in place of brick as a face material gave great decorative advantages to the rowhouse because the stone could be carved. Ornamental stone at every level of a building showed wealth, taste, and pride. The kind of stone used was an economic consideration as well as an aesthetic preference.

Many well-preserved soft stone facades are now in a good state of repair because they were painted early in the life of the building. Since the stone was porous, the paint was absorbed and sealed the surface, preserving the details while presenting a color sympathetic to the stone.

**Granite**   Granite is an igneous rock, formed under high, volcanic heat. It is without doubt the stone best suited for facade construction, since it will resist decay caused by weather. Granite is rare except on institutional structures because it is very expensive to quarry and difficult to work, carve, and erect.

**Limestone**   Limestone is a brilliant white sedimentary rock formed under water, and is also suited to facade construction. It is much softer than granite, and easy to cut, shape, and erect. Limestone has a grainy surface texture that can catch airborne dirt and will stain and wear away in the rain and corrosive elements of the city's industrial atmosphere. It is most commonly used for lintels, window sills, and water tables, but is also found as a face material on institutional buildings or on homes built by the late nineteenth-century wealthy of this neighborhood. In some cases front steps and rail walls of limestone show how wear and tear has weathered away edges and carving.

**Sandstone (Brownstone)**   Sandstone is nature's own terra cotta or brick. Found under hard clay, it is a sedimentary rock made up of fine mineral grains of quartz or arkosic (granite and feldspar) sand, ranging in color and hardness from light pink (hard) to reddish brown (soft). Easy to quarry, cut, shape, and erect, brownstone was

91. *Decomposing brownstone edge (Photo by Bernie Cleff)*

used for the facades of whole blocks by the architects and builders of late nineteenth-century Rittenhouse. Brownstone and other facing stones (limestone and serpentine) were generally not used for structural building parts.

Natural erosion, aided by acid pollutants in the air, will wear away soft stone (fig. 91). Corrosive elements in our atmosphere are carried by rain or wind and deposited on stone work. They dissolve into the grains of the stone surface, etching the external layer of the stone. For as much as this process accelerates decay and disfigurement, it is not always structurally dangerous.

The more porous stones allow moisture penetration and saturation. In freezing weather the water expands and causes splits along the weakest lines of the stone. Moisture will also cause the metal wall ties or cramps to rust and rot away, weakening the connection between the face material and the backup brick. Moldings, lintels, and sills are visibly melting because of rain wear. Natural rifts in the stone are opening, allowing layers of sediment to separate.

A New York geologist in the late nineteenth century criticized builders there for erecting brownstone on building facades with no regard for the bedding plane. The sedimentary stone is formed in horizontal planes under water and is strongest when it lies with its layering lines horizontal, in the position in which it was formed. Laying the stone in an upright position and adding weight by piling other stones on top will cause it to fracture and delaminate over time. This explains some of the many problems apparent in brownstone facades of Rittenhouse.

Solutions are numerous, depending on the nature of the problem. On a painted facade where new stone will have to be placed next to existing, the old and new may be painted with a common color. On an unpainted brownstone front it is almost impossible to match colors. Dirt and age have mellowed and changed the hue of the stone so that new, freshly cut stone will look obvious.

Tinted cement patching is often used where details have broken down or corners or edges have chipped off. Such patching is a continuing maintenance trial and never achieves a good match in color, texture, or shape.

If deterioration and damage have progressed to such a serious stage on a brownstone facade that certain stones are beginning to crumble, they must be replaced. The best way to do the job properly is to perform a kind of macro-dentistry. Have a length of stone cut exactly to match the existing profile, then cut out only the area where natural damage has occurred. Place the new material in the cavity prepared and anchor it to the backup wall with steel pins or cramps and grout. This may have to be done in several areas of a facade at the same time, and repeated in other areas in the future, until much of the wall has been refaced. The process is costly, but unlike patching, will look right, be sound, and last a long time.

Never stucco a brownstone facade. It may look reasonable at first but it will invariably change color and stand out next to the old stone. In frustration some brownstone owners have resorted to having the entire wall stuccoed. This method is the very worst reaction to the problem: it dulls all the detail when finished, and obscures the good parts of the wall as well as the damaged parts. Once the wall is scarified or lathed to receive the stucco there is no hope of future restoration.

One very cheap but questionable method of dealing with the problem is to mix sand with a paint tinted to match the brownstone or green serpentine and trowel it on with wide brushes. Though not highly recommended, it can make the wall look better than shaggy flaking old brownstone in decomposition.

Green serpentine stone melts away and decays from within. It is attractive material used for facades during the latter part of the last century but restoration is almost impossible. Green oriental art stucco applied over bad areas may be the only way to correct defects.

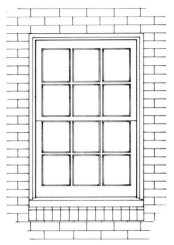

6-over-6 Colonial window,
popular since 18th century

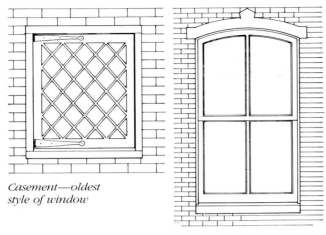

Casement—oldest
style of window

2-over-2 Victorian window,
late 19th century

92. Windows: Sash types

93. Windows on Pine St. (Photo by Hugh McCauley)

94. Section through double-hung window.
Air drafts can be sealed with weatherstripping.

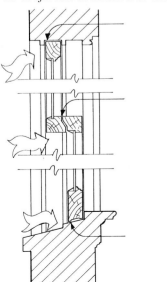

# Windows

Windows allow light to enter and afford a view of the street, while keeping weather out. The simple double-hung wooden window is a fragile mechanism that should be inspected and maintained more often than most other parts of the building. As seen in the illustrations (figs. 92 and 93), windows give evidence of style, and there are various designs belonging to different periods which should not be misapplied.

Practically speaking, wooden windows are the best for homes in this neighborhood. Wood is a natural insulating material that will not allow easy transmission of cold from outdoors. When an old wooden window sash is worn out by exposure to the elements it is usually due to lack of paint and putty over many years. If properly maintained, a wooden sash will last at least seventy-five years.

Even with reasonable maintenance problems will occur in wooden windows where the bottom rail of the sash meets the window sill. Rain water may be trapped in the joint when absorbed by capillary action. The longer water is trapped in the space the more opportunity it has to seep into the wood and eventually cause rot where the side stiles meet the bottom rail. Paint, properly applied, will stave off this damage and good weather stripping will keep excess moisture out of the sill area (fig. 94).

Storm windows protect the painted sash and save energy by reducing heat loss, but they can detract from the appearance of a fine nineteenth-century facade and window ensemble. Modern storm windows can be mounted on the interior of the frame where the energy-saving advantage will not detract from the overall exterior design. Shutters and blinds also, if used properly, will help protect windows and save on energy (see below).

New wooden replacement window sash matching existing ones can be ordered at reasonable prices from most area lumber and building supply companies. Prepainting and installation are a simple weekend do-it-yourself job. Try to maintain the original architectural detail and character of the building by keeping the original

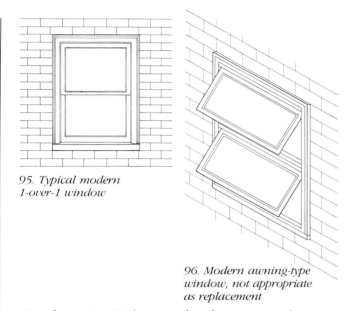

95. *Typical modern
1-over-1 window*

96. *Modern awning-type
window, not appropriate
as replacement*

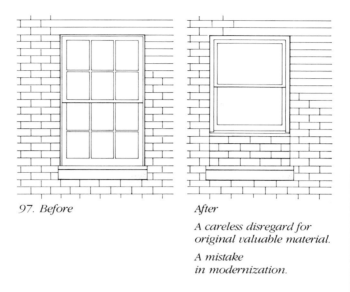

97. *Before*   *After*

*A careless disregard for
original valuable material.*

*A mistake
in modernization.*

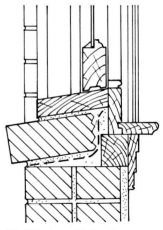

98. *Window sill detail*

size of opening. Modern metal replacement windows are hard to find in sizes that match the original opening. Smaller windows placed in an oversized frame where the lintel has been lowered or the sill built up is damaging to the streetscape in general and mars the appearance of the building in particular. They are also more difficult to install. Metal replacement sash allow condensation on the interior in the winter, and this leads to more complicated maintenance headaches. With windows and other significant exterior details or appurtenances use the principle of same-for-same when replacement becomes necessary (figs. 95, 96, 97).

## Window Sills

Window sills are important but vulnerable protective elements of a building. They are designed to shield the masonry under the window opening, and should slope away from the opening to shed water as quickly as possible.

The window sill is one of the most likely places where structural damage can begin to weaken the wall of a building. A lack of timely maintenance will allow rain water to seep into and rot a wooden sill, dissolve the old mortar in warm weather and expand and split the masonry joints in freezing weather (fig. 98). Proper care of window sills will prevent this kind of damage. The sill should be examined every year to monitor its wear and condition and it should be painted at least every five years. If a wooden window sill has decomposed (this can be determined by probing with a very sharp knife), it can be replaced with a new piece of hard red pine or cedar timber cut to match the original and secured to the remainder of the undamaged sill. If the wear is serious but replacement is not yet possible, a piece of sheet metal, preferably copper, or lead coated stainless steel, may be used to cover the sill to extend its life for many years. Wood putty, plastic resins, and epoxy coatings are available to make repairs where the wood has begun to open, crack, and splinter.

Doors Throughout the last century designers and carpenters paid a great deal of attention to the entry. Doors and their surrounds were expressive of the times, styles, and tools of craftsmen and machines. In many buildings there are very few places to show architectural character. The special attention to detail and beauty at the entry allows form and function to blend. When looking at a building from the street, one is drawn to focus on the entry.

Wood panels, cut or stained glass, iron grills, bright brass hardware in many styles can be seen in original condition at entry doors in this neighborhood. It is very hard to understand building owners who would throw away a fine set of doors simply because they need repair and paint. A wooden door maintained properly will last for many generations and should be retained if replacement is necessary so that the original can be given to the mill where a new one can be made to match it. This may sound expensive but the truth is that several lumber dealers in the city have made a reputation for this kind of replacement work, and the cost is nothing in relation to the many years it will endure. The value of the property can be enhanced if original doors are kept and cared for (fig. 99).

Wood is a natural insulation material. It is easy to shape and is strong but lightweight. Various pine woods were used in the last century to build doors, red hard pine was a favored material because it would not dry out and shrink or warp like softer pine. When fitted to a sturdy frame of the same material or hemlock it could be made almost draftproof. This not only kept out weather but the noise and dust of the street as well. After many years of hard use, especially on large houses that have become apartment buildings, these doors may have pulled away from the frames and hinges may have broken. The fancy locksets may have been taken as collector's items and the moving of furniture may also have scratched and broken the edges of fine old doors. Abuse has left them in disgraceful condition and shabby appearance, but neglect by the owner is often the culprit.

Follow the principle of same-for-same when the entry doors and surrounds must be overhauled. Improve the situation with weatherstripping that is not seen from the outside, light the entry area to discourage vandals and night collectors. If storm doors are a must, select full-view safety glass with frames of compatible color. In this way the door can still be seen as a part of the architecture and modern protection and energy conservation can be incorporated at the same time.

*99. Types of doors*

*Six-panel Colonial, or Christian, door, popular since 18th century*

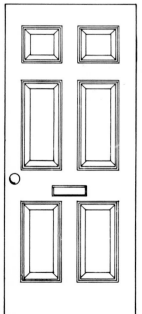

*Two-panel Greek door, 1840s–60s*

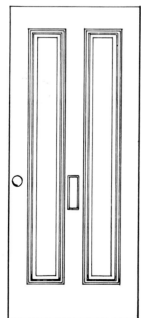

*Four-panel Commandments door, 1850s–70s*

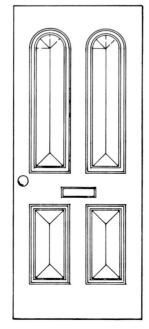

*Modern replacement door, not appropriate*

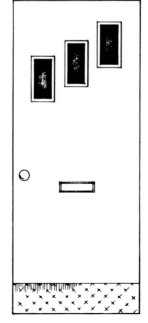

## Shutters and Blinds

Shutters and blinds are made of wood. Shutters have solid panels; blinds have louvers in the panel openings (fig. 100). Most houses in Rittenhouse were built with external shutters on the first and second floors and blinds on the third and/or attic floors. In winter the shutters were used to keep the warmth of the house inside, especially at night, while in summer the shutters were left open at night to allow cool air into the building and closed during the day to keep out the heat of the sun. This very successful climate control also involved the use of blinds on the upper floors where the windows behind the louvers could be left open in warm weather allowing breezes to flow and providing a privacy and sunlight screen.

The same maintenance rules apply to shutters and blinds as to window sash. Since shutters and blinds are exposed to weather, they are usually built to be very sturdy, and their top end is covered with thin sheet metal or copper to keep direct rain from entering the wood. As with windows, the style of shutter should match the style of building. If correctly made and maintained, a pair of wooden shutters will last the life of the windows, depending on exposure.

When water is allowed to enter the joints where the rails and stiles are connected, the joints rot and weaken so that eventually the shutter falls apart. Frequent inspection, painting, and repair is the only way to keep these parts of the building in good condition and working order.

There is a tendency to use shutters only as decorative and ornamental items which are secured to the building wall. Often they are of the wrong size and have strap hinges mounted on the wrong side of the leaf (fig. 101). Plastic and aluminum imitation shutters seriously detract from the appearance of a fine nineteenth-century building. These fake shutters can never be made to operate, and cost far more than they are worth. Having new wooden shutters made with proper working hardware is

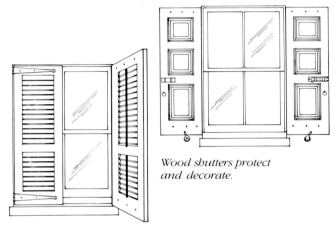

*Wood shutters protect and decorate.*

*100. Blinds appropriate above first floor.*

expensive, but it is a once-in-a-lifetime investment that will enhance and protect the building.

A low-cost do-it-yourself method of building shutters is to make them from A-A exterior grade plywood (fig. 102). Each leaf is made of two ¾-inch-thick layers, with the back solid and the front plunge-cut to make panels. Lath strips and simple base cap molding make up the trim. When all the parts are glued and screwed together, primer-sealed and painted, and hung with the proper hardware, it is hard to distinguish them from more expensive custom-milled shutters. Many hardware stores in this area stock strap hinges, bar latches, and dogs or hold backs. These pieces are made of mild steel because wrought iron is rare, but a good coat of red zinc oxide primer before installation and painting will keep the metal from rusting. If the original shutters are still stored in the basement or attic and can be repaired and painted, restore and reinstall them. If one or two badly worn shutters can be found, use them as the models to make up new ones.

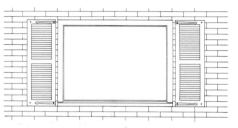

*101. Picture window is suburban; shutters would never cover glass area.*

*102 Do-it-yourself shutters*

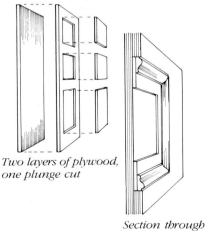

*Two layers of plywood, one plunge cut*

*Section through shutter, showing plywood and molding*

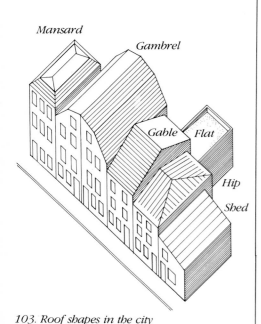

*Mansard*

*Gambrel*

*Gable* *Flat*

*Hip*

*Shed*

*103. Roof shapes in the city*

*104. Roof with dormer and chimney*

*Valley flashing at dormer gable and step flashing at cheeks*

*Brick chimney with step flashing and spark arrestor*

## Roofing

No matter how beautiful the interior or how well built the masonry structure of a building, the roof is the weakest link; without a sound and watertight roof the building and its contents are threatened.

The buildings of Rittenhouse have an amazing variety of roof shapes and materials (fig. 103), but in all cases under structure (roof deck) is wooden planking, which must be kept dry and sound. Roof leaks will cause rot and weakening of the deck, rafters, ceilings, walls, and floors if they are not repaired.

The earliest houses in Rittenhouse were built with a gabled roof covered with wooden shingles. These roofs were almost watertight for several decades of weather but were eventually covered with sheet iron, galvanized metal, tin plate, or terne metal. The metal roofing ultimately developed pin holes from rust and was covered with felt paper and hot tar. Eventually four old roof surfaces were buried under another new one. In this kind of

piled-up roof, leaks may develop that can never be traced and corrected.

In the late nineteenth century the most expensive buildings with steep slope roofs were built with sheet copper or slate roofing, installed very carefully by expert craftsmen and designed to last the life of the building. As newer, so-called flat-roofed houses were built, the use of felt paper and hot tar provided cheaper, faster, waterproof roof surfaces. (No roof is really flat; the surface must be pitched in one or more directions so the water drains off the roof as soon as possible.)

Eventually every roof will develop a leak somewhere and patching will be necessary to hold off for as long as possible the large costs involved in reroofing. When it becomes apparent that a new roof is necessary, pick the material carefully, since in some cases it is very much a part of the design, intended to be seen. Listed here, in order of value and applicability for different roof shapes, are materials that may be expected to make a roof surface watertight.

High-cost original roofing materials for steep roofs include the following: red clay tiles; slate shingles; wood shingles; standing-seam copper; standing-seam terne metal; galvanized folded seam. Lower-cost replacement materials for such roofs include the following: mineral-surface asphalt shingles or more costly simulated standing-seam aluminum. Weights of modern asphalt roof shingles are specified in pounds per 100 square feet. The higher the number, the longer they will last and the higher the cost for material and labor.

High-cost modern roofing materials for flat roofs include the following: vulcanized sheet rubber; five-ply hot asphalt with gravel ballast; four-ply felt with steep asphalt; three-ply fiberglass-backed sheet asphalt. A lower-cost replacement material for such roofs is mineral surface ninety-pound cold-roll asphalt.

It is always expensive but wise to remove all old roofing material before installing new. When the deck of the

105. Slate roofs and metal roofs

Roof planks with
felt paper and
slate shingles

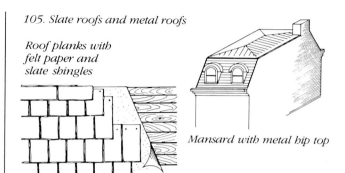

Mansard with metal hip top

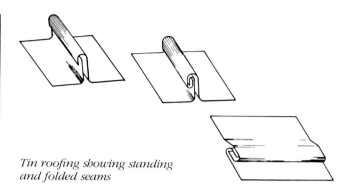

Tin roofing showing standing
and folded seams

Installing a metal roof,
1896 Chicago catalogue

roof is exposed, repairs can be made that will make the new material last longer. This also allows installation of new deck insulation, which will replace the insulation value of the old layers of material. Examine the proposed material before allowing it to be installed on your roof.

The tools, equipment, and heavy labor involved in re-roofing should discourage all but the most dedicated do-it-yourselfer from taking on the project alone. When interviewing roofing contractors always ask for an estimate with specifications and a particular manufacturer's guarantee of materials. Every roofing materials manufacturer has a guaranteed system which is spelled out in a set of specifications that tells the roofer just how to install the material. The roofing contractor must follow the specifications in order for the guarantee to be valid.

If a roof leak occurs, an inspection should be made to determine whether a whole new roof is necessary or if a patch is all that is needed. Often an owner goes into panic and agrees with the first roofer who visits the building to replace the entire roof. On very steep roofs the leaking may simply be caused by a worn-out gutter or valley flashing. There are hundreds of roofing contractors in the yellow pages, but with luck and some skill you may be able to find the right one. Ask for a list of local satisfied customers who can vouch for the quality of work. Costs are so various for roofing of domestic buildings in Center

City that the only way to come to a decision is to get at least three estimates based on the same specifications. Remember that the low bidder is not always the most reliable. You get what you pay for. An added cost but a wise investment may be a maintenance agreement that will bring the original roofer back to examine and recoat the new roof after a year of wear. At this time any problem areas can be dealt with. Ice, rain, and wind can do great damage in a short time. It is wise to inspect your roof each year in early winter to check for wear and to clear gutters and drains of debris.

Only minor repairs are necessary each year to keep a good roof from becoming a problem. Never put hot or cold tar sealant on a painted tin roof; it will cause rust. The petroleum-base product will only accelerate damage and obscure the area where patching is necessary. Never mix materials; use the basic principle of same-for-same in making repairs. Never join two dissimilar metals if it can be avoided. In a humid atmosphere there could be electrolytic action in which aluminum and copper (for example) will destroy each other. Never walk directly on a slate roof. The roof should be covered with wide planks so that the slates will not be cracked. Roofing, as it is done today, is probably the least exact of the building trades. Learn all you can about methods and materials before signing a contract.

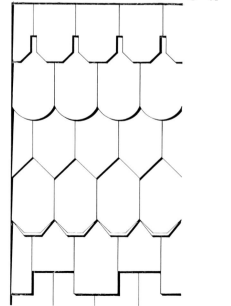

106. Various Victorian vintage shingle types

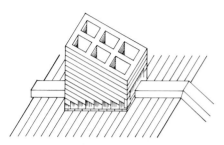

*107. Cluster (with many flues) chimney with metal step flashing and metal parapet cover*

*108. New metal chimney liner details*

Many buckets of concrete give stability and seal up voids

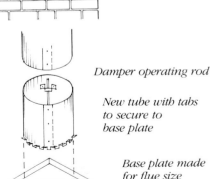

Damper operating rod

New tube with tabs to secure to base plate

Base plate made for flue size

If sheet metal rusts away, the concrete acts as flue

## Chimneys

A brick chimney passing through the roof, exhausting a fireplace or a heat plant (furnace) has three important attributes: a watertight seal between the roof and the masonry, structural stability, and fireproof construction. The roofer is responsible for the flashing that creates the water seal, a brick or cement mason may be necessary for the structural integrity, and a good old-fashioned chimney sweep for the safe operation of the flue. Take no chances with an old brick chimney; have it inspected at least every five years by a sweep so that it can be cleaned and repaired if necessary. Weather cap and spark arrestor equipment should be installed to prevent rain from pouring down the open flue and deteriorating the masonry and to keep hot sparks from rising out of the flue and onto the roof. Top-hatted women and men with dirty morning coats are in the neighborhood each fall working on rooftops and standing on high brick chimneys. Thanks to the energy crisis in the last decade, the sweeps have returned to Rittenhouse.

Alterations to old brick chimneys or lack of maintenance may create problems that eventually will cost trouble and money. Typical problems include eroded mortar which permits the brickwork to crumble. One brick at a time may fall down the flue or onto the roof; rain can get into the structure behind flashing and cause unseen rot or serious visible roof leaks. Repointing a brick chimney is one of the easiest jobs to do and needs doing only about every twenty-five years. Crooked chimneys can often be solidified by parging with stucco if it will not be seen. But for an ornamental brick chimney viewed from the street, this easy repair may not look right.

Some brick chimney flues were built with no interior liner, thus allowing fire and smoke to leak into the building at openings and faults between floors or in attic spaces. This is dangerous and must be corrected if you plan to use an old fireplace or to vent an oil burner through an old brick flue. Relining will make the old flue fireproof and will solidify the structure of the chimney. One method is to insert prefabricated stainless steel tube sections, lowered from the top of the chimney (fig. 108). Each section should be secured to the next and the first, or bottom, section should have a metal flange which fits snug against the inside of the old flue. When the new metal flue is in place and secured at the top, lightweight concrete is poured all around the metal flue liner, filling the space between the old bricks and the new metal. The process should be done slowly, filling no more than one floor height per day, lest too much heavy wet concrete push the old brick shaft walls and possibly collapse the chimney.

Top-mounted dampers can easily be installed on a chimney where there is no damper at the throat. Installing throat dampers is very hard to do without opening the masonry from the interior and making a mess of the house.

The burning of soft wood should be discouraged no matter what the flue is like because it leaves a tar residue on the flue which will build up over time. This residue may ignite and shoot flames into the room or out onto the roof, causing a fire. It is safer to burn hard wood and hard coal in an open hearth fireplace.

## Parapets

The masonry party wall between buildings should project above the roof line to about one foot above the highest adjacent building. The mission of this projection, or parapet, is to act as a fire barrier between the structures on either side. In case of a serious fire the houses without parapets separating them will share the damage more than those with a full parapet. The masonry parapet should be covered and flashed to protect it from weather. The roofing from one structure should not lap over the parapet and contact the adjacent roofing material.

Parapets are most common on two- and three-story flat-roofed houses in this neighborhood built since the 1860s. Older rows of gable- and shed-roofed structures were often built without parapets, with common roofing boards spanning over several houses. The party walls stop at the underside of the roof deck. In several examples the party wall stops at the third floor ceiling, so that the attic space above is common to all of the adjacent structures.

Knowing the nature of a problem or hazard allows for choices in precautions and protection. Complete replacement of a missing parapet can be done only at vast expense, while a good fire prevention program, including a first-class detection system, is much cheaper. Certain very old fire insurance companies in Philadelphia (the home of such companies) will not today insure a house without a parapet. Most ordinary insurance carriers who do not inspect before covering will write a policy and disregard the construction characteristics.

Like any other part of the building, the parapet will need regular inspection and maintenance. If the bricks or mortar joints are exposed to the weather, they may wear and leaking could occur. Where the roofing material meets the parapet, flashing may rust and pit, allowing rain to enter the structure. As with a chimney, the parapet must be flashed and sealed where it passes through the roof to prevent leaks leading to structural as well as interior finish damage.

## Cornices and Gutters
Where an exterior wall meets the roof at the top of a building there is a cornice of some kind (fig. 109). Wood, metal, and masonry were and still are used to make the connection between the roof and wall structurally sound, weather-tight, and architecturally attractive. Styles of cornices are probably more various than any other architectural treatment in this neighborhood.

Their practical aspects are just as important as their aesthetics—perhaps more so—when it comes to maintenance and preservation of a building. Since this part of the structure is hard to reach without a tall ladder, it may

be neglected. Unchecked damage to the cornice could allow rain water to permeate and weaken the whole facade below. If the roofing is also faulty, leaks in the interior of the house could result as well. Such damage can be very expensive to repair.

Wooden cornices are put together with nails that will corrode and need replacement, masonry cornices will need pointing, and tin cornices will have to be patched (if only to keep the pigeons from nesting). If the rain gutter is part of the cornice assembly, the wear will be greater because of overflowing storm water and winter ice action.

On a gable roof the cornice is usually attached to the tail end of the rafters. The assembly closes the joint between the roof and wall and seals the spaces between the rafters. The soffit of the cornice is usually at the attic floor line. Venting the soffit or frieze to allow air flow will help keep the material from retaining moisture that may cause rot.

Gutters can be either attached to or built into the cornice assembly. The gutter conducts the water it catches to one or more drains so that the water will not fall at random from the roof and spill all over the wall of the building. Many centuries of practical experience have given us the standard methods used to protect and prolong the life of our buildings. Gutters are just another important element needing attention in the annual maintenance list.

In the fall the leaves of trees will be blown and washed into the gutters. We cannot see them but we know that they are there and that they will form a dam around the drain, causing water to back up and pool on the roof. In addition, the gutter will overflow and send water sheeting down the front or rear wall, washing away mortar and seeping into the structure. At the end of each fall, when most of the trees are bare, gutters should be cleaned of all leaves. If necessary, the drain should be cleared with a wire to make sure water will not be blocked. Wire strainers are normally used to prevent blocking of the drain and downspout.

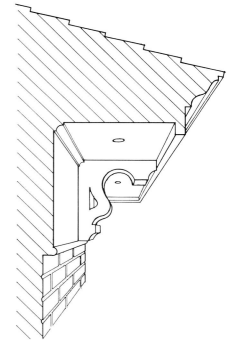

*109. Typical bracketed cornice over brick wall. Soffit has spaced vent holes.*

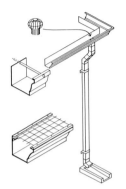

Metal basket strainer in gutter

K type gutter secured to cornice with spike

Continuous metal screen will keep out debris

*110. Gutter and downspout system for yard with drain*

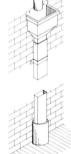

*111. Leader head or collector box secured to wall. Downspout connects to house sewer pipe.*

*112. Downspouts: do not allow water to enter foundations; direct water away from building.*

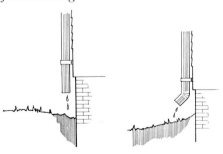

# Downspouts

The pipe that is connected to the low end of a gutter is the downspout, conductor, or leader. Sometimes attached to a collector box below the cornice, the pipe is also clamped to the wall of the building at each floor line (figs. 110 and 111). This is to prevent the wind from blowing it away. Some leaders spill water on the ground near a drain in a yard (fig. 112), while most evacuate it into the sanitary soil system. The downspout should be large enough to drain the roof area.

Downspouts are made of galvanized iron or sheet metal, aluminum, or copper. They may be round or square, with or without fluting. Every manufacturer has a different system of fabrication and of securing the material together. The most recent designs are made of plastic but look exactly like the aluminum that is now the standard of the trade.

Problems with old downspouts include damage from winter freezing, which can go unnoticed for a long time. When wind cools already cold metal, wet slushy snow pouring into the downspout will freeze solid and expand in the pipe, causing it to split on the seam facing the wall. This will block the draining action and allow water to spill out onto the building wall and freeze into the brickwork. Repair is usually impossible. Replacement is not too expensive but it must be done before the spring rains pour vast quantities of water onto the wall. Old iron downspouts that have rusted through on the side against the wall will produce the same damage. Replacement with a better material is recommended.

The connection of the leader to the iron soil line at pavement level is another vulnerable spot. Vandals or auto bumpers may crush the pipe, cutting off the water flow. When this occurs the line will block, joints will leak, and the gutter will eventually overflow. Correction is easy, but the inspection is important. Look carefully at these things and keep alert to small problems before they become large expensive ones.

*114. Iron foot scraper in marble block (Photo by Hugh McCauley)*

*113. Decorative detail (Photo by Bernie Cleff)*

*115. Old brick paving (Photo by Hugh McCauley)*

# STREETSCAPES

The Rittenhouse neighborhood has a nineteenth-century character that derives from the collection of buildings lining its streets. The streets constitute almost one half of the real estate of the neighborhood. They are not just empty space or a government-owned no man's land. They are rooms, with walls, floors, and open ceilings, and they affect and reflect our attitude toward them and ourselves. The relationship between real estate values and the quality of the streetscape cannot be ignored.

The outdoor room that is the streetscape is defined by the flanking facades from door stoop to cornice line. In the outdoor room are simple elements: iron and brass

*116. Street games (Photo by Hugh McCauley)*

handrails; foot scrapers; basement window grills; shutters and flowerboxes or planters; trees; the brick, slate, or concrete footway; the curb and cartway. As each building or block of buildings has character, so do the streets, the spaces between and around the buildings.

The streetscape has elements and aspects that can be dealt with and improved by individuals and groups of

*117. Brick paving patterns, more appropriate than concrete*

| *Herringbone* | *Parquet pattern* | *Running bond* |
|---|---|---|

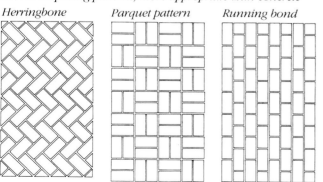

neighbors. The Center City Residents' Association has for many years had a street tree program that has enhanced the entire neighborhood with green, cool, and friendly shade on streets that were absolutely blank. This program has offered an umbrella under which neighbors can work on other important details that make these streets more livable and handsome.

If, for example, the sidewalk in front of the building you own is scheduled by the city for replacement because of heaving and cracked concrete, you have to bear the cost. Think of using red brick pavers instead of the concrete (fig. 117). Check costs with various contractors and let it be known to the city authorities that you want to do this. Get the support of your neighbors, who were probably also given notices depending on the condition of their footway or pavement and curb. The new pavers may cost one hundred to three hundred dollars more than ordinary concrete, but the great change would enhance your property by a greater factor.

Another example of improving the streetscape may be in using a large square flue tile adjacent to the front steps for evergreens, seasonal flowers, or climbing ivy vines. These are not expensive, and masonry supply companies in the city have them and will deliver and place them. The only problem may be the city ordinances. Check with the local building inspector first and talk it over with your neighbors. If several people work on such projects at the same time the change for the better will be that much faster and easier.

Previous chapters have given the historical background of the neighborhood as well as descriptions of architectural styles. All of this information may help give a feeling of pride in the community. That pride will show in the understanding and care for the buildings as well as for the spaces we take for granted while walking along Delancey Place or Waverly Street. Each street should have its own identity; careful examination today will reveal the potential of the streetscapes of Rittenhouse.

*118. Railing detail (Photo by Bernie Cleff)*

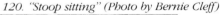

*119. Keep up with repairs*
*(Photo by Hugh McCauley)*

*120. "Stoop sitting" (Photo by Bernie Cleff)*

# METHODS FOR PRESERVATION

## TRINA VAUX

*Academy of Music and Academy House*
*(Photo by Bernie Cleff)*

Introduction    In 1875 when a Rittenhouse resident, Mrs. Elizabeth Duane Gillespie, was directing the Centennial Women's Committee, she might well have assumed that the buildings she lived and worked in would last forever, that the monuments going up in Fairmount Park would form a legacy to be cherished by generations of Americans. A century later only one of the major centennial buildings is left, and the house in which Mrs. Gillespie lived has been replaced. Decay, changing tastes, and progress have altered much that was taken for granted in previous eras.

Yet the 1876 Centennial Exposition, while it celebrated progress, also marked a revival of interest in the colonial and post-Revolutionary past. Not too long afterward, the Mount Vernon Ladies' Association of the Union mounted its successful effort to preserve George Washington's home. And as the twentieth century dawned, some Americans became conscious that resources were finite—even in the United States. Theodore Roosevelt advocated preservation of public lands and, in the Antiquities Act of 1906, public buildings as well. Frederick Law Olmsted, the great park designer, predicted that the national parks would soon be so crowded that appointments to see them would have to be made a year in advance.

In the first half of the twentieth century, citizens' groups organized to restore and maintain historic houses as museums. Almost every area of the country spawned an old homestead preserved as a monument to its favorite native son. In the 1950s Philadelphia embarked on the revitalization of Society Hill, which became a model of urban renewal as well as preservation of eighteenth-century buildings. In the 1970s interest in nineteenth-century architecture began to grow, and the popularity of neighborhoods such as Rittenhouse boomed.

While interest in nineteenth-century architecture has increased over the last decade, so has concern for preservation generally. This concern has been reflected in more legislation and in the expansion of national, state, and local programs encouraging preservation of historic buildings. Recognition of buildings of state and local, as well as national, importance has widened. Tax incentives are available to assist preservation efforts. Review processes have been established to discourage damage to historically important structures.

In addition to public programs, there are measures that individuals and groups can take on their own to pre-

*121. Northwest corner, Rittenhouse Square, with Holy Trinity Church and Plaza Apartments (Photo by George E. Thomas)*

serve buildings. The use of such techniques as easements and adaptive reuse has gained in sophistication and frequency in the last few years. Community groups throughout the country are increasing their efforts in planning for preservation and in establishing historic districts and commissions and protective zoning.

In Rittenhouse a survey of architectural resources was conducted as part of a federally mandated statewide program. A Rittenhouse National Register Historic District has been established based on the survey and the boundaries it recommended. National Register status now affords protections and tax benefits, as well as distinction, to the neighborhood.

The following section describes basic preservation programs and methods currently practiced. It is designed to be used with the Procedures section, which gives specific details on inspection and research methods and applying for federal, state, and local programs. Addresses for all the agencies mentioned and reprints of federal guidelines for grants and tax advantages may be found in the Appendix.

## Planning
Forethought is an effective deterrent to destruction of valuable buildings. It is usually too late for discussion when the wrecker's ball arrives at a site. Preservation of historic buildings is often difficult, but it becomes easier when preservation goals are included in overall community plans.

The planning process is a continuing one, the aim of which is to deal rationally with the future, based on solid information from the past and present. Knowing which buildings in a community are of value is a fundamental tool for physical planning. Over the past few years a comprehensive historic architectural survey of Philadelphia has been carried out under the auspices of the State Bureau for Historic Preservation and the Philadelphia Historical Commission. The survey, which includes Rittenhouse, shows existing buildings, their age, physical state,

use, and an assessment of their significance. These data are now filed at the bureau and commission offices and are available to the public.

The object of the survey is not to embalm Rittenhouse in amber to remain untouched by developers forever. It is designed as a tool to guide development and change. Using the survey, the community and the city can set priorities and determine goals that take into account the historical significance and character of the neighborhood and individual areas in it. Thus, general development can be encouraged while truly valuable historic elements are preserved.

Planning requires constant communication between state and local authorities, such as the State Bureau for Historic Preservation and the City Planning and Historical commissions, and community groups and individuals. It entails awareness of what is going on in the community and a sense of neighborhood goals. Reasoned discussion in advance based on solid information, and an ability on all sides to compromise, can be more effective in furthering preservation than leaflets and protests at the eleventh hour.

## Federal Laws and Programs
Preservation at the federal level began with the Historic Sites Act of 1935, which established a national policy of preserving for public use historic sites, buildings, and objects of national significance. The Secretary of the Interior was designated to carry out this policy by surveying and preserving data on properties of exceptional value, and to acquire them as National Parks.

Prior to 1935, the Historic American Buildings Survey had been established as part of the Works Progress Administration to give architects employment measuring and drawing historic buildings. Some commemorative sites had been placed under the jurisdiction of the Department of the Interior. The Historic Sites Act served to expand this kind of activity and to establish national recognition of historically significant buildings.

Some thirty years later, passage of the National Historic Preservation Act of 1966 with subsequent amendments, plus enactment of successive tax laws starting in 1976, has expanded federal policy and programs to include a range of activity beyond documentation and acquisition of memorials. Programs established since 1966 have reflected an increasing awareness of the value of historic buildings to community life across the nation. Generally, they encourage preservation through recognition procedures, tax incentives, grants, and review processes. The recognition programs (National Landmarks and National Register), tax laws, and grants are discussed later in this section.

Federal law is designed to encourage preservation not only in the private sector but in the public arena as well. There are a number of provisions that require federal agencies to survey, record, and nominate to the National Register appropriate buildings, sites, and structures under their control. Moreover, Section 106 of the Historic Preservation Act requires review of any project carried out with federal assistance that may affect a property listed on or eligible for the National Register. This includes activity of a federal agency or of any public or private organization licensed by the government or using federal funds. The review is executed by the Advisory Council on Historic Preservation, which determines whether the effect of the project on the historic property will be adverse. While the council does not have the authority to veto projects, it can propose, in consultation with other parties involved, alternative solutions which may lessen any adverse effect on the property. Any individual or organization may request such a review, either through the state or directly from the Advisory Council.

In Rittenhouse this procedure was followed at one stage in the development of the Wanamaker House on Walnut Street. In that case it was required because the house was eligible for (and was ultimately placed on) the National Register, and the developer had a federally insured loan to do the work.

The chief agencies within the federal government responsible for preservation are the Advisory Council and the Department of the Interior. The council serves as an adviser to the president and Congress and fosters studies and publishes reports on preservation issues, as well as carrying out Section 106 reviews. The Department of the Interior, with assistance from appropriate federal, state, and local agencies, administers all other programs, sets guidelines and standards for preservation work, and gives advice and information to the public. (For a list of subdivisions and duties within the department, see Appendix, Resources—Federal.)

It should be noted that although on paper there is a fairly comprehensive array of federal programs encouraging preservation, actual execution depends on the philosophy of the executive and Congress in power at any given time. Funds may be cut back, regulations revised, emphases shifted. And since state and local programs are in many ways dependent on federal appropriations and guidelines, they are affected as well. Many changes have occurred in Washington since passage of the Historic Preservation Act of 1966. There will undoubtedly be more changes that will affect preservation programs for better or worse.

## State Laws and Programs
Federal law directs the Secretary of the Interior to encourage state activity in historic preservation, specifically in surveys and nominations to the National Register. The Secretary of the Interior in turn has required each state to designate an Historic Preservation officer in order to participate in Department of the Interior programs. Each Office of Historic Preservation must conduct a statewide survey of historic resources and nominate all eligible districts, structures, objects, and sites to the National Register. It

must also establish a statewide preservation plan, be equipped to receive and administer Department of the Interior grants-in-aid, and review certification applications for tax benefits.

Different states have reached varying degrees of development in conforming with Department of the Interior guidelines and in providing legislation and guidance for preservation generally. Some states, such as Maryland, have had strong preservation programs and legislation for a long time. New Jersey has a law that provides for review, similar to the federal Section 106 review, of any state or municipally funded projects affecting structures on the National and State Registers. Pennsylvania's Office of Historic Preservation was established within the State Historical and Museum Commission in 1968, and has since become a bureau.

The State Bureau for Historic Preservation operates under the state Historic Preservation Act of 1978, which directs it to prepare a comprehensive plan for preservation within the commonwealth and to coordinate a statewide survey to identify and document historic resources. Documentation from the survey becomes a part of a permanent data base maintained in Harrisburg. The bureau must also provide information and technical and financial assistance to public officials and private individuals and organizations. In addition, it administers federal programs, such as the National Register, grants-in-aid, and certification for tax benefits, and is qualified to receive easements in historic resources. It also consults on Section 106 reviews. Generally, the bureau does not itself prepare National Register nominations but encourages and reviews those submitted by others. Within the Bureau for Historic Preservation there is a Historic Preservation Board which acts in an advisory capacity. It reviews National Register nominations and the bureau's preservation plan.

Although the bureau has a fairly wide role in preservation throughout the state, and does review and com-

ment upon activities undertaken by state agencies that affect historic resources, there is no legislation at the state level that affords solid protection for those resources, such as Section 106 of the federal act and Philadelphia's review procedure. (See below, Historic Districts and Commissions.)

## Historic Districts and Commissions

As concern for architectural preservation has grown over the last twenty years, communities throughout the country have established increasing numbers of historic districts and commissions to watch over those districts and the significant buildings in them. A historic district is a specific geographic area having a concentration of historically or architecturally important buildings and structures, a large proportion of which have a common heritage or aesthetic. Districts may be National Historic Landmarks, may be listed on the National Register, a state or local inventory, or all of the above. Such designations give all significant buildings in the district the privileges of the particular categories in which the district is listed.

Historic district designation has several purposes: to recognize historically important buildings, to preserve the architectural heritage and aesthetic value of a particular area, and to prevent unwanted incursions into it. The elements such designation seeks to preserve are usually exterior ones: facades, paving, lighting fixtures, plantings—pleasant streetscapes. Generally, districts, commissions, and accompanying regulations are not as concerned with interiors and other features not visible from the street, although these may be valuable to each building individually and to its relative standing among buildings in the district.

In some cities historic districts are strictly regulated by local zoning ordinances especially designed to preserve the aesthetics of the district. Such ordinances restrict development and limit the alterations allowed on significant buildings. In addition to standard use, density,

*122. Frank Samuel House, 2136 Locust St.
(Photo by Bernie Cleff)*

mass, and height regulations, they cover definitions of boundaries, architectural values to be preserved, and specific design controls.

A historic district commission is a body that regulates change within a historic district, enforces zoning regulations, and reviews and decides on proposed alterations, demolitions, and new construction within the district. Its criteria are generally based on zoning regulations, the existing design vocabulary, and relationships between structures. Criteria should be objective, flexible, and understandable, taking into account social and commercial needs as well as design considerations. They should not limit change to purist reproductions and restorations, but should require that alterations and new construction be compatible in scale and design with the surrounding structures.

Throughout the country there is great variety in the kinds of historic district legislation and powers of commissions. Newport and Providence, Rhode Island, Annapolis, Maryland, and Savannah, Georgia, all have particularly strong historic district ordinances and commissions. The Philadelphia Historical Commission, established in 1955, was the first such body in the nation to have jurisdiction over an entire city.

On April 1, 1985 a new historic preservation ordinance, expanding the powers of the commission, is expected to take effect. As revised, Section 2007 of Title 14 of the Philadelphia Zoning Code authorizes the City Historical Commission and redefines its powers and responsibilities. The commission is made up of certain city officials, plus eight other people "learned in the historic traditions of the city and interested in the preservation of the historic character of the city." All are appointed by the mayor. Their overall purpose is to "preserve buildings, structures, sites, and objects which are important to the education, culture, traditions, and economic values of the city." To that end the commission may designate historic districts as well as buildings, et al., and must encourage their restoration and rehabilitation and discourage their alteration and demolition.

The Historical Commission also plays a coordinating and informing role, assisting in developing solutions to the city's preservation problems, and providing information and advice to the public on preservation issues and programs.

It is anticipated that some portions of the new ordinance may be amended; furthermore, specific procedures have yet to be established. For up-to-date information and guidance, consult the Historical Commission.

## Recognition Programs
Recognition programs at the local and federal levels have been established to designate and, in some cases, protect, significant districts, sites, buildings, and objects. In Philadelphia there are three possible designations: National Historic Landmarks, National Register, and Philadelphia designation.

***Landmarks*** In 1935 when the Historic Sites Act authorized the National Park Service to survey and preserve historic sites, buildings, and objects, the intention was to locate properties for inclusion in the National Park System. Over time it became clear that there were numerous eligible properties that could never become part of that system, and in 1960 the National Historic Landmark program was established to recognize private property of particular historical architectural distinction.

The designation National Historic Landmark is the highest honor given by the federal government to a building, site, object, or district. Landmarks are important to the nation as a whole, as well as to a state or locality. In order to qualify, a property must "possess exceptional value or quality in illustrating or interpreting the historical heritage of our nation." Above all, it must have, and continue to maintain, "integrity," that is, "original workmanship, original location, and intangible elements of feeling and association." In addition to physical and historical integrity, a landmark must also have an appropriate use and relationship with its surroundings. Landmarks are visited periodically by Department of the Interior staff to assure that they remain eligible. Landmarks are generally nominated by National Park Service staff in Washington, although state offices of Historic Preservation or other agencies or individuals may suggest appropriate buildings to the National Park Service.

National Landmark status gives a building or site a number of advantages in addition to prestige. Matching grants-in-aid (up to 50 percent of the total cost of a project) may be available for acquisition, surveys, and restoration of landmark properties. Grants are administered by the states in cooperation with the Department of the Interior. In Pennsylvania the Bureau for Historic Preservation is the agency responsible for grant administration. (See below, Grants-in-Aid, and Procedures—How to Apply for a Grant-in-Aid.)

Landmarks are protected from demolition or harm by Section 106 of the National Historic Preservation Act of 1966. They also are protected in certain cases by tax laws that provide advantages for rehabilitation of commercial landmark structures. (See below, Tax Incentives, and Procedures—How to Apply for Tax Advantages.) Further information on the National Historic Landmarks program may be obtained from the State Bureau for Historic Preservation in Harrisburg or the Office of Cultural Resources, Department of the Interior, in Washington.

As of March 1984 there are two National Historic Landmarks in Rittenhouse: the Academy of Music and the Edward Drinker Cope House at 2102 Pine Street.

***National Register*** The 1966 National Historic Preservation Act, in an effort to extend recognition beyond the level of the nationally significant, authorized the establishment of the National Register of Historic Places. The National Register recognizes historic buildings, sites, objects, and districts that have state, regional, and local significance, in addition to those that have national significance. (All National Landmarks are automatically listed on the National Register.) It is the official list of the nation's cultural resources considered worthy of preservation.

Amendments to the 1966 act require that all properties eligible for the National Register be nominated to it. Such properties are identified through surveys coordinated by state offices of Historic Preservation. In Pennsylvania, nominations to the National Register are made through the State Bureau for Historic Preservation. If approved by the bureau's Preservation Board, they are forwarded to the Office of Cultural Resources in Washington for consideration and official designation. Anyone, with the owner's consent, may nominate a property to the National Register. A district nomination must be approved by at least 50 percent of the owners of property within the district boundaries.

Registered properties are entitled to the same assistance as landmarks, namely, grants-in-aid, Section 106 review of adverse effect, and tax advantages. No restrictions of use or disposition are placed on owners of registered properties, and changes may be made to them without federal review, so long as no federal funds are used. A building that is severely damaged or demolished will, however, be taken off the register. Further information on national registration is available from the State Bureau for Historic Preservation in Harrisburg or the Office of Cultural Resources in Washington.

In 1983 a district of some 140 acres in Rittenhouse was placed on the National Register of Historic Places (fig. 123). The nomination was based on the inventory done some years before under the statewide survey plan, and the district boundaries were laid out to include most of the historically or architecturally important properties in the neighborhood. Also within the boundaries are a number of "intrusions"—buildings without historical value, deemed not significant to the district. Only significant properties are eligible for federal benefits and protection. Copies of the National Register district nomination and the survey, identifying significant buildings and intrusions, are on file at the Philadelphia Historical Commission and the State Bureau for Historic Preservation in Harrisburg. Any building of historical significance outside the district can be nominated individually to the National Register if the owner so desires.

***City Designation*** At the local level the Philadelphia Historical Commission designates buildings, structures, sites, objects, and districts as significant. Criteria used are similar to those of the National Register, but are more localized. All National Landmarks and National Register properties and districts are reviewed for city designation. Historic designation is obtained by applying to the Philadelphia Historical Commission.

Designated buildings and significant buildings within designated districts cannot be altered or demolished without prior review by the commission. (Alteration includes any changes for which a permit may be needed.) Commission review is automatic upon application for a building permit for a designated structure or structure within a designated district. Criteria for alteration are based on the Secretary of the Interior's Standards for Rehabilitation (see Appendix). The commission may approve the permit, approve it on certain conditions, deny the request, or postpone a decision for six months in order to search for alternative solutions. Appeals of commission decisions are made to the Board of Licenses and Inspections Review. The Department of Licenses and Inspections is responsible for inspection of designated historic properties and for assuring compliance with commission regulations. Information on local designation of historic buildings and districts and requirements for permit applications may be obtained from the Philadelphia Historical Commission.

Grants The federal government has several financial aids specifically for preservation and some programs that are primarily geared to general development or housing purposes, but that are also applicable to historic buildings and surveys. Although these programs are established by law, and thus are generally permanent, it should be noted that funds to carry them out are appropriated annually. The actual amount of money available at any given time is dependent on the current congressional philosophy.

Of most use to preservationists is the Historic Preservation Grant-in-Aid program, authorized by the National Historic Preservation Act of 1966 as amended, and administered by the National Park Service through the state offices of Historic Preservation. The grant program gives matching funds of up to 50 percent of the costs of surveys, acquisition, and development of properties listed in the National Register. Grants may be given to local governments, private organizations, or individuals.

Currently in Pennsylvania most of the limited funds available are dispersed for surveys, planning, and feasibility studies. A grant is rarely given for acquisition, and then only to a nonprofit agency in an emergency case.

Grants for acquisition and development of buildings are divided into seven categories: acquisition, protection, stabilization, preservation, rehabilitation, restoration, and reconstruction. The categories cover a broad range of preservation activity and allow for sequential development of a project. It may be possible, if funds are available, to apply for several grants over a period of time. (See Appendix, Guidelines for Acquisition and Development Projects, for definitions of the seven categories.)

Specific criteria for work done with a grant-in-aid are set forth in the Secretary of the Interior's Standards for Rehabilitation and Guidelines for Acquisition and Development Projects (see Appendix). These standards and guidelines generally require that the basic structure be protected from weather, fire, and deterioration, and that the historic character of the building be retained. For specific information on applying for a Historic Preservation Grant-in-Aid see Procedures. Further information is available from the State Bureau for Historic Preservation in Harrisburg.

Other federal funding programs that can be applied to historic preservation efforts include: Housing and Urban Development 701 funds, Comprehensive Employ-

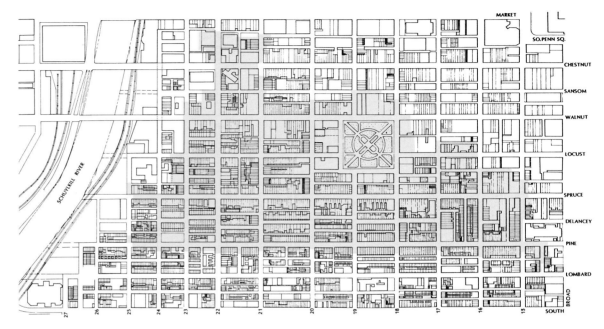

*123. Rittenhouse National Register Historic District Boundaries (City Planning Commission map redrawn by Richard Tatara and Hugh McCauley, with boundaries approved by the National Register of Historic Places)*

ment and Training Act manpower programs, and Community Development Block Grants, among others, all of which come and go from time to time. They are generally administered through the city government. Further information on eligibility may be obtained from the City Office of Housing and Community Development, the Planning Commission, and the managing director's office.

## Tax Incentives
Economics govern all our lives, and taxes are a continual burden. Tax incentives, therefore, have become a most effective support to preservation. Since 1976 the Federal Internal Revenue Code has encouraged preservation by giving incentives for rehabilitation and disincentives for demolition of recognized historic structures and by allowing benefits for charitable

donations of partial property interests (such as ease-ments) for preservation purposes. Unfortunately, tax laws and regulations are particularly subject to change; conse-quently, it is difficult to present information that is not likely to be obsolete and misleading almost immediately. The following is a very general summary of the law in effect as this book goes to press.

The most advantageous preservation-oriented tax provisions allow investment credits for rehabilitations of income-producing properties listed individually on the National Register or certified by the National Park Service as important to a National Register District. In order to qualify, both the building and rehabilitation must be cer-tified as historic by the National Park Service.

The law also allows a tax deduction for donation to a charitable organization or government agency of a lease on, option to purchase, easement, or remainder interest in certified historic property. Such a donation (except for an option to purchase) must be given in perpetuity for conservation or preservation purposes. (See below, Easements.)

The tax laws are subject to challenge in the courts and revision, as well as to clarifying rulings set down, in this case, by the Internal Revenue Service. Procedures for es-tablishing eligibility may also be changed from time to time by the Department of the Interior.

Nevertheless, anyone in Rittenhouse contemplating renovation, particularly of a commercial building, should investigate current tax provisions. Up-to-date information may be obtained from the Bureau for Historic Preserva-tion in Harrisburg and the National Park Service. Instruc-tions for applications for certification of historic build-ings and rehabilitations are included in Procedures, How to Apply for Tax Advantages. In most cases a lawyer, ac-countant, and possibly an architect should be consulted.

## Revolving Funds
Revolving funds have been re-sponsible for the restoration and rehabilitation of numer-ous historic buildings throughout America. Although the uses to which revolving funds may be put are diverse, one approach is as follows. A public or private nonprofit agency buys and rehabilitates an endangered historic property. It then sells to a buyer willing to preserve the property's historic character. The money originally in-vested is thus recouped and is reused to acquire or im-prove another property, which is then sold, and so on.

This recycling of funds is economically efficient and can make the difference between demolition and survival for individual buildings, and, indeed, entire neighbor-hoods. In some cases it has turned an "eyesore" with a potential that few wanted to gamble on into an attractive and successful property. Often revolving funds are simply used to "hold" a property until a buyer sympathetic to its historic character can be found. In some cities, such as Pittsburgh, they have been used to revitalize neighbor-hoods for low-income residents.

In Philadelphia revolving funds for preservation is a mechanism in search of a sponsor. The National Trust for Historic Preservation and the recently formed Pennsyl-vania Preservation Fund both raise and administer re-volving funds.

## Adaptive Reuse
Buildings often outlast the original purpose for which they were built. Social and economic patterns change, people and businesses move, and the buildings, still strong and usable, are left empty. Adaptive reuse is the rehabilitation of a building that no longer serves its original purpose in order that it can serve a new purpose. Whenever the function of a building changes from dwelling to shop, warehouse to living space, from single-family residence to apartments and offices, or back again, adaptive reuse is at work. More dramatic examples in Rittenhouse are the Jayne House at Nineteenth and De-lancey (fig. 124), formerly the Heart Fund headquarters, now law offices; the Van Rensselaer Mansion at Eigh-teenth and Walnut, now Urban Outfitters; the Deaf and

*124. Center Hall, Jayne House, 318–22 S. 19th St.
(Photo by Tom Crane)*

Dumb Asylum and the Arco Building on Broad Street, now used by Philadelphia College of Art; and the Lea Mansion at 1622 Locust, now law offices.

Adaptive reuse encompasses a broad range of degrees, depending on finances, tastes, and needs. As a preservationist's tool its basis lies in the philosophy that it is better to alter a valuable historic building, if that will ensure its survival, than to demolish it; and that old buildings should be integral parts of our daily life, not rele-

gated to museum status in the interests of historical accuracy.

Adaptive reuse is a method commonly used for economic as well as aesthetic reasons. Whether it is cheaper to renovate than to demolish and rebuild depends on the condition of the building and the kind of reuse. Clearly it would be impractical to attempt to reuse a residence as a warehouse for heavy machinery, although warehouse lofts are now popular as residences. A complete restoration of a building that has suffered great change and damage is very costly. But a reuse that does not put great stress on the building and does not demand perfection in historical detail is almost always cheaper than new construction. Basic elements such as walls, floors, and foundations already exist and do not have to be built from scratch. In Rittenhouse, with its mixture of residential, institutional, and commercial uses, and virtually no industry, adaptive reuse is generally a practical and economical option.

Adaptive reuse can be controversial because it entails value judgments and compromises. How far the adaptation can go before it does drastic aesthetic damage to a building is often a hotly debated matter of opinion. In most cases, however, it is possible to retain original distinctive features of a building while still serving the needs of modern life. Cornices, moldings, paneling, and mantelpieces are all amenities as pleasant for a twentieth-century office or studio as they were for the bedroom that preceded it, and they do not impinge on the basic functioning of the office. The Horn Mansion in the 2400 block of Pine Street (fig. 125), originally built as a house, has since successfully accommodated ARA Services and an architectural office with only minor physical alteration. Other former dwellings now house the Curtis Institute and the Art Alliance.

In considering a building for adaptive reuse, imagination is as important as economics. Converting a large late

125. Horn Mansion, 2410 Pine St. (Photo by Bernie Cleff)

nineteenth-century residence to condominiums is not the only solution. In an area such as Chestnut or Walnut Street, which already has an abundance of mixed use, adapting such a building or buildings to a combination of offices or studios and living spaces may be practical. The objective in any case is to find uses that will offer the investor a reasonable return while maintaining the building as an amenity for all.

## Easements
An easement is a right of less than total ownership in a property that an owner sells or, more often, gives, by deed or will to an organization qualified to hold and administer it. Easements generally restrict alterations, development, and demolition, and can be used to protect open space or buildings or portions of them for a period of years. The donor retains all other rights and privileges, including the right to rent or sell the property, and the responsibility for maintenance and improvements. Easements are binding on the donor and any lessee, as well as on future owners.

The most common kinds of easements in an urban area are for air rights above a building, the exterior, or a particular facade of the building, and open space. An air rights easement prevents additions higher than the existing structure; a facade easement limits changes to the face of a building. An open space easement prohibits construction on a site. Air rights can also be sold or transferred from one building to another for development purposes. The case of Academy House is a good example in Rittenhouse, where the air rights over the Academy of Music were transferred to Academy House to afford the apartment building more height than otherwise would have been allowed (fig. 126).

Open space easements have been effectively employed in rural areas to protect watersheds and landscapes for ecological as well as aesthetic reasons. In Rittenhouse an imaginative use of both open space and facade easements protects the exterior and garden of the Bishop Mackay-Smith House, now Chandler Place, on Twenty-Second Street (fig. 127).

Easements are complex documents that must follow local, state, and national legal precedent in order to be effective, and each one must be individually written. In theory they can vary widely in the protections and requirements they guarantee, and in the length of time they cover. For historic easements fulfilling certain criteria there can be federal tax benefits. A charitable deduction may be claimed for the donation of an easement in perpetuity on a building, structure, or land area listed on the National Register or certified as significant to a National Register district. This applies to both commercial and non-income-producing property. The easement must be given to a qualified government or nonprofit agency, such as the Philadelphia Historic Preservation Corporation. The amount deductible is the difference between the fair market value of the property before granting and the fair market value after granting the easement. It takes into account the obligation to maintain the facade, as well as the development potential lost. (See Tax Incentives, above, and Procedures, How to Apply for Tax Advantages.)

A disadvantage of an easement is that it may affect the attractiveness of the property for sale purposes. A prospective buyer or lessee may view the limiting of development potential and the maintenance obligation as undesirable. However, a house on a block full of protected facades may attract buyers appreciative of the value of a historic streetscape.

Care should be taken in writing an easement that it is not impractical, but still gives the required protection. It may be wise to include a method of arbitration to allow for unforeseen changes in circumstances. Further information on easements is available from the Philadelphia Historic Preservation Corporation and the State Bureau for Historic Preservation. A lawyer and/or tax adviser should be consulted by anyone considering donating an easement.

## Restrictive Covenants

A restrictive covenant is another legal mechanism used to ensure protection for a property. It takes the form of a document attached to the deed restricting the use or ability to alter or demolish the property, and is binding on future owners of the property. In its effect a restrictive covenant is similar to an easement. It is not, however, held by a party other than the property owner, nor does it qualify for tax advantages. Furthermore, there is considerable recent precedent in law for breaking covenants, particularly if they impose burdens that become unrealistic as times, needs, and society change. As with an easement, a restrictive covenant should be very carefully written by a lawyer.

126. *Academy of Music and Academy House*
*(Photo by Bernie Cleff)*

127. *Chandler Place, 251 S. 22nd St. (Photo by Bernie Cleff)*

# PROCEDURES

### TRINA VAUX

*Railings in the snow (Photo by Bernie Cleff)*

# How to Inspect a Building
Whether you are buying a building or trying to maintain one, the following checklist should be helpful. A building is the single most important and expensive investment for most people. Buying one is almost like marrying. And once you have it, a building, like a spouse, requires regular attention. When inspecting a building remember that any defect can be corrected if there is sufficient time and money. But make sure the building you fall in love with will satisfy your needs with a minimum of alteration. Carefully measure your pocket and capabilities against the task, so as not to tax your patience and deplete your savings.

The following inspection checklist is reproduced courtesy of *The Old-House Journal* (69A Seventh Avenue, Brooklyn, N.Y., 11217. Subscriptions $16 a year).

Go Prepared: When setting out on an old-house inspection, you should have with you: flashlight, small magnet, plumb line (string with small weight will do), penknife, a marble, pair of binoculars, pad and pencil, and an inspection checklist. Wear old clothes so you can closely inspect important places like the cellar and underneath porches.

***The Roof*** A sound, tight roof is the first line of defense against the No. 1 enemy of an old house: water. If the roof is in bad shape, you should plan on repairing—or replacing—it right away.

1. Type of roof on house (arranged in approximate order of longevity): (1) slate; (2) copper; (3) ceramic tile; (4) tar and gravel; (5) asbestos tile; (6) wood shakes; (7) wood shingles; (8) galvanized steel; (9) asphalt shingles; (10) roll roofing.
2. **Pitched roof**: Any sign of missing, broken, or warped shingles or tiles? (This could mean roof will have to be replaced soon. It can also mean that there is water damage inside.) *Note: Binoculars can give you a good close-up view if it is impossible to actually get up on the roof.*
3. **Asphalt shingles**: Are the mineral granules getting thin and do edges of shingles look worn?
4. **Asphalt shingles**: Does roof look new but lumpy? (New roof may have been applied directly over old shingles. No way to tell what sins may have been covered over.)
5. **Flat roof**: Any sign of bubbles, separation, or cracking in the asphalt or roofing felt? (Roofing should be flat and tight to roof; it shouldn't feel squishy under foot.)
6. **Flashing around chimneys and valleys**: Any sign of rusty, loose, or missing flashing? (Flashing is the weakest part of any roof. Copper is the best flashing and will show a green patina.)
7. **Chimneys**: Is the masonry cracked or crumbling?
8. Do the old chimney flues have a tile lining? (If not, they could be a fire hazard in conjunction with wood-burning fireplaces.)
9. **Gutters**: Are there any loose, rotted, or missing gutters?
10. Does the ridge of the roof sag? (This could be normal settling that comes with age—or it could be caused by rotted rafters. Check further.)
11. **Cornice**: Is there badly peeling paint on the cornice—especially the underside? (This can signal a roof leak that is spilling water into the cornice.)

***Exterior Walls***

1. Do exterior walls seem plumb? (You can check with a plumb line. Out-of-plumb walls can be a sign of serious foundation problems.)
2. Sight along exterior walls. Any sign of major bulges? (This could signal major structural flaws.)
3. Do doors line up squarely in their frames? (Out-of-square doors can be another sign of possible foundation trouble.) *Note: Almost all old houses settle in a haphazard manner. So signs of sag are not necessarily a major drawback. But they do require a thorough investigation to find the root causes. Some sags*

*require no remedy; others can be cured with a few extra support posts. Still others may require major foundation surgery.*

4. Is decorative woodwork firmly attached to house and tightly caulked to prevent water penetration?

5. Is exterior paint fresh and in good condition?

6. If paint is not new, is it powdering and chalking to a dull powdery surface? (This is the way old paint should look.)

7. Is paint peeling, curling, and blistering? (This could mean a serious water problem—either a leak or lack of sufficient vapor barrier in wall.)

8. Are there open joints around door frames, window frames, and trim? (These will have to be caulked.)

9. Are joints between dissimilar materials (e.g., wood and masonry) well protected with flashing or caulk?

10. Is putty around window glass sound and well painted?

11. **Masonry walls**: Any signs of cracks? (Horizontal cracks and hairline cracks in bricks are not a major problem; cracks that run vertically through bricks and mortar are more serious.)

12. Is mortar soft and crumbling; are bricks missing or loose? (Loose masonry is vulnerable to attack by water, and having a masonry wall repointed with fresh mortar is expensive.)

13. Has masonry been painted? (It will have to be repainted about every five years, or else stripped—a major task.)

14. **Stonework (especially sandstone)**: Any sign of spalling, cracking, or crumbling of the stone? (This can be expensive to repair.)

15. **Clapboards**: Are many loose, cracked, or missing? (This is an open invitation to water—and rot.)

16. **Shingles**: Are they thick and well nailed? (Thin, badly weathered shingles may have to be replaced.)

17. Do shingles have a natural finish? (Natural finishes are easier to reapply to shingles than is paint.)

***Termites and rot:***

1. **Termites**: Any sign of veins of dirt on interior or exterior walls? (These are termite mud tunnels. Look for them on foundation, under porches, steps, and on cellar walls.)

2. Does wood near the ground (both outside and inside) pass the "pen knife test"? (Wood should be probed with pen knife to test for soundness. Check areas such as cellar window frames, sills, floor beams and posts, porches, and steps.) *Note: Unsound wood can be caused by either termites or rot. Rot can be arrested by shutting off the source of moisture. Termites call for chemical warfare. If at all unsure about the cause of bad wood, call in the experts.*

3. Is all exterior wood at least six to eight inches above the ground? (If not, this is an inviting target for termites and/or rot.)

4. Is there any vegetation close to the house? (Vegetation holds moisture in wood; be sure to check behind it for rot.)

5. Any signs of rot in cornice or attic beams? (Leaking roofs and gutters often spill water into top of house where it goes undetected for long periods.)

***Attic***

1. Any sign of leaks (such as dark water stains) on the underside of roof, especially around chimneys, valleys, and eaves?

2. Is attic adequately vented? (Check especially for signs of mildew on underside of roof boards.)

***Insulation*** *Note: Most houses before 1940 had no built-in insulation. However, some old houses will have had insulation added. Houses with brick or stone walls rarely have any wall insulation. With cost of fuel soaring, a well-insulated house is a big asset.*

1. **Attic**: Any loose fill insulation visible between attic floor joists? (This is best place for attic insulation.)
2. Has insulation been blown into side walls? (You may have to take owner's word for this. In cold weather you can tell how good wall insulation is by feeling the inside of an exterior wall and comparing with temperature of an interior partition. They should feel about the same.)

### Interior spaces

1. Are there any signs of damp plaster? (This means leaks coming either from roof or internal pipes. Check especially top-floor ceilings, the inside of exterior walls, and ceilings and partitions under bathrooms.)
2. Is there any loose plaster in walls or ceilings? (Cracks in plaster are par for the course—but plaster that is spongy when you push on it will have to be repaired or replaced.)
3. Is there a noticeable bounce to the staircase when you jump on it? Are there any noticeable gaps between treads, risers, and side stringers? (Substantial vibration may mean structural problems that will be quite costly to correct.)
4. Is flooring original and in good repair? (Floors covered with carpet or linoleum can harbor many problems—especially if you want to restore the original flooring.)
5. Do floors have a pronounced sag or tilt? (Simple test: Place a marble on the floor and see if it rolls away. This could just be normal settling or serious structural flaws. Check for cause.)
6. Do floors vibrate and windows rattle when you jump on floors? (This is symptom of inadequate support. Among possible causes: undersized beams, inadequate bridging, cracked joists, rotted support posts. Often this can be cured fairly simply with a few new support posts.)
7. **Windows**: Do sash move up and down smoothly?

8. Do window frames show signs of substantial water leakage? (Look for chipped and curling paint at bottom of sash and sills. Although quite unsightly, this can be cured with caulk, putty, and paint.)
9. Are fireplaces operational? (Evidence of recent fires in the fireplace is a reassuring sign. Peek up the chimney; if you can see daylight you at least know the flue is clear.)
10. Are there smoke stains on front of mantel? (This is a sign of a smoky fireplace. It can be cured—but it is a bother.)

### Foundation

1. Is there a dug cellar with wood sills resting solidly on a masonry foundation well above ground level? (Some old structures have "mud sills"—heavy beams resting directly on the ground. These eventually have to be replaced, which is a major undertaking.)
2. Is mortar in foundation soft and crumbling? (This is not necessarily serious as long as there is no sign of sag in the structure; ditto for foundation walls laid dry—without mortar.)
3. Are there any vertical cracks in the foundation wall? (This could be serious, or it could be from settling that stopped years ago. Have an engineer check it.)
4. Does ground slope away from foundation so that rain water drains off?
5. Do downspouts have splash blocks to divert water away from house? (If downspout goes into ground, be sure it isn't pouring water into the earth next to the foundation—a flooded basement is the likely result.)

### Cellar

1. Do sills (the wood beams at the top of the foundation walls) show signs of rot or termites? (Probe with penknife.)
2. Any sign of dampness on the underside of floors

around pipes? (If leaks have gone undetected for some time, there could be substantial wood rot.)
3. Does basement show signs of periodic flooding? (It's a good sign if current owner stores important tools and papers on cellar floor. Bad signs: rust spots, efflorescence or mildew on walls, material stored on top of bricks to raise it above floor level.)
4. Any sign of sagging floors, rotted support posts or jury-rigged props to shore up weak flooring?

## Electrical system

1. Does wiring in cellar appear to be a rat's nest of old frayed wires?
2. Does main power box in cellar have a capacity of at least one hundred amperes? (An up-to-date installation will have capacity marked on it. An old fuse box with only three or four fuses in it means there may only be thirty to forty amperes—far too little. A re-wiring job will be needed.)
3. Do all ceiling light fixtures have wall switches?
4. Is there at least one electrical outlet on each wall in every room?
5. Is there any sign of surface-mounted lampcord extension wiring? Multiple cords plugged into a single outlet? (This is a telltale of underwiring. Expect to hire some electricians.)

## Plumbing

1. Are water pipes copper or brass? (If they are, magnet won't stick to them. Copper or brass is longer-lasting than galvanized iron. Magnet won't stick to lead piping either. Lead will be soft and silvery when scratched with penknife. Lead piping will probably have to be replaced shortly.)
2. Is water pressure adequate? (Test by turning on top floor sink faucets; then turn on bathtub and flush toilet. If water slows to a trickle, piping may be inadequate or badly clogged with scale.)
3. Is plumbing connected to a city sewer system?
4. If there is a septic tank, was it cleaned in the last three or four years? (Overloaded septic tanks are a common source of trouble. It's best to call the serviceman who did the last cleaning and get his opinion of the system. Repairs can easily run over $1,000.)
5. Is water supply from: city main? drilled well? shallow well? Are the water pipes and large waste pipes in good condition? (The cellar is the best place to evaluate the overall condition of the plumbing. For example, look for patches on the waste pipes; it's an indicator of advanced age. Replacement is expensive.)

*Notes on water supply: City main is the most dependable source; shallow (dug) well is the least desirable. If water is from a well it is best to get it analyzed by the county agent for fitness. If water is from a spring, beware of claims that "spring never runs dry" unless you can verify it. You may end up paying to drill a well during a long dry summer.*

## Heating system

1. Was heating plant originally designed to burn coal? (If so, it is probably more than twenty-five years old and may be a candidate for replacement.)
2. Does heating system operate satisfactorily? (You can test system even on a summer day: Move thermostat setting above room temperature. Heat from a hot-air furnace should appear at registers within a few minutes; in a steam or hot water system radiators should heat up in fifteen to twenty minutes.)
3. Will fuel bills present you with any unpleasant surprises? (Copies of fuel bills from the last heating season are the best measure of the heating system's efficiency.)
4. Is capacity of hot water heater at least forty gallons? (This is minimum required by a family of four with an automatic clothes washer.)

*128. "Philadelphia Library" by
George B. Wood, 1880
(Library Company of Philadelphia)*

5. Any sign of leaks or rust spots on the hot water heating tank? (Check by peeking through small door that gives access to the pilot light.)
6. On steam heating systems, do floorboards around radiators show signs of black stains and rot? (This comes from leaks and indicates system hasn't been well maintained.)

## How to Research a Building
Once you have a building, or even before you buy, you may want to find out its architectural history—when it was built, what alterations may have been made since then, and at what dates. This is important if you are doing any physical preservation work on the building: Know what is and is not original. Research is required for National Register nominations and applications for grants-in-aid. For your own interest, you may want to investigate the social history as well—who owned the building, what sort of people they were, and how they used the structure. Potential sources for all this information exist in varying degrees of accessibility. The City Records and Archives, insurance companies, newspapers, and the various private and public repositories in the city have historical documents that may be helpful. Family papers of previous owners are invaluable but rare and often hard to find. Professional architectural historians and restoration architects can advise on the basis of physical evidence in the building itself.

Public records in City Hall are the first place to go to research your deed. Through them you should be able to trace the property back to the grant by William Penn or his representatives. In the process, you can find out when your building was built and the names and, in some cases, professions of all the owners. The *Real Estate Record and Builders' Guide*, published from 1886 to 1940, has information on all aspects of the building trade. City newspapers used to publish lists of new construction contracts. If you know an approximate date of construction, you may be able to find the names of the builder and architect in the *Real Estate Record and Builders' Guide*, *Ledger*, *Record*, *Inquirer*, or *Bulletin*. (The *Real Estate Record* is available at the Athenaeum of Philadelphia. The Historical Society of Pennsylvania, the Free Library of Philadelphia, and other institutions have other newspapers.) Plans and specifications are harder to come by, although a limited number of files and drawings of some "name" architects survive in the Athenaeum, the Historical Society of Pennsylvania, the University of Pennsylvania Library, and some architectural firms. If your building was built after 1858, you may be able to find it on one of the City Survey atlases. This will show the outline of the building and the type of construction. The City Archives also has some records of builders' contracts starting in the 1880s, but they are cataloged only for the period after 1902.

Most insurance companies in Philadelphia have kept meticulous records on clients' properties over the years, some of which are cataloged and accessible to the public at the Historical Commission, the Historical Society, and the Insurance Company of North America Archives. Such records often give a physical description of both the interior and exterior of the building insured. By this means you may be able to find out how the structure was arranged when it was originally built and discover any changes made to it over the years. (Terms used in these records are sometimes obscure. Ask the archivist to give you the definitions as they were understood at the time of writing.)

Pictorial evidence of Philadelphia's history abounds, although whether your building or lot is shown anywhere depends on its location, importance, visual interest, and luck. The Library Company, the Historical Society, the Athenaeum, the Free Library, and various other repositories have collections of photographs, drawings, lithographs, watercolors, and so forth showing various parts of the city at various times. Other sources periodically come to light, but all are not yet cataloged, so finding a specific item, if it exists, is difficult.

Discovering the social history of a building beyond the names of owners is also a matter of serendipity, unless the owner was prominent. Profession, race, marital status, and number of people in a household may be found in census records (at the Historical Society), but these were not taken every year. (Beware of comments on social status—they tend to be subjective.) City directories (in the City Archives and the Historical Society) give names, addresses, and occupations. Wills usually give some basic information, and knowing a death date will help in finding an obituary. Beyond these public records and newspapers, the chance discovery of a family diary, letters, memoir of a neighbor, or other chatty ephemera is a historian's dream seldom fulfilled.

The following is a procedure for tracing title to your building in the City Department of Records. Go prepared with time and good eyesight. You will be competing with many other people looking for information, and you will be reading microfilm copies of documents, which is sometimes difficult, particularly when the originals are handwritten. Depending on the extent of your search, you may be confronted with several different kinds of microfilm, each of which fits a different machine. Be sure you use the right one. If you get lost or stuck, ask until you find a workable answer. Some of the clerks are knowledgeable, some are not. A friendly researcher may be able to advise. Above all, use your best Sherlock Holmes instinct and enjoy the chase.

1. Find your property on the maps posted in the Department of Records, and get the code (a number, letter, and number) for your area. Ask to see the plan corresponding to that code. Your property, as shown on the plan, will have a lot number.
2. Write the plan code and lot number on one of the orange cards provided (one card for each lot number), and give it to a clerk. (Usual practice is to call out "jacket" to attract the clerk's attention. Clerks are busy.)

129. George P. Rowell and Company's Newspaper Pavilion (Frank Leslie's Illustrated Historical Register of the Centennial Exposition, 1876)

3. You will be given a strip of microfilm or "jacket" for your lot, which shows a series of deed abstracts. These are summaries of the transactions of your lot that have taken place from the present time back to the middle of the nineteenth century. Each abstract gives the date of the transaction, names of grantor (seller) and grantee (buyer), and location and dimensions of the property. If you are lucky, the series will be complete. If not, or if you want to see the full deeds, you will have to consult the index.

4. Most Philadelphia deeds are indexed by date, grantor, and grantee. Each entry gives the initials, book, and page number of the deed book in which the deed is recorded. (The initials are those of the Recorder of Deeds at the time of the transaction.) Most indexes and deed books are on microfilm. Originals not microfilmed are in the City Archives in City Hall Annex.

5. Fill out an orange card in the Registry Unit with the initials, book, and page number to request a microfilm of the deed you want. The deed, or indenture, gives the date of the transaction, names of the parties, often with their occupations and places of residence, and price paid. It also gives the dimensions of the property, possibly with the address, and sometimes refers to structures, rights of way, covenants, or other restrictions on the property. It may show who owns the adjoining properties as well. Finally, it will show how, from whom, and when the grantor got the land, and the book and page number where that prior deed is recorded. (Sometimes the deed book reference is not written in the actual deed. In this case look for it noted in pencil in the margin.)

6. By following these references to previous owners you can trace your property back to its origin, always looking for the first mention of a building, structure, or "messuage," or significant rise in value, indicating an approximate period of construction.

7. You may be able to find a full record this way, encountering only an occasional lack of deed book reference, which will send you back to the index. From time to time your property may be part of a larger transaction. The mention of the previous grantor will usually appear immediately after the description of your lot and any others conveyed along with it by that grantor. If not, you will have to look up all the deed book references to find which one concerns your lot.

8. If you come to a point at which the deed books and index have no record of your property, it may be an indication of some other kind of conveyance. The most common of these are: wills, in City Hall, indexed by testator; administrative records (for people dying intestate), in City Hall Annex, indexed by name of decedent (the index is in City Hall); sheriff's deeds, in City Hall Annex, cross indexed by names of defendant and purchaser; patents (used when the grantor is the government), in the Office of Land Records in Harrisburg (some copies and indexes are in City Hall).

## How to Work with Architects and Contractors

An architect is trained to design buildings. He or she may also supervise and coordinate their construction. Although some architects specialize in restoration and rehabilitation, few specialize in the restoration of Victorian buildings. A contractor is responsible for the performance of construction work, including provision of labor and materials. Contractors work in accordance with plans and specifications, under a contract fixing the costs and schedule for the completion of the work. An architect and contractor can be very helpful working with you. Advice on selection of a qualified restoration architect may be secured through the Philadelphia Chapter of the American Institute of Architects and the Philadelphia Historical Commission.

Before making a commitment with any professional, ask questions and explain your needs. Ask to see examples of work similar to the work needed. If you are working with an architect, you will choose a contractor together; if not, you must choose the contractor yourself. A contractor should also be questioned carefully. Some have more experience in restoration than others. Don't be rushed into a contract.

Contracts, bids, liens, laws, and bonds: When dealing with a contractor, always ask for a complete breakdown of costs based on clear specifications. A complete breakdown of costs is an itemized list of work to be done which shows materials, labor, profit, overhead, insurance costs, and any contingency.

If a contractor will not provide a cost breakdown, do not engage him. Always get a minimum of three bids, all based on the same specifications. Shop around. It is best to get five bids. One will be too high, one too low, and three will be in the mid-range where the price is right and competitive. The high bidder doesn't really want the job. The low bidder may use lower quality materials, cause problems for you, and not be able to live up to the estimate. Pick one of the mid-range bidders. Deal with a company with experience and reasonable prices.

When a project has been agreed upon, the bids opened, and the contractor selected, the owner or architect will examine the contractor's insurance and ask for a bond (usually 10 percent of the total cost) to be deposited in escrow at a bank. The bond is placed by the contractor in good faith; the money will be returned only when the work is finished in accordance with the agreement and specifications. A binding legal contract is then drawn up by the architect, owner, or contractor during the preliminary discussions; the parties must agree to sign and follow the directions in the agreement.

The contract is filed with the local prothonotary with a waiver of liens, a document that holds the property owner harmless from any claims against his or her property by a worker on the job, a subcontractor, or a supply company.

*130. Architects Preparing Plans and Drawings of Centennial Buildings (*Frank Leslie's Illustrated Historical Register of the Centennial Exposition, 1876*)*

1. Examine the building. Decide what you really want and need. Write specifications or have an architect do it.
2. Choose an architect. Talk with more than one. Find out preliminary project costs. Revise the plans to fit your budget.
3. Ask at least three bidders to submit itemized cost breakdowns based on the same specifications and/or drawings.
4. Evaluate the bids and select the one that seems to fit your needs. Begin to negotiate a fair contract. Ask about the contractor's insurance and make sure bond money is deposited and a waiver of liens is signed. The contractor should also agree to secure all necessary permits from local authorities.
5. Sign the contract when every detail has been explained and understood by all parties.
6. Begin work. A previously agreed-upon schedule may have to be adjusted for a variety of reasons.
7. Inspect the quality and progress of the work.
8. Any changes made after work gets underway should be carefully negotiated. Be careful of on-job changes which could increase expenses; look for those that could reduce costs.

*131. Local Applications*

9. Make progress payments based on the amount of work in the construction schedule.
10. Check completed work. If you aren't satisfied, negotiate a change.
11. Release final payment to the contractor. Notify the bonding institution of the project completion. Be sure there is a guarantee by the contractor in case there is a problem with workmanship not visible at the time of final payment. Finally, always read what you sign, and sign only what you understand.

## Do It Yourself

You may decide, for financial reasons, or for personal satisfaction, to do your own maintenance and repair work. Be careful. Many jobs look easy but are complicated. You may end up spending more when you have to call in a professional to redo the job. Generally, a professional has the proper tools and can do the work more efficiently. A professional knows what shortcuts can and can't be taken. You may have adequate experience in construction. If so, go ahead, if city codes allow you to do the work yourself (see below, How to Apply for Building Permits). If you don't have experience, and are still determined, do some reading first. Even painting requires special techniques that make the job easier. A number of "how to" books explain methods. The *Reader's Digest* and the *Mechanics Illustrated* series are particularly good; *The Old-House Journal* deals specifically with old buildings.

## How to Apply for Building Permits

If you are planning to alter, renovate, or restore your building in any way except for routine repairs, you should be aware of the city regulations governing what you may or may not do, what permits may be necessary, and whether you are required to have a licensed contractor do the work. Buildings in Philadelphia, their use, mass, and construction, are governed by six codes designed to protect the public health, safety, and welfare. The Housing Code sets minimum standards for basic equipment and facilities in city dwellings. The Zoning Code restricts the location, size, bulk, and use of buildings and open space, and establishes zoning districts within the city. The Building Code and Electrical Code set standards in their respective areas, and the Fire Code establishes regulations for fire prevention and protection. Each of the codes includes provisions for permits, licenses, inspections, and appeals. All are administered by the Department of Licenses and Inspections (L&I) in cooperation with other city departments and boards. The codes are available in public libraries and for sale by L&I.

There is no special provision for historic buildings in the Building, Plumbing, Housing, or Electrical codes. If repairs or alterations are made to a building at a cost more than 50 percent of the assessed market value of the building, the entire building must conform to the code. In some cases this provision may require alteration of valuable historical architectural elements. By all means seek a variance if you are asked to destroy an important historical piece of your building.

In the case of historic buildings and significant buildings in a district designated by the city, the permit application process includes Historical Commission review. The commission may deny or postpone for up to six months granting of any permit that may allow harm to be done to the exterior of a historically significant building. If you plan a full or partial restoration of the exterior of a designated building or a significant building in a designated district, you will do well to check with the commission for their requirements and present your plans in advance. The Historical Commission's guidelines for restoration and rehabilitation are based on the Secretary of the Interior's Standards for Rehabilitation (see Appendix), and are concerned with the maintenance of original exterior features of the structure.

Code requirements vary, depending on the nature of the building (commercial, residential, single-, or multifamily). Generally if you are changing the size, bulk, or use of your building, you will need a zoning permit, or possibly a variance (see below, How to Apply for a Zoning Variance). If you are doing major rehabilitation work, you may need one or more permits.

The easiest way to deal with the city regulations and officials is to make sure that any work you do complies with the appropriate code. Building officials are primarily concerned with life and safety, so they pay most attention to plumbing, especially waste and water lines, and electricity. These are the areas in which you are most likely to need permits and/or expert work. Specifically, changes in drainage vent and water supply systems require a permit and a master plumber to do the job. For electrical work costing over $100 you must have a permit; for over $2,500 you must have a licensed electrician. Plumbing permits are issued only to master plumbers. Electrical permits for jobs costing over $2,500 are issued only to licensed electricians. Some areas of the Building Code require that plans and specifications be drawn up and stamped by a registered architect, in which case he or she may apply for the permit. Except for these items, a permit can usually be acquired by the owner or contractor.

It is best at the outset to estimate carefully the extent of work you are doing and its cost, and not to apply for a permit unless you are certain you have to. You should check the code first, then, if necessary, get L&I advice. When you present your plans and application, L&I will inform you of what you need for the work you are doing. The codes and permit requirements are all subject to interpretation by L&I staff. Likewise, all staff decisions may be appealed.

1. When you visit L&I allow plenty of time. Your plans and application may have to be reviewed by a number of different people while you wait.
2. Take your plans and specifications to the L&I Plan Examiner. You will be given an application form on which you must describe and draw your plans and es-timate costs for the work. You must also include your name, address, the ward, lot, and block numbers of the property, and names and addresses of any contractors employed.
3. Hand in your application and get a number.
4. Wait. You will be called by your number and address.
5. The plan examiner will compare your plans with your zoning file. If your changes to the building do not conform with zoning regulations in your area, you will have to apply for a zoning variance before proceeding further (see below, How to Apply for a Zoning Variance).
6. If your building is certified by the city as historical, your plans will have to be approved by the Historical Commission.
7. Assuming there are no problems with zoning or Historical Commission review, the plan examiner will check your plans against the code to determine whether you are in compliance with it and what permits you need. He will also check your cost estimate for accuracy.
8. If your plans are not approved, ask why and get the relevant code chapter. You may appeal on the basis that you are in line with the spirit and intent of the code, or on the basis of hardship. Appeals must be made to the Board of Licenses and Inspections Review within ten days of notification of the decision.
9. If all goes well, your plans will be approved and you will be issued the necessary permits. For each permit you must pay a fee based on the cost estimate for the job.
10. Establish an inspection schedule. The schedule will vary according to the kind of work you are doing.
11. If your building has a low value for tax purposes you may be eligible for a real estate tax exemption on the improvement over a period of five years. Be sure to ask about it and apply for it when you get your permits. Application is made to the Board of Revision of

Taxes through L&I. (Buildings with low assessments are now rare in Rittenhouse, but there may be some that qualify for this provision.)

12. Post your permits in a visible place and start work. All permits have an expiration date, so try to get your work done expeditiously. If you run over the time allowed, you may have to apply for a renewal or extension.

13. Inform the appropriate city departments when you are ready for inspections.

14. If your building is used by the public (office, apartment, etc.) you will have to get a Certificate of Occupancy after the work has been completed and inspected.

## How to Apply for a Zoning Variance   The Philadelphia Zoning Code covers the size, mass, and use of buildings and open space throughout the city. It also regulates outdoor advertising and signs, has special controls for Rittenhouse Square (among other areas), and sets guidelines for the Historical Commission to encourage historic preservation.

If you put up a sign, change the use of your building, or change it in such a way that a neighbor is deprived of light and air, or that the ratio on your lot of open area to built-up area is altered, you must get approval from the Department of Licenses and Inspections (L&I). The application form requires information similar to that required for a building permit application, and will be given to you automatically if you go to L&I for any kind of building permit. Zoning permits have a deadline of one year for construction, during which time the work must be started and continued without interruption. If you are changing the use of your building, you must establish the new use within three months of getting the permit. If you fail to meet the deadline in either case, you may be required to apply for a new permit.

If your request for a zoning permit is not approved, you may apply for a variance. You cannot apply for a variance until your application for a permit is formally refused. Requests for variances are usually based on hardship or on the spirit and intent of the code. Specific criteria for granting variances are laid out in the Zoning Code. They include, among other things: unique condition of the property; there will be no injury to adjoining property; there will be no overcrowding of the land; there will be no adverse effect on public health, safety, and general welfare.

1. Obtain from L&I a refusal in writing of your plans. They will also send you instructions on applying for a variance.

2. Your appeal must be made within ten days of the refusal of your permit. It must include your name and address and the name and address of your attorney if you have one; your interest in the controversy; a brief description of the property; your original application number and the date of refusal of it; a statement of the factual and legal grounds for appeal and for relief sought.

3. Submit your application to the Zoning Board of Adjustment.

4. The board will inform you of the date and place set for your hearing, and will send you yellow notice-of-appeal cards. The cards must be prominently posted on all street fronts of the building for at least twelve consecutive days before the hearing. An inspector will make sure your cards are posted. If they are not, you will be denied a hearing.

5. Anyone may come to your hearing, including neighbors, and testify for or against your variance.

6. Ask to meet with the Center City Residents' Association (CCRA) Zoning Committee. Counsel for the CCRA is usually present at City Zoning Board hearings and may be asked to comment on your proposal. Gener-

ally a variance that is not opposed by the CCRA Zoning Committee will not be opposed by the City Zoning Board.

7. At the Zoning Board of Adjustment hearing you must show the following: proof of your interest in the property (deed, lease, agreement of sale); clear five-by-seven photos of each side of the property, showing the zoning notice. You may also be required to submit two copies of plans drawn to scale showing the dimensions of the lot and the location, elevation, dimensions, and uses of all existing and proposed structures. You must inform the board of any applications made concerning the property to any government agency. (All the preceding information should also be produced for the CCRA Zoning Committee if you have a meeting with them.)

8. At the Zoning Board hearing you will be asked to describe your situation and answer any questions.

9. Comments are then made by board members and anyone else who wishes to make them.

10. You will be informed by mail of the board's decision.

11. Appeals to board decisions are made either by requesting a rehearing or through the Court of Common Pleas.

## How to Apply for a Grant-in-Aid
The National Historic Preservation Act of 1966 authorized the Department of the Interior to disperse funds to the states for, among other things, acquisition and development of National Register properties, including significant structures within a National Register Historic District. In fact, grants are rarely given for acquisition, and availability of funds in general depends on congressional appropriation. In Pennsylvania the Bureau for Historic Preservation of the State Historical and Museum Commission is the agency administering grants-in-aid.

Historic Preservation grants-in-aid are "reimbursing" grants of up to 50 percent of the costs of an approved project. Application must be made in advance of actual work, and no costs incurred prior to Department of the Interior approval of the project are allowed. Upon completion of the work, a request is made for reimbursement of the amount approved.

Although administered by the states, grants are subject to guidelines, reviews, and approvals from the National Park Service. They are given to eligible public and private agencies and individuals for projects conforming to the Secretary of the Interior's Standards for Rehabilitation and Guidelines for Acquisition and Development Projects (see Appendix). It is particularly important that application be made under the appropriate category from the Guidelines for Acquisition and Development, since actions allowable under one category may not be appropriate under others. For instance, changing the size of a room or removing a hallway may be a legitimate action for the rehabilitation category, but not for restoration.

Among the costs generally allowed for a grant-in-aid are: exterior restoration, structural work, improvements in utilities; interior restoration if the public has access to the building; burglar and fire protection; landscaping—either a restoration or to protect the building; historical, archaeological, and architectural research necessary to the project; signs acknowledging federal assistance; costs of architects, and plans, specifications, and other documentation required by the Department of the Interior.

Since funds for the grant-in-aid program are limited, not all applications can be approved. Priorities are set by the Department of the Interior and by the State Bureau for Historic Preservation according to its own statewide preservation plan.

1. Check with the State Bureau for Historic Preservation for the most up-to-date information and ask for a preliminary application and guidelines.

2. Unless your project is a very small one, enlist the services of an architect to advise you and draw up plans and specifications for the project. (See Maintenance and Restoration, Architects and Contractors.)

*132. Federal Applications*

The state and Department of the Interior review processes are technical, including consideration of historical appropriateness and conformance with accepted preservation technology. It is important that plans and specifications be professionally done.

3. Prepare, with the assistance of your architect, a historic structures report. This will be helpful in determining the parts of your building that are of particular value and what work is needed. It will also be useful in preparing your grant application. The report should have a section on the chronological architectural development of the structure—description with dates of the main structure and any additions or changes, and a section showing preservation objectives—how the building is to be used, what changes must be made and why. (Guidelines for historic structures reports are available from the Department of the Interior.)

4. Determine how the work you want to do fits with the Secretary of the Interior's Standards and Guidelines for Acquisition and Development.

5. Fill out a preliminary application, which includes the following information: names and addresses of property and owner; present and intended use; National Register status; description and justification of proposed project; cost breakdown; eight-by-ten black and white glossy photos of the property and major areas of work.

6. Bureau personnel will review your preliminary application and either turn it down or suggest that you file a more detailed application.

7. The second application must include the following information and materials: name, address, and telephone number of person or organization applying; name of property and owner; category in which the project falls; itemized breakdown of all work with estimated costs; plans and specifications with corroborating historical documentation; three current eight-by-ten black and white glossy photos of the structure, and, where appropriate, additional photos showing the area to be restored; source of matching (nonfederal) share of project costs; names, addresses, and telephone numbers of project personnel; resume of primary supervisor.

8. In the application you must also include the following documents: qualified professional appraisal of any donated property or services used to match federal funds; certification that the property is not in a designated flood zone, or if it is, that flood insurance covering at least the amount of the proposed grant has been purchased.

9. If you receive the grant, you will be required to encumber your deed with two covenants for a number of years, depending on the amount of the grant. Your application should include a letter stating your willingness to comply with these restrictions. A Maintenance and Administration Covenant requires the owner and successors to repair, maintain, and administer the premises and to preserve their historic integrity, materials, workmanship, and appearance. A Public Benefit Covenant, for grants covering interior work, requires the owner to open the building to the public at least twelve days each year. If the funds are for exterior work visible from the public street, no Public Benefit Covenant is required. If your grant is for acquisition of a property, you must also have a covenant giving the state first right of refusal in case of sale or other disposal of the property.

10. Submit your application to the State Bureau for Historic Preservation. It will be reviewed by the bureau, and if approved, passed on to the Department of the Interior. If your application is in any way incomplete or unclear, either of these agencies may ask further questions.

11. Do not start work until you receive notice that your grant has been approved by the Department of the

Interior and you are authorized to proceed. Any work done prior to approval of the grant is not eligible for reimbursement.

12. When your grant is approved you must send the state a copy of your deed encumbered by the required covenants.

13. Actual money is not usually dispersed until the project, or a major stage of it, is completed. Requests are made to the state for reimbursement of the federal share of the amount spent.

14. Bureau for Historic Preservation staff may, from time to time, make on-site inspections to ensure that your project is proceeding as authorized.

15. While work is in progress, you must post a sign giving credit to the Bureau for Historic Preservation and the Department of the Interior for assisting the project. Credit must also be given in any publications, films, exhibitions, and so forth about the project.

16. Grantees must conform to all equal opportunity employment and federal and state contract regulations.

# How to Apply for Tax Advantages
Current tax law gives investment credits for certified rehabilitations of certified historic properties and allows charitable deductions for donations of easements on such properties. (See Methods for Preservation, Tax Incentives.)

A certified historic property is one that is on the National Register or considered significant to a National Register district. (See Appendix, Standards for Evaluating Structures within Registered Historic Districts.) A certified rehabilitation is one that conforms to the Secretary of the Interior's Standards for Rehabilitation (see Appendix) and is approved by the National Park Service. In order to obtain a tax credit, you must have both certifications. Certification of significance is required to claim a deduction for an easement.

If you intend to do a certified rehabilitation, it may be wise to consult an architect and have him draw up plans and specifications for the project and fill out the Description of Rehabilitation form. (See Procedures, How to Deal with Architects and Contractors.) The National Park Service has rigorous guidelines for historical appropriateness and use of technology. Moreover, its forms and review procedures require technical detail. An architect knowledgeable in preservation may help you avoid problems. The regulations governing certification procedures change from time to time. The following are the most current as this book goes to press.

## Evaluation of Significance

1. Ask the State Bureau for Historic Preservation for up-to-date information and a Historic Preservation Certification Application. This form is in two parts: (1) evaluation of significance, for the building certification; (2) description of rehabilitation, for rehabilitation certification.

2. Find out if your building is listed on the National Register of Historic Places or if it is in a National Register district. National Register listings are available at local libraries, the Philadelphia Historical Commission, and the State Bureau for Historic Preservation.

3. If your building is on the National Register, it is automatically certified. If it is in a National Register district, you must apply for designation as a certified historic structure by filling out the evaluation of significance section of the certification application. This requires the name and address of the owner; name and address of the structure; name of the historic district; current photographs of the structure; a brief description of the property, including mention of alterations, distinctive characteristics and spaces, and dates of construction; a brief statement of historical and/or ar-

chitectural significance; and a sketch map showing the structure's location within the district.

4. Send your completed application to the State Bureau for Historic Preservation. They will review it and forward it, with a recommendation, to the National Park Service. The Park Service will send you either a certification of significance or notice that the structure is not historically significant.

5. If you are denied certification of significance, you may appeal in writing to the National Park Service. Your appeal must be made within thirty days of receipt of the notice of denial, and a decision on your appeal will be made within thirty days. This decision is final.

### *Description of Rehabilitation*

1. At any time during the course of the rehabilitation work, you may apply for designation of your work as a certified rehabilitation. It is best, however, to apply before starting work, or at least before the work is finished, in case you are directed to make changes to comply with the Secretary of the Interior's Standards for Rehabilitation. Application should be made on part two of the Historic Preservation Certification Application form, available from the State Bureau for Historic Preservation. The form requires a description of the existing condition of the building; a description of the rehabilitation work and its effect on existing architectural features; and photographs and drawings showing existing conditions and the proposed or completed work.

2. Send your completed application to the State Bureau for Historic Preservation. They will review it and send it on, with a recommendation, to the National Park Service.

3. The National Park Service will notify you whether the project conforms to the Secretary of the Interior's Standards for Rehabilitation. It will also ask you to pay a fee for processing your request for rehabilitation certification. The fee is $250 for proposed or ongoing projects worth over $20,000. For completed projects fees range from $500 to $2,500, based on the cost of the project. If the project is not yet completed, and does not conform to the secretary's standards, the Park Service or state bureau will advise you of necessary revisions, and, on occasion, make consultants available to help in developing acceptable plans.

4. When you have completed your work, you must notify the National Park Service, through the state bureau, stating that you believe it meets the Standards for Rehabilitation. You should include photographs or other materials showing the completed project.

5. If, in the opinion of the National Park Service, the completed project meets the secretary's standards, it will be certified.

6. If your application for certification is denied, you may appeal in writing to the National Park Service. An appeal must be made within thirty days of receipt of denial of certification, and you will be advised of the decision on the appeal within thirty days of filing it. This decision is final.

7. File the appropriate certification forms with your tax return.

# APPENDIXES

*Railing detail (Photo by Bernie Cleff)*

# 1. BIOGRAPHICAL LIST OF ARCHITECTS REPRESENTED IN RITTENHOUSE

*Compiled by* JEFFERSON MOAK

**Chandler, Theophilus Parsons (1845–1928)** A Boston native with Philadelphia ancestry, Chandler studied at the Atelier Vandremer in Paris after spending a year at Harvard University. He returned to Boston after his Parisian studies, where he trained in the offices of several city architects. Chandler moved to Philadelphia in 1872 to work on the development of Ridley Park, a suburb in Delaware County, Pennsylvania. Six years later, *Godey's Lady's Book* published several of his designs. He belonged to both the Philadelphia chapter and the national American Institute of Architects, becoming president of the former in 1888. This position assisted him in his efforts to convince the University of Pennsylvania to establish its Department of Architecture. He then served as the department's first head. His completed buildings appear throughout the Middle Atlantic states, including ecclesiastical designs in Darlington, Maryland, Pittsburgh, Pennsylvania, and Washington, D.C., as well as in Philadelphia. Although many of Chandler's buildings have gone, much of his work in Rittenhouse still stands, principally the Church of the New Jerusalem at Twenty-Second and Chestnut streets, and residences at 2136 Locust Street, 1912 Rittenhouse Square, 2006 and 2032 Walnut Street, and 133 and 251 South Twenty-Second Street.

**Cope and Stewardson (1884–1912)** Walter Cope (1860–1902) and John Stewardson (1857–1896) met while employed by Theophilus P. Chandler, having traveled different roads to that meeting. Cope was a product of the Germantown Friends School; Stewardson was a graduate of Harvard University and several years' study at the Ecole des Beaux-Arts in Paris. Leaving Chandler's office in 1884, they established their own firm with John Stewardson's younger brother Emlyn (1863–1936). First working in the popular Queen Anne style, the firm soon developed the Jacobethan, or "Collegiate Gothic," style, which it employed extensively on the campuses of Bryn Mawr and Haverford colleges, Princeton University, the University of Pennsylvania, and Washington University,

St. Louis. Like their contemporary and friend Wilson Eyre Jr., the firm received favorable reviews from the various architectural journals and was the subject of a photo essay in the *Architectural Record*. Cope and Stewardson designed many town houses throughout Rittenhouse, including 1630, 1631–33, and 1718 Locust Street, 1921–23 Walnut Street, and 306 South Nineteenth Street. The Lady Chapel of St. Mark's Episcopal Church also owes its design to this firm.

**Cret, Paul Philippe (1876–1945)** Paul Cret's chief contribution to Philadelphia's architectural world is the training and discipline he acquired at the Ecoles des Beaux-Arts in both Lyons and Paris, and transmitted to his students during a thirty-four-year teaching career at the University of Pennsylvania. He thereby influenced an entire generation of architects. Cret did not limit his activities to education. He designed many buildings, bridges, and memorials, not only in Philadelphia but throughout the United States and Europe. His chief commissions include the Folger Shakespeare Library in Washington, D.C., the Federal Reserve Bank in Philadelphia, the Detroit Institute of Arts, many major components of the University of Texas at Austin, and the Benjamin Franklin and Henry Avenue bridges, both in Philadelphia. His contribution to the Rittenhouse neighborhood was the redesign of the Rittenhouse Square landscaping in 1913.

**Day, Frank Miles (1861–1918)** Day received much of his early training in the offices of George T. Pearson and Addison Hutton while he attended classes at the University of Pennsylvania. After his graduation in 1883, he spent three years in Europe furthering his studies, which included courses at the Royal Academy School of Architecture in London. Upon his return he gained immediate recognition when he won the competition for the Philadelphia Art Club on Broad Street below Walnut. In 1893 he invited his elder brother, H. Kent Day, to become his partner, forming the firm of Frank Miles Day and Brother.

In the early twentieth century this firm again changed names with the elevation of Charles Z. Klauder to a partnership (Day Brothers and Klauder, Day and Klauder). Although most of the firm's work exists within the immediate vicinity of Philadelphia, important commissions stand on the campuses of Princeton and Cornell universities and Wellesley College. Day designed a number of buildings in Rittenhouse, including 235 and 245–47 South Seventeenth Street, 1920–30 Pine Street, 1922 Spruce Street, and 251 South Eighteenth Street (presently the Philadelphia Art Alliance).

***Eyre, Wilson, Jr. (1858–1944)*** Born in Florence, Italy, of American parents, Eyre attended the Massachusetts Institute of Technology in 1876–77. After graduation he moved to Philadelphia and entered the office of James P. Sims, whose sudden death in 1881 allowed Eyre to assume control of the firm. In 1888 he helped found the T-Square Club with Walter Cope, John Stewardson, and others, to assist in the architectural training of the younger practitioners in the field and to help them obtain a broader outlook on their profession. It soon rivaled the local chapter of the American Institute of Architects, although many architects belonged to both organizations. The majority of Eyre's work appeared in the Philadelphia metropolitan area in the form of country houses. However, examples of his designs exist throughout the United States. The *Architectural Record* devoted a full article to his career in 1905 and another one, showcasing his office at 1003 Spruce Street, in 1913. Eyre designed the St. Anthony's Club at 32 South Twenty-Second Street, the Bradsbury Bedell House at 101 South Twenty-Second Street, and the Neil and Mauran Houses at 315–17 South Twenty-Second Street, among others.

***Furness, Frank (1839–1912)*** A native Philadelphian, Furness trained in the New York office of Richard Morris Hunt before returning to this city to form a partnership with John Fraser and George W. Hewitt. The various firms he either headed or in which he acted as a partner include Fraser, Furness, and Hewitt (1867–71); Furness and Hewitt (1871–76); Frank Furness (1876–81); Furness and Evans (1881–86); and Furness, Evans, and Company (1886–1912). Unfortunately, much of his major commercial and institution work failed to survive past the mid-twentieth century; the Furness Library at the University of Pennsylvania and the Pennsylvania Academy of the Fine Arts are exceptions. Many Rittenhouse commissions still exist, including 235 South Twenty-First Street, 318–22 South Nineteenth Street, and the First Unitarian Church at 2121 Chestnut Street. His office also produced the design for 1804 Rittenhouse Square under the direction of George W. Casey.

***Hahn, Frank Eugene (1879–1962)*** Hahn received his early training as an engineer with the Philadelphia and Reading Railroad and the Philadelphia Rapid Transit Company. He subsequently studied architecture under Paul Cret. He formed two partnerships during his career: the first with Andrew J. Sauer (Sauer and Hahn) from 1906 to 1916, the other with Hamred Brian Baylinson (Hahn and Baylinson) from 1923 to 1928. Otherwise he practiced alone. His works generally have been undistinguished. With Baylinson he designed the Westbury on the northeast corner of Fifteenth and Spruce. The Warwick Hotel at Seventeenth and Locust streets, a 1925 creation, is his masterpiece of architectural design.

***Haviland, John (1792–1852)*** John Haviland, a native of Sussex, England, studied under the London architect James Elmes from 1811 to 1815. He then traveled first to Russia and later to the United States, choosing to settle in Philadelphia in September 1816. He issued a three-volume work entitled *The Builder's Assistant* between 1818 and 1821. He started to receive a number of important commissions in Philadelphia, including the Franklin

Institute (now the Atwater Kent Museum) on Seventh Street below Market, and St. Andrew's Episcopal Church (now St. George's Greek Orthodox Church) on Eighth Street below Locust. He achieved an international reputation with Eastern State Penitentiary, a design copied by prison architects throughout the world. Of the several designs he executed in Rittenhouse, only the Pennsylvania Institution for the Deaf and Dumb (now the Philadelphia College of Art) at Broad and Pine streets remains.

***Hazelhurst and Huckel (1881–1900)*** Edward Hazelhurst (1853–1915) was a native of Kentucky. He entered the University of Pennsylvania in 1872 but left before graduating to train in the offices of T. P. Chandler and Frank Furness. He joined Huckel in partnership in 1881. Samuel Huckel, Jr. (1858–1917), a native of the Frankford section of Philadelphia, graduated from Central High School in 1879 and trained with Benjamin D. Price until 1881. Known primarily for its late Victorian and Richardsonian Romanesque style, the firm's ecclesiastical work includes Mother Bethel A.M.E. Church at Sixth and Lombard streets and the Union Methodist Church on Diamond Street. Examples of work in Rittenhouse are 2017 Locust and 28–30 South Twenty-Second Street.

***Hewitt, G. W. and W. D. (1878–1907)*** George Watson Hewitt (1841–1916) and his brother William Dempster Hewitt (1847–1924) joined forces in 1878 to form this distinguished firm. George Hewitt had trained in the offices of Joseph C. Hoxie, John Notman, and John Fraser before Fraser elevated him to a partnership in 1867 (Fraser, Furness, and Hewitt). He continued in partnership with Frank Furness until 1875–76, executing many church designs which marked him as one of the preeminent architects working in this specialized field. The Hewitt firm after 1878 became one of the most versatile of architectural offices, designing buildings for residential, ecclesiastical, commercial, and industrial clients. Its influence was primarily local, with a large amount of resi-

dential work executed for upper-class clients in the suburbs of the city, numerous church buildings throughout the city and suburbs, and a number of major buildings, including the Philadelphia Bourse, the Wissahickon Inn, and the Bellevue-Stratford Hotel. In Rittenhouse, residences for Lucien Moss at 2100 Spruce Street, John C. Bullitt at 125 South Twenty-Second Street, and Travis Cochran at 129–31 South Twenty-Second Street are examples of its town house commissions. George Hewitt also designed the tower of the Church of the Holy Trinity facing Rittenhouse Square.

***Huston, Joseph M. (fl. 1892–1929)*** Huston's relatively short career as one of Philadelphia's prominent architects began with his training in the office of Furness, Evans, and Company from 1892 to 1894. After forming an independent practice he received several commissions in center city, including the Witherspoon Building at Walnut and Juniper streets and two houses at 1913 and 1917 Walnut Street. He then entered and won the competition for the Pennsylvania State Capitol Building in Harrisburg. Becoming embroiled in the scandals surrounding its construction, he served a short term in prison. After his release he continued his practice but received no major commissions.

***Hutton, Addison (1834–1916)*** Hutton spent his early life in Westmoreland County, Pennsylvania, coming to Philadelphia in 1857 to work in the office of Samuel Sloan. He maintained a professional association with Sloan off and on for almost ten years, first as an assistant (1857–60) and later as a partner (1864–68). With two exceptions, Hutton spent the remainder of his career without partners. The first partnership occurred in 1877 with John Ord, a draftsman in his office. One commission survives from this short relationship: 2200 Walnut Street. Not until 1904 did he consent to join another partnership: this time with his two nephews Addison and Albert Savery, and William Cramp Scheetz. Often called the "Quaker Architect," Hutton designed a speculative row of houses at 20–30 South Twenty-First Street in 1890 and the Hipple House at 244–46 South Twenty-First Street in 1882. Other surviving Center City buildings include the Philadelphia Savings Fund Society Building at 700 Walnut Street, the Arch Street Methodist Church at Broad and Arch streets, and the Historical Society of Pennsylvania at 1300 Locust Street.

**Keen, Charles Barton (1868–1931)**    A graduate of the University of Pennsylvania, Keen spent his career working in his native city, first in the offices of Theophilus P. Chandler and Frank Miles Day, then in partnership with Frank Mead from 1893 to 1900. He specialized in residential architecture, devoting his later career to the design of large country houses throughout the Atlantic seaboard. He did produce a number of town house designs in Rittenhouse during the first decade of the twentieth century, including six houses at 2125–43 Locust Street, 1827 Delancey Street, and 228 South Twenty-First Street.

**Le Brun, Napoleon (1821–1901)**    Le Brun, a native Philadelphian, was trained in the office of Thomas U. Walter. His first recorded commission was in Rittenhouse: Saint Patrick's Church (1841, no longer standing). A few years later he received Philadelphia's mid-century architectural plum, the design of the Roman Catholic Cathedral of Saints Peter and Paul on Logan Square. The twenty-year history of the building's construction awaits a final accounting but Le Brun was in charge from 1846 to 1851 and again from 1860 to its completion in 1864. Le Brun's best known design is the Academy of Music (1854–57). For this building, he formed a short-lived association with the German-born Gustav Runge. Le Brun moved to New York City in the mid-sixties and by 1868 was a member of the New York Chapter of The American Institute of Architects, later serving as its president. His firm became the official architect for the New York City Fire Department and was responsible for such "tall build-

ings" as the Metropolitan Life Insurance Company Building (1890–93) and the Home Life Insurance Company Building (1893–94). Le Brun is believed to have designed additional buildings in Philadelphia but they are so far undocumented.

**McArthur, John (1823–1890)**    McArthur, a native Scot, moved to Philadelphia with his uncle and received his training as an architect from the Carpenters' Company and the Franklin Institute. His surviving works are few; residential commissions for Dr. David Jayne, George W. Childs, and the Repplier family have fallen to the wrecking ball, along with the old Post Office at Ninth and Chestnut streets and the old Public Ledger Building at Sixth and Chestnut streets. Lanning Hall, a part of the U.S. Naval Home, is scheduled to fall soon. However, some of his work still exists, forming landmarks throughout the city: First Presbyterian Church in Frankford, the Tenth Presbyterian Church in Rittenhouse, Wagner Free Institute of Science in North Philadelphia, and Philadelphia City Hall.

**McLanahan and Bencker (1919–1925)**    A short-lived partnership between M. Hawley McLanahan (1865–1929) and Ralph Bowden Bencker (1883–1961) contributed a major element to the Rittenhouse Square streetscape: the Rittenhouse Plaza at 1901 Walnut Street. McLanahan, a native of Hollidaysburg, Pennsylvania, worked in the shadow of two architects generally considered to have had greater talent: William L. Price (Price and McLanahan, 1903–19) and Bencker (McLanahan and Bencker, 1919–25). Bencker, a Philadelphia native, trained in the offices of Wilson Eyre, Jr., Paul A. Davies, and Price and McLanahan before McLanahan elevated him to partnership status. He practiced alone after the breakup of McLanahan & Bencker. A noted architect working principally in the Art Deco style, he gained recognition with his many designs for the Horn and Hardart Baking Company and the N. W. Ayer and Son Building on Washington Square.

**Newman, Woodman, and Harris (1900–1907)**
Frank E. Newman (fl. 1898–1919), Henry Gillette Woodman (1873–1902), and James Russell Harris (1874–c. 1936) practiced together for only two years, 1900–02, when Woodman died. Newman and Harris continued the firm until Newman moved to New York in 1907. Little is known of Newman, although he is thought to have met Harris while both worked in the office of Frank Miles Day in the late 1890s. Harris received a B.S. degree in architecture from Harvard in 1896. After Newman's departure he practiced with Louis H. Rush from 1907 to 1913, and later joined Magaziner and Eberhardt. Between about 1900 and 1907 the Newman (and Woodman until 1902) and Harris firm designed the Corn Exchange National Bank at Second and Chestnut streets and the Fels mansion at Thirty-Ninth and Walnut. In Rittenhouse they were responsible for the Rittenhouse Club, the Armory at Twenty-Third and Ludlow streets, and renovations to 2107 Spruce and 2014 Delancey.

**Notman, John (1810–1865)**  Born in Edinburgh, Scotland, Notman received his architectural training before emigrating to the United States. This training may have included courses at the Royal Academy of Scotland and employment in the office of William Henry Playfair, a noted Edinburgh architect. Notman's selection as the architect of Laurel Hill Cemetery over local notables, including William Strickland, propelled him to the forefront of Philadelphia architectural circles, a status later enforced when he won the competition for the Athenaeum of Philadelphia on Washington Square. With this building he introduced the Italianate style to America. His lifelong efforts to elevate the status of the architectural profession cost him not a few clients. Nevertheless, ecclesiastical, residential, and landscape designs existing in Pennsylvania, New Jersey, Delaware, and Virginia attest to the talent of this man. Representative samples of his work in and near Rittenhouse include St. Mark's Episcopal Church and several Italianate brownstone houses in the 1600 block of Locust Street, the Church of the Holy Trinity facing Rittenhouse Square, and St. Clement's Episcopal Church at Twentieth and Cherry streets.

**Ritter and Shay (c. 1917–1934)**  This partnership between Versus Taggart Ritter (1883–1942) and Howell Lewis Shay (1884–1975) produced some of the handsomest buildings in Center City, including the Market Street National Bank (now One East Penn Square), the Packard Building (Fifteenth and Chestnut streets), the U.S. Customs House (Second and Chestnut streets), the Drake Hotel (1512 Spruce Street), and the National Society, Colonial Dames of America (1630 Latimer Street). Unfortunately, detailed information about Ritter does not exist, except that he moved to Philadelphia from Williamsport to form a partnership with Shay. The latter had achieved a local reputation by resolving an impasse between his employer, Horace Trumbauer, and Zantzinger and Borie over the design of the Philadelphia Museum of Art. Prior to working with Trumbauer, Shay, a Washington, D.C., native, had worked in the New York office of McKim, Mead, and White and the Philadelphia office of John T. Windrim.

**Sloan, Samuel (1815–1844)**  Sloan's impact upon architecture exceeded the effects of his own executed work. Although his various buildings for residential, governmental, and institutional uses achieved a quality emulated by many, Sloan more widely affected and reflected mid-nineteenth-century architectural thought and taste through his many publications, including *The Model Architect* and *City and Suburban Architecture*. Although he practiced alone for most of his career, he did form partnerships twice: with John Stewart from 1853 to 1855, and Addison Hutton from 1864 to 1868. He designed a number of houses for the Harrison family on Rittenhouse Square and along the 1700 block of Locust Street, none of which exists today.

***Trumbauer, Horace (1868–1938)*** Philadelphia-born, Trumbauer received his architectural training in the offices of G. W. and W. D. Hewitt. At first specializing in residential architecture, Trumbauer began accepting commercial and institutional commissions about 1900. His work may be found throughout the eastern United States. Perhaps his most spectacular design outside Philadelphia is the Duke University Chapel in North Carolina. He designed some of the major landmarks in Philadelphia, including the Free Library of Philadelphia on Logan Square, Irvine Auditorium of the University of Pennsylvania, and the Benjamin Franklin Hotel at Ninth and Chestnut streets. In Rittenhouse diverse examples of his work remain: 1720 Locust Street (now part of the Curtis Institute of Music), the Chateau Crillon at 222 West Rittenhouse Square, 2145 Locust Street, and the E. C. Knight, Jr. house at 1629 Locust.

***Walter, Thomas Ustick (1804–1887)*** Walter learned the architectural profession in the office of William Strickland and in the classrooms of the Franklin Institute. He became a major force in American architecture, designing residential, ecclesiastical, and monumental buildings, including Ivy Lodge in Germantown, Portico Row in Philadelphia, the Spruce Street Baptist Church (now the Society Hill Synagogue), Founder's Hall at Girard College, and the addition of the wings and dome on the United States Capitol Building in Washington, D.C. (1851–65). After resigning his post with the U.S. government, he returned to Philadelphia and assisted John McArthur in the design and construction of Philadelphia's City Hall. Walter designed several town houses in the Rittenhouse area, including 1504–38 Pine Street.

***Webber, Frederick (fl. 1899–1920)*** Renowned for his design of apartment houses throughout Philadelphia, Webber formed a partnership with Samuel C. Milligan from 1899 to 1910, executing such major commissions as Hamilton Court at Thirty-Ninth and Chestnut streets, the Coronado at Twenty-Second and Chestnut streets, and the Belgravia Hotel at 1811–17 Chestnut Street. Webber continued practicing alone after the breakup of his partnership, contributing to the Rittenhouse neighborhood such landmarks as 1830 Rittenhouse Square and the Touraine at 1520 Spruce Street. He also designed Sprucemont at 257 South Sixteenth Street, 1530 Locust Street, and 250 South Seventeenth Street.

***Zantzinger, Borie, and Medary (1911–1929), Zantzinger and Borie (1910, 1929–1943)*** Clarence Clark Zantzinger (1872–1954), Charles Louis Borie, Jr. (1870–1943), and Milton Bennett Medary, Jr. (1874–1929), all attended the University of Pennsylvania in the 1890s. As individuals and as a firm, these men became some of the most influential architects of their generation. Zantzinger attended the Ecole Nationale et Speciale des Beaux-Arts in Paris after his graduation. Borie left the university before his graduation to work in his father's banking office. In 1902 he entered Zantzinger's office and achieved partnership status by 1910. Medary dropped out of the university to work in the office of Frank Miles Day and Brother. In 1895 he formed the firm of Field and Medary with Richard L. Field, a firm responsible for several buildings in Rittenhouse, including the Butcher House at 2200 Locust Street. After Field's death in 1905 Medary practiced alone before joining Zantzinger and Borie in 1911 as a full partner. The firm of Zantzinger, Borie, and Medary executed several notable designs throughout Philadelphia, including the Fidelity Mutual Life Insurance Company Building at Pennsylvania and Fairmount avenues, and St. Paul's Episcopal Church in Chestnut Hill. They assisted in the designs of the Benjamin Franklin Parkway and the Philadelphia Museum of Art. The firm also designed one of the landmarks on Rittenhouse Square: the Penn Athletic Club Building, now the Rittenhouse Regency, at 229 South Eighteenth Street.

# 2. RESOURCES

## FEDERAL

**Advisory Council on Historic Preservation**
Suite 530, 1522 K St., N.W., Washington,
    D.C., 20005.

*Advises the president and Congress on historic preservation matters. Advises on coordination of activities of federal, state, and local agencies and private institutions. Encourages public interest and participation in preservation, supports studies, training programs, and publications. Reviews and comments on federally assisted projects that may "adversely affect" a Landmark or National Register property, or property eligible for such designation.*

**Department of Housing and Urban Development,**
    **Office of Community Planning and Development**
Washington, D. C., 20410 (Philadelphia area office, 625
    Walnut St., Philadelphia, Pa., 19106).

*Administers all HUD programs for grants and loans to local agencies and individuals for Community Development Block Grants, Section 202 housing for the elderly, Section 8 rental assistance, and so on.*

**Department of the Interior, National Park Service,**
    **Office of Cultural Resources**
Washington, D.C., 20240 (Mid-Atlantic regional office,
    600 Arch St., Philadelphia, Pa., 19106).

***Archaeological Services Division***
*Administers archaeological surveys and reviews.*

***HABS/HAER Division (Historic American Buildings
Survey, Historic American Engineering Record)***
*Supervises measuring, drawing, researching of historic buildings and structures. Documentation becomes a permanent record deposited in the Library of Congress, Washington, D.C.*

***History Division***
*Administers National Landmarks program.*

***Inter-Agency Resources Division***
*Supervises National Register, Natural Landmarks, and Planning and Surveying programs.*

***Preservation Assistance Division***
*Administers preservation grants-in-aid and reviews requests for certifications under the Tax Reform Act.*

**Department of Labor, Employment and Training**
    **Administration**
Patrick Henry Building, 601 D. St., N.W., Washington,
    D.C., 20213.
(regional office, 3535 Market St., Philadelphia, Pa.,
    19104).

*Administers CETA and Manpower programs.*

## NATIONAL—PRIVATE

**American Association for State and Local History**
1400 Eighth Ave., S., Nashville, Tenn., 37203.

*Membership association for historians and other interested persons. Holds an annual meeting and seminars, publishes technical leaflets and a monthly magazine.*

**American Institute of Architects**
The Octagon, Washington, D.C., 20006.

*Professional architects' association, has publications, exhibitions, and a Committee on Historic Preservation.*

**Association for Preservation Technology**
Box 2487, Station D, Ottawa, Ontario, K1P 5W6,
    Canada.

*Canadian-American association of professional preservationists, curators, educators, craftsmen, and other interested persons. Publishes a quarterly technical journal on restoration techniques, and a regular preservation news bulletin.*

**Committee for the Preservation of Architectural**
    **Records**
c/o Prints and Photographs Division, Library of
    Congress, Washington, D.C., 20540.

*National clearinghouse of information relating to American architectural documents.*

**National Center for Preservation Law**
2101 L St., N.W., Washington, D.C., 20037.

*Coordinates a national litigation strategy for the preservation movement. Cooperating attorneys around the country assist local preservation organizations and individuals with advice on law and economic development and community conservation techniques.*

**National Trust for Historic Preservation**
1785 Massachusetts Ave., N.W., Washington, D.C.,
    20036 (regional office, Cliveden, 1641
    Germantown Ave., Philadelphia, Pa., 19144).

*Private, nonprofit membership organization chartered by Congress to protect the built environment. Assists groups and individuals through membership, library, consultant services, and publications. Also operates its own historic properties.*

**Preservation Action**
2101 L St., N.W., Washington, D.C., 20037.

*A national lobby for preservation. Membership organization.*

**Society for Industrial Archaeology**
Room 5020, National Museum of History and
    Technology, Washington, D.C., 20560.

*International membership organization promotes study and preservation of physical survivals of the technological and industrial past. Has publications, meetings, field trips. Publishes an illustrated newsletter six times yearly, and a journal.*

**Society of Architectural Historians**
Room 716, 1700 Walnut St., Philadelphia, Pa., 19103.

*Association of architectural historians and others interested in the field. Programs for members include lectures and tours in this country and abroad. Publishes a quarterly scholarly journal and a bimonthly newsletter.*

**Victorian Society in America**
c/o The Athenaeum of Philadelphia, East Washington
    Square, Philadelphia, Pa., 19106.

*Membership organization specializing in architecture, arts, and general culture of the Victorian era. Holds annual seminar on nineteenth-century culture. Publishes seminar proceedings and a monthly bulletin.*

PENNSYLVANIA—PUBLIC

**Pennsylvania Historical and Museum Commission,
    Bureau for Historic Preservation**
William Penn Memorial Museum Building, Box 1026,
    Harrisburg, Pa., 17120.

*Administers State Historic Preservation Plan, handles applications and recommendations to the Department of the Interior for National Register properties and evaluation of properties for tax purposes. Administers Historic Preservation Grants and Section 106 reviews. Maintains data base compiled from statewide survey.*

PENNSYLVANIA—PRIVATE

**Pennsylvania Committee for the Preservation of
    Architectural Records**
c/o The Athenaeum of Philadelphia, East Washington
    Square, Philadelphia, Pa., 19106.

*Volunteer clearinghouse for information relating to architectural documents. Concerned with locating, recording, indexing, and helping in the preservation of architectural drawings, photographs, manuscripts, and so on.*

**The Preservation Fund of Pennsylvania**
2470 Kissel Hill Road, Lancaster, Pa., 17601.

*Acquires and administers revolving funds for historic preservation of endangered historic, archaeological, and maritime properties in Pennsylvania.*

PHILADELPHIA—PUBLIC

**City Planning Commission**
13th floor, City Hall Annex.

*Responsible for guiding the physical development of the city. Designs comprehensive development plan and modifications. Proposes zoning ordinances and amendments and subdivision regulations. Sets capital program and budget for public improvements.*

Department of Licenses and Inspections
720 Municipal Services Building.

*Administers and enforces Zoning, Planning, Building, Electrical, Plumbing, and Fire codes. Issues permits, collects fees, and inspects buildings. Zoning Board of Adjustment deals with appeals on zoning matters.*

Department of Public Property
Art Commission, 1329 City Hall Annex.

*Reviews design of signage, art work, and architecture on public property. In Rittenhouse, its jurisdiction includes streets, Rittenhouse and Fitler squares, Schuylkill River Park.*

Department of Records
156 City Hall, 523 City Hall Annex.

*Keeps all records, current and archival, of the city and county of Philadelphia. Includes deeds, wills, sheriff's records, atlases, directories, and so on.*

Department of Recreation
1450 Municipal Services Building.

*Is responsible for maintenance of Fitler Square (among other areas citywide) and for recreation programs in public spaces, including play equipment and performances.*

Fairmount Park Commission
Memorial Hall, Fairmount Park.

*Responsible for the maintenance of Fairmount Park, including Rittenhouse Square and Schuylkill River Park.*

Free Library of Philadelphia
Logan Square.

*Public library, includes large collection of newspapers, photographs, prints, and survey maps.*

Managing Director's Office
1620 Municipal Services Building.

*Administers Clean Streets program, among others.*

Office of Housing and Community Development
703 City Hall Annex.

*Administers community and economic development pro-grams, including funds from U.S. Department of Housing and Urban Development.*

Philadelphia Historical Commission, 1313 City Hall Annex.

*Designates buildings, structures, objects, sites, and districts historically significant to the city and administers laws and procedures protective of them. Keeps records on designated and National Register buildings and historical architectural survey of the city. Has some insurance records. Supports and encourages preservation activity in the city.*

Streets Department
840 Municipal Services Building.

*Administers city-owned streets.*

PHILADELPHIA—PRIVATE

American Institute of Architects, Philadelphia Chapter
Architects' Building, 17th and Sansom sts., Philadelphia, Pa., 19103.

*Local branch of professional architects' association. Has exhibitions, publications, Committee on Historic Preservation, bookstore, file of local members indexed by specialty.*

Athenaeum of Philadelphia
East Washington Square, Philadelphia, Pa., 19106.

*Independent research library with outstanding architectural and nineteenth-century collections. Open to researchers and others, as well as members. Has lecture series and other programs of literary, historical, and architectural interest. Reprints architectural pattern and paint books and publishes monographs on specific architects.*

Center City Association of Proprietors
1704 Walnut St., Philadelphia, Pa., 19103.

*Membership organization for businesses. Promotes Center City business, both locally and for tourists. Aims to improve quality and public visibility.*

**Center City Residents' Association**
2027 Chestnut St., Philadelphia, Pa., 19103.

*Community membership organization for Rittenhouse area. Makes recommendations to city on planning and zoning matters. Encourages and assists in developing community resources. Holds annual house tour and public meetings.*

**Foundation for Architecture**
Architects' Building, 17th and Sansom sts., Philadelphia, Pa., 19103.

*Promotes appreciation and understanding of architecture through public education for adults and children. Sponsors lectures, tours, workshops, and schools program. Holds smaller, more specialized events for members.*

**Friends of Rittenhouse Square**
1818 Market St., Philadelphia, Pa., 19103.

*Membership organization initiates and supports maintenance and improvements to Rittenhouse Square, also public programs.*

**Historic Rittenhouse, Inc.**
2027 Chestnut St., Philadelphia, Pa., 19103.

*Nonprofit organization promotes historic preservation in and recognition of the Rittenhouse neighborhood through planning and public programs.*

**Historical Society of Pennsylvania**
1300 Locust St., Philadelphia, Pa., 19107.

*Research collection of books, manuscripts, art works, and objects dealing with Pennsylvania history from its founding to the present. Includes extensive newspaper file, insurance and census records, city directories, photographs, prints, and genealogical records. Mounts exhibitions and holds meetings for members, publishes quarterly* Pennsylvania Magazine of History and Biography.

**Library Company of Philadelphia**
1314 Locust St., Philadelphia, Pa., 19107.

*Rare book research library, includes books to 1880 and large collection of nineteenth- and twentieth-century photographs and prints. Mounts exhibitions and holds special programs for members.*

**Philadelphia Historic Preservation Corporation**
Suite 1400, 1 East Penn Square, Philadelphia, Pa., 19107.

*Promotes preservation and restoration of historic buildings by holding facade easements, developing historic buildings, and assisting public and private agencies and individuals in restoration projects.*

**Preservation Coalition of Greater Philadelphia**
1629 Locust St., Philadelphia, Pa., 19103.

*Consortium of agencies, neighborhood organizations, and individuals dedicated to maintaining the historic heritage of greater Philadelphia.*

**Society of Architectural Historians, Philadelphia Chapter**
(Check national office for most recent address.)
*Local chapter of national organization. Holds tours and lectures dealing with architecture. Assists in Delaware Valley preservation efforts as needed.*

**University of Pennsylvania Fine Arts and Architecture Library**
Furness Building, 34th and Walnut sts., Philadelphia, Pa., 19104.

*Collection of architectural and rare books. Has some architects' drawings.*

**Victorian Society in America, Philadelphia Chapter**
(Check national office for most recent address.)
*Local chapter of national organization. Holds tours, lectures, and other programs on nineteenth-century life and culture.*

# 3. THE SECRETARY OF THE INTERIOR'S STANDARDS FOR EVALUATING STRUCTURES WITHIN REGISTERED HISTORIC DISTRICTS

# 4. THE SECRETARY OF THE INTERIOR'S STANDARDS FOR REHABILITATION

The following standards are used to determine eligibility for grants and tax incentives of buildings within National Register Districts. (Reprinted courtesy of the National Park Service.)

1. A structure contributing to the historic significance of a district is one that by location, design, setting, materials, workmanship, feeling, and association adds to the district's sense of time and place and historical development.
2. A structure not contributing to the historic significance of a district is one that detracts from the district's sense of time and place and historical development; or one where the integrity of the original design or individual architectural features or spaces have been irretrievably lost; or one where physical deterioration and/or structural damage has made it not reasonably feasible to rehabilitate the building.
3. Ordinarily structures that have been built within the past fifty years shall not be considered eligible unless a strong justification concerning their historical or architectural merit is given or the historical attributes of the district are considered to be less than fifty years old.

The Secretary of the Interior's Standards for Rehabilitation are the basic guidelines for work done under the Historic Preservation Grants-in-Aid program and for certified rehabilitations under the tax law. Although there is some flexibility in interpreting the Standards for Rehabilitation, an owner who does not follow them, at least in spirit, is unlikely to get a grant-in-aid or tax credit.

The Department of the Interior has also prepared more specific Guidelines for Rehabilitating Historic Buildings which elaborate on these standards, but are too lengthy to be reprinted here. Copies are available from the Office of Cultural Resources in Washington, or from the Bureau for Historic Preservation in Harrisburg. (The following is reprinted courtesy of the National Park Service.)

Rehabilitation means the process of returning a property to a state of utility, through repair or alteration, which makes possible an efficient contemporary use while preserving those portions and features of the property which are significant to its historic, architectural, and cultural values.

The following Standards for Rehabilitation shall be used by the Secretary of the Interior when determining if a rehabilitation project qualifies as "certified rehabilitation" pursuant to the Tax Reform Act of 1976 and the Revenue Act of 1978. These standards are a section of the secretary's "Standards for Historic Preservation Projects" and appear in Title 36 of the Code of Federal Regulations, Part 1208 (formerly 36 CFR Part 67).

1. Every reasonable effort shall be made to provide a compatible use for a property which requires minimal alteration of the building, structure, or site and its environment, or to use a property for its originally intended purpose.
2. The distinguishing original qualities or character of a building, structure, or site and its environment shall not be destroyed. The removal or alteration of any historic material or distinctive architectural features should be avoided when possible.
3. All buildings, structures, and sites shall be recognized as products of their own time. Alterations that have no historical basis and which seek to create an earlier appearance shall be discouraged.
4. Changes which may have taken place in the course of time are evidence of the history and development of a building, structure, or site and its environment. These changes may have acquired significance in their own right, and this significance shall be recognized and respected.
5. Distinctive stylistic features or examples of skilled craftsmanship which characterize a building, structure, or site shall be treated with sensitivity.

6. Deteriorated architectural features shall be repaired rather than replaced, wherever possible. In the event replacement is necessary, the new material should match the material being replaced in composition, design, color, texture, and other visual qualities. Repair or replacement of missing architectural features should be based on accurate duplications of features, substantiated by historic, physical, or pictorial evidence rather than on conjectural designs or the availability of different architectural elements from other buildings or structures.

7. The surface cleaning of structures shall be undertaken with the gentlest means possible. Sandblasting and other cleaning methods that will damage the historic building materials shall not be undertaken.

8. Every reasonable effort shall be made to protect and preserve archaeological resources affected by or adjacent to any project.

9. Contemporary design for alterations and additions to existing properties shall not be discouraged when such alterations and additions do not destroy significant historical, architectural, or cultural material, and such design is compatible with the size, scale, color, material, and character of the property, neighborhood, or environment.

10. Wherever possible, new additions or alterations to structures shall be done in such a manner that if such additions or alterations were to be removed in the future, the essential form and integrity of the structure would be unimpaired.

In addition to the Secretary of the Interior's Standards for Rehabilitation, there are more specific guidelines for acquisition and development under the grants-in-aid program for National Register buildings. They consist of a series of definitions of various levels of preservation, and standards for work done under each category. These guidelines, together with the Standards for Rehabilitation, are used by all grants officers in planning, undertaking, and supervising grant-assisted projects. All grant applications must specify the particular category under which the work to be done falls. (The following is reprinted courtesy of the National Park Service.)

***Acquisition***   Is defined as the act or process of acquiring fee title or interest other than fee title of real property (including the acquisition of development rights or remainder interest).

1. Careful consideration shall be given to the type and extent of property rights which are required to assure the preservation of the historic resource. The preservation objective shall determine the exact property rights to be acquired.

2. Properties shall be acquired in fee simple when absolute ownership is required to insure their preservation.

3. The purchase of less than fee interests such as open space or facade easements shall be undertaken when a limited interest achieves the preservation objective.

4. Every reasonable effort shall be made to acquire sufficient property with the historic resource to protect its historical, archaeological, architectural, or cultural significance.

***Protection***   Is defined as the act or process of applying measures designed to affect the physical condition of a property by defending or guarding it from deterioration, loss, or attack, or to cover or shield the property from danger or injury. In the case of buildings and structures,

# 5. GUIDELINES FOR ACQUISITION AND DEVELOPMENT PROJECTS

such treatment is generally of a temporary nature and anticipates future historic preservation treatment. In the case of archaeological sites, the protective measure may be temporary or permanent.

1. Before applying protective measures which are generally of a temporary nature and imply future historic preservation work, an analysis of the actual or anticipated threats to the property shall be made.
2. Protection shall safeguard the physical condition or environment of a property or archaeological site from further deterioration or damage caused by weather or other natural, animal, or human intrusions.
3. If any historical material or architectural features are removed, they shall be properly recorded and, if possible, stored for future study or reuse.

*Stabilization*    Is defined as the act or process of applying measures designed to reestablish a weather resistant enclosure, and the structural stability of an unsafe or deteriorated property, while maintaining the essential form as it exists at present.

1. Stabilization shall reestablish the structural stability of a property through the reinforcement of loadbearing members, or by arresting material deterioration leading to structural failure. Stabilization shall also reestablish weather resistant conditions for a property.
2. Stabilization shall be accomplished in such a manner that it detracts as little as possible from the property's appearance. When reinforcement is required to reestablish structural stability, such work shall be concealed wherever possible so as not to intrude upon or detract from the aesthetic and historic quality of the property, except where concealment would result in the alteration or destruction of historically significant material or spaces.

*Preservation*    Is defined as the act or process of applying measures to sustain the existing form, integrity, and material of a building or structure, and the existing form and vegetative cover of a site. It may include initial stabilization work, where necessary, as well as ongoing maintenance of the historic building materials.

1. Preservation shall maintain the existing form, integrity, and materials of a building, structure, or site. Substantial reconstruction or restoration of lost features generally are not included in a preservation undertaking.
2. Preservation shall include techniques of arresting or retarding the deterioration of a property through a program of ongoing maintenance.

*Rehabilitation*    Is defined as the act or process of returning a property to a state of utility through repair or alteration which makes possible an efficient contemporary use while preserving those portions or features of the property which are significant to its historic, architectural, and cultural values.

1. Contemporary design for alterations and additions to existing properties shall not be discouraged when such alterations and additions do not destroy significant historical, architectural, or cultural material, and such design is compatible with the size, scale, color, material, and character of the property, neighborhood, or environment.
2. Wherever possible, new additions or alterations to structures shall be done in such a manner that if such additions or alterations were to be removed in the future, the essential form and integrity of the structure would be unimpaired.

*Restoration*    Is defined as the act or process of accurately recovering the form and details of a property and its setting as it appeared at a particular period of time, by means of the removal of later work or by the replacement of missing earlier work.

1. Every reasonable effort shall be made to use a property for its originally intended purpose, or to provide a compatible use which will require minimum alteration to the property and its environment.
2. Reinforcement required for structural stability or the installation of protective or code-required mechanical systems shall be concealed whenever possible so as not to intrude or detract from the property's aesthetic and historic qualities, except where concealment would result in the alteration or destruction of historically significant materials or spaces.
3. When archaeological resources must be disturbed by restoration work, recovery of archaeological material shall be undertaken in conformance with current professional practices.

***Reconstruction*** Is defined as the act or process of reproducing by new construction the exact form and detail of a vanished building, structure, or object, or a part thereof, as it appeared at a specific period of time.

1. Reconstruction of a part or all of a property shall be undertaken only when such work is essential to reproduce a significant missing feature in a historic district or scene, and when a contemporary design solution is not acceptable.
2. Reconstruction of all or a part of a historic property shall be appropriate when the reconstruction is essential for understanding and interpreting the value of a historic district, or when no other building, structure, object, or landscape feature with the same associative value has survived, and sufficient historical documentation exists to insure an accurate reproduction of the original.
3. The reproduction of missing elements accomplished with new materials shall duplicate the composition, design, color, texture, and other visual qualities of the missing element. Reconstruction of missing architectural features shall be based upon accurate duplication of original features, substantiated by historical, physical, or pictorial evidence rather than upon conjectural designs or the availability of different architectural features from other buildings.
4. Reconstruction of a building or structure on an original site shall be preceded by a thorough archaeological investigation to locate and identify all subsurface features and artifacts.
5. Reconstruction shall include measures to preserve any remaining original fabric, including foundations, subsurface, and ancillary elements. The reconstruction of missing elements and features shall be done in such a manner that the essential form and integrity of the original surviving features are unimpaired.

133. The Parthenon in Athens[1]

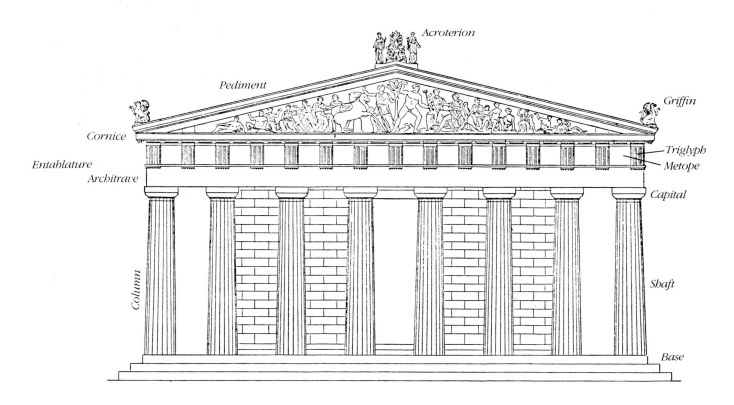

Acroterion

Pediment

Griffin

Cornice

Triglyph

Entablature

Metope

Architrave

Capital

Column

Shaft

Base

**ACROTERION**   Originally in Greek architecture the plinth or base of a statue at the apex and ends of a pediment. By extension an ornament at the same location.

**ANTHEMION**   A symmetrical ornamental design based on honeysuckle flowers and leaves used in Greek and Roman architecture.

**ARCHITRAVE**   The lowest component of the entablature that spans an opening in the classical orders. Also applied to door and window design.

**ASHLAR (COURSED)**   The stone facing of a wall set with continuous horizontal joints.

**BALUSTRADE**   A row of small columns topped by a rail, serving as a fence for balconies, parapets, and stairs.

**BARGE BOARD**   A piece of wood trim at the juncture of wall and roof, also called a vergeboard.

**BASE**   The lower projecting part of a wall or the part of a column below the shaft.

**BAY WINDOW**   A window projecting out from a wall. Also called an oriel.

**BONDING**   Refers to various patterns of laying up and tying together brick masonry. (See figs. 80–83.)

**BOSS**   An ornamental projection at the convergence of ribs in a ceiling. By extension any ornamental projection.

**BRACKET**   A piece of wood or stone (sometimes carved) projecting from a wall, designed to support an element above. (See fig. 109.)

**BROWNSTONE**   Buff-colored sandstone popular for facing exterior walls and for sills and lintels, 1860–90. Often richly shaped.

**BUTTRESS**   A projecting support to the exterior of a wall.

**BUTTRESS, FLYING**   On the exterior, a full or half arch of stone, wood, or metal designed to resist the tendency of a roof to push the supporting walls outward, as in a Gothic cathedral.

**CAPITAL**   The uppermost part of a classical column or pilaster below the entablature.

**CASEMENT WINDOW**   A window hinged at the side or designed to act as if hinged at the side so it opens like a book.

**CHAMFER**   A diagonal cut or bevel at the corner of a squared piece of masonry or wood.

**CLASSICAL ORDERS**   The architectural canons of ancient Greek and Roman column design.

**COLUMN**   A cylindrical support for roofs, ceilings, etc. May be composed of base, shaft, and capital.

**COLUMN, ENGAGED**   A column recessed into and attached to a wall.

**CORBEL**   A bracket executed as successive courses of brick with the uppermost course projecting farthest.

**CORNICE**   The projection, often decorated, that protects the joint between a wall and a roof. (See fig. 109.)

**CRENELATION**   The vertical slits at the top of a battlement wall.

**DENTIL**   An ornamental square block or projection in a cornice.

**DORMER**   An enclosure and window in a vertical plane emerging from an inclined roof. (See fig. 104.)

**DOUBLE-HUNG WINDOW**   A window made up of separate upper and lower parts, each of which can slide up or down.

**DRESSED STONE**   Stone that has been smoothed and cut.

**DUTCH-STEPPED GABLE**   The end wall of a double sloping roof in which the masonry rises in a series of stepped tiers.

**EAVE**   The edge or lower part of a roof projecting beyond the wall to throw off water.

**ENGLISH BASEMENT**   First floor of a building that is a few steps below sidewalk level.

*134. anthemion*

*135. boss*

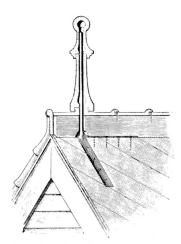

*136. finial*

*137. half-timbering*

**ENTABLATURE**   The horizontal member supported by classical columns.

**FANLIGHT**   A semicircular window over a door.

**FINIAL**   The upper extremity of a pinnacle in Gothic architecture.

**GABLE**   A gable end is formed by a roof that has a single slope on each of two opposing sides. (See fig. 103.)

**GAMBREL**   A roof that has two slopes on each of two opposing sides—the lower slope being steeper than the upper. (See fig. 103.)

**GARRETT**   An attic space.

**HALF TIMBER**   Refers to medieval construction in which heavy framing members are exposed with infill of brick or stucco.

**HIP**   A roof having sloping ends and sides. (See fig. 103.)

**HOOD**   A projecting molding over the top of an arched opening.

**IMPOST**   The base of an arch.

**KEYSTONE**   The masonry block at the top of an arch without which all other components would fail.

**LANCET**   An elongated and narrow window pointed at the top.

**LIGHT**   In construction, an individual piece of glass in a door or window.

**LIMESTONE**   All stones containing lime, usually gray or buff. Marble is a crystallized limestone.

**LINTEL**   A piece of wood, stone, or steel set horizontally over an opening.

**MANSARD**   A type of roof of two slopes in any one direction, the lower slope being more steep than the upper. (See fig. 103.)

**METOPE**   The section of flat stone or wood between two triglyphs.

**MOLDING**   A decorative member of a door or window surround or column.

**PALLADIAN WINDOW**   Two rectangular windows flanked by an arched window.

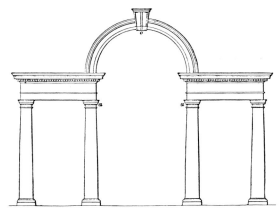

*138. palladian opening*

**PEDIMENT, SEGMENTAL**   An ornamental facing in the shape of a segment of a circle, used over a portico or any opening.

**PEDIMENT, TRIANGULAR**   An ornamental facing in the shape of a triangle over a portico or any opening.

**PENDANT**   A hanging ornament.

**PIER**   A load-bearing column, engaged or free-standing.

**PILASTER**   A column with two square corners set within a wall, usually projecting a fourth or fifth of its diameter.

**QUATREFOIL**   An ornamental pattern consisting of four pointed or round shapes.

*139. pediments*

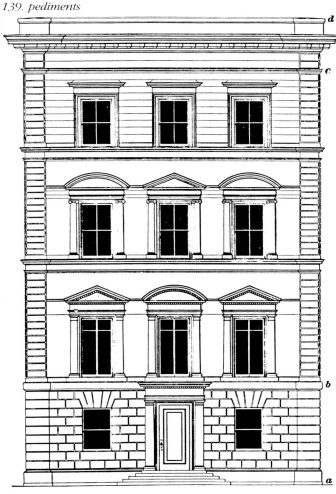

**QUOIN**   The corner stones of a wall, often of a contrasting material or finish to make them stand out.

**REVEAL**   The area between a door or window frame and the surrounding wall.

**RUSTICATION**   A rough stone finish with deeply recessed joints, usually at basement or street level.

**SPALLING**   A condition affecting stone or brick in which moisture penetration and subsequent freezing cause the outer face to fall away. (See fig. 91.)

**SPANDREL**   A panel below a window or the triangular area between two arches.

**STOOP**   A flight of entrance steps to a house (from New York Dutch usage).

**STRINGCOURSE**   Horizontal bands of stone, brick, or terra cotta extending across a facade.

**STUCCO**   An exterior finish made up of Portland cement, lime, and sand mixed with water.

**TERRA COTTA**   A ceramic material made of clay, poured into molds and fired. Glazed when for exterior use.

**TRANSOM**   The horizontal crossbar over a door or window, by extension the upper window.

**TREFOIL**   An ornamental pattern consisting of three pointed or round shapes.

**TRIGLYPH**   A decorative ornament in the Greek Doric order having three vertical channels on its surface.

**TURRET**   A small tower attached to a building and rising above it.

**VIGA**   The end of a wood beam projecting through and beyond the exterior of a wall in Spanish Colonial architecture.

**WATER TABLE**   The projecting base of a wall. Also called a plinth.

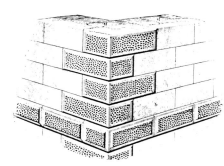

*140. quoins*

This bibliography is divided into topical sections related to the chapters of this book. It has been noted that not a great deal of research has been done heretofore on the Rittenhouse neighborhood, and there are few secondary sources on the subject. The bibliography on History and Development can therefore be fairly comprehensive in limited space. The literature on styles, maintenance, and preservation programs, on the other hand, is large and growing larger. The bibliographies on these topics are designed to be suggestive rather than complete, and to lead the reader to further sources according to interest and need.

## HISTORY AND DEVELOPMENT

Andrews, Wayne. *Architecture, Ambition, and Americans*. Rev. ed. New York, 1978.

Aspinwall, Marguerite. *A Hundred Years in His House: The Story of the Holy Trinity on Rittenhouse Square, 1857–1957*. Philadelphia, 1956.

*A View of a Hundred Years: 1875–1975 at Trinity Memorial Church, Philadelphia*. Philadelphia, 1975.

Baltzell, E. Digby. *Philadelphia Gentlemen: The Making of a National Upper Class*. Glencoe, Ill., 1958.

Biddle, Cordelia Drexel. *My Philadelphia Father*. Garden City, N.Y., 1955.

Brinton, Mary Williams. *Their Lives and Mine*. Philadelphia, 1972.

Burt, Nathaniel. *The Perennial Philadelphians*. New York, 1963.

Campbell, William E. *One Hundred Twenty-Fifth Anniversary, St. Patrick's Church*. Philadelphia, 1965.

Clark, Dennis. *The Irish in Philadelphia: Ten Generations of Urban Experience*. Philadelphia, 1973.

Cohen, Charles J. *Rittenhouse Square: Past and Present*. Philadelphia, 1922.

Davis, Allen F., and Mark Haller, eds. *The Peoples of Philadelphia: A History of Ethnic Groups and Lower-Class Life, 1790–1940*. Philadelphia, 1973.

DuBois, William E. B. *The Philadelphia Negro*. Philadelphia, 1899.

Finkel, Kenneth. *Nineteenth-Century Photography in Philadelphia: 250 Historic Prints from the Library Company of Philadelphia*. New York, 1980.

Gillette, Howard, and William Cutler, eds. *The Divided Metropolis: Social and Spatial Dimensions of Philadelphia, 1800–1975*. Westport, Conn., 1980.

Gowans, Alan. *Images of American Life: Four Centuries of Architecture and Furniture as Cultural Expression*. Philadelphia, 1964.

Greiff, Constance M. *John Notman, Architect*. Philadelphia, 1979.

"Historic Philadelphia: From the Founding until the Early Nineteenth Century." *Transactions of the American Philosophical Society* 23, pt. 1 (1953) (reprinted 1965).

Jacobs, Jane. *The Death and Life of Great American Cities*. New York, 1961.

King, Moses. *Philadelphia and Notable Philadelphians*. New York, 1902.

Looney, Robert F. *Old Philadelphia in Early Photographs, 1839–1914*. New York, 1976.

Lukacs, John. *Philadelphia Patricians and Philistines, 1900–1950*. New York, 1980.

O'Gorman, James. *The Architecture of Frank Furness*. Exhibition catalogue, Philadelphia Museum of Art. Philadelphia, 1973.

Peterson, Charles E., ed. *Building Early America*. Radnor, Pa., 1976.

Philadelphia Museum of Art. *Philadelphia: Three Centuries of American Art*. Exhibition catalogue. Philadelphia, 1976.

Scharf, J. T., and T. Westcott. *History of Philadelphia*. 3 vols. Philadelphia, 1884.

Scully, Vincent. *American Architecture and Urbanism*. 4th ed. New York, 1975.

Snyder, Martin P. *City of Independence: Views of Philadelphia Before 1800*. New York, 1975.

Tatman, Sandra L., and R. W. Moss, Jr. *The Athenaeum Biographical Dictionary of Philadelphia Architects*. Boston, 1984.

Tatum, George. *Penn's Great Town*. Philadelphia, 1961.

Teitelman, Edward, and Richard W. Longstreth. *Architecture in Philadelphia: A Guide*. Cambridge, Mass., 1974.

Wainwright, Nicholas B. *Philadelphia in the Romantic Age of Lithography*. Philadelphia, 1958.

Warner, Sam Bass, Jr. *The Private City: Philadelphia in Three Periods of its Growth*. Philadelphia, 1968.

Watson, John F. *Annals of Philadelphia and Pennsylvania*. Philadelphia, 1844.

Webster, Richard. *Philadelphia Preserved: Catalog of the Historic American Buildings Survey*. Philadelphia, 1976.

Weigley, Russell F., ed. *Philadelphia: A 300-Year History*. New York, 1982.

White, Theo. B., ed. *Philadelphia Architecture in the Nineteenth Century*. 2d rev. ed. Philadelphia, 1973.

White, Theo. B. *The Philadelphia Art Alliance: Fifty Years, 1915–1965*. Philadelphia, 1965.

Wilson, George. *Yesterday's Philadelphia*. Seemann's Historic Cities Series No. 13. Miami, Fla., 1975.

Wolf, Edwin, 2nd. *Philadelphia: Portrait of an American City*. Harrisburg, Pa., 1975.

## STYLES

Ames, Kenneth L. "What is the Neo-Grec?" *Nineteenth Century* 2, no. 2 (Summer 1976): 12–21.

Blumenson, John J.-G. *Identifying American Architecture*. 2d rev. ed. New York, 1983.

Burchard, John, and Albert Bush-Brown. *The Architecture of America*. Boston, 1966.

Collins, Peter. *Changing Ideals in Modern Architecture*. London, 1965.

Foley, Mary Mix. *The American House*. New York, 1980.

Harris, Cyril M., ed. *Historic Architecture Source Book*. New York, 1977.

Jordy, William H. *American Buildings and Their Architects*. Garden City, N.Y., 1976.

Kidney, Walter C. *The Architecture of Choice: Eclecticism in America 1880–1930*. New York, 1974.

Poppeliers, John S., S. Allen Chambers, and Nancy B. Schwartz. *What Style Is It?* 2d ed. Washington, D.C., 1983.

Rifkind, Carol. *A Field Guide to American Architecture*. New York, 1980.

Roth, Leland M. *A Concise History of American Architecture*. New York, 1979.

Van Zanten, David, and George H. Marcus. "Second Empire Architecture in Philadelphia" and "Philadelphia and the Second Empire." *Philadelphia Museum of Art Bulletin* 74, no. 322 (1978).

## MAINTENANCE AND PRESERVATION

Creative Homeowner Press. *Heating*. Passaic, N.J., 1981.

———. *Plumbing*. Passaic, N.J., 1981.

———. *Wiring*. Passaic, N.J., 1981.

Harris, Cyril M., ed. *Dictionary of Architecture and Construction*. New York, 1975.

Insall, Donald. *The Care of Old Buildings Today*. London, 1972.

Johnson, Ed. *Old House Woodwork Restoration*. Englewood Cliffs, N.J., 1983.

McKee, Harley J. *Introduction to Early American Masonry: Stone, Brick, Mortar and Plaster*. Washington, D.C., 1973.

Moss, Roger. *Century of Color: Exterior Decoration for American Buildings, 1820–1920*. Watkins Glen, N.Y., 1981.

National Trust for Historic Preservation. *New Energy from Old Buildings*. With introductions by John C. Sawhill and Neal R. Peirce. Washington, D.C., 1981.

———. *Old and New Architecture: Design Relationship*. Washington, D.C., 1981.

The Old-House Journal. *The Old-House Journal New Compendium*. New York, 1983.

———. *Yearbooks*. 7 vols., 1976–1982. Brooklyn, N.Y., 1982/83.

### NATIONAL PARK SERVICE PUBLICATIONS

*Preservation Briefs: 1. Cleaning and Waterproof Coating of Masonry Buildings*. By Robert C. Mack.

*Preservation Briefs: 2. Repointing Mortar Joints in Historic Buildings*. By Robert C. Mack and de Teel Patterson Tiller.

*Preservation Briefs: 3. Conserving Energy in Historic Buildings*. By Baird M. Smith.

*Preservation Briefs: 4. Roofing for Historic Buildings*. By Sarah M. Sweetser.

*Preservation Briefs: 6. Dangers of Abrasive Cleaning to Historic Buildings*. By Anne E. Grimmer.

*Preservation Briefs: 7. The Preservation of Historic Glazed Architectural Terra Cotta*. By de Teel Patterson Tiller.

*Preservation Briefs: 9. The Repair of Historic Wooden Windows*. By John E. Myers.

*Preservation Briefs: 10. Exterior Paint Problems on Historic Woodwork*. By Kay D. Weeks and David W. Look.

*Preservation Briefs: 11. Rehabilitating Historic Storefronts*. By H. Ward Jandl.

*Respectful Rehabilitation: Answers to Your Questions about Old Buildings*.

### U.S. GOVERNMENT PUBLICATIONS

Chambers, J. Henry. *Cyclical Maintenance for Historic Buildings*.

Gayle, Margot, and David Look. *Metals in America's Historic Buildings: Uses and Preservation Methods*. Part 1.

Kleyle, Frederec Ellsworth. *Rehabilitation of Historic Buildings: An Annotated Bibliography*.

Waite, John. *Metals in America's Historic Buildings: Uses and Preservation Methods*. Part 2.

**METHODS AND PROCEDURES**

Andrews, Gregory E., ed. *Tax Incentives for Historic Preservation*. Washington, D.C., 1981.

Boasberg, Tersh. *A Primer on Historic Preservation Law in Pennsylvania*. Washington, D.C., 1982.

Coughlin, Thomas. *Easements and Other Legal Techniques to Protect Historic Houses in Private Ownership*. Washington, D.C., 1981.

International Centre for Conservation and National Trust for Historic Preservation. *Preservation and Conservation: Principles and Practices*. Washington, D.C., 1976.

Maryland Historical Trust. *Preservation Easements*. Annapolis, Md., n.d.

Morrison, Jacob H. *Historic Preservation Law*. Washington, D.C., 1974.

National Center for Preservation Law. *A Handbook on the Law of Preservation*. Washington, D.C., 1982.

National Trust for Historic Preservation. *Conserve Neighborhoods Notebook*. Washington, D.C., 1980.

————. *Economic Benefits of Preserving Old Buildings*. Washington, D.C., 1976.

————. *Information: A Preservation Sourcebook*. With supplements. Washington, D.C., 1979, ff.

————. *Preservation: Toward an Ethic in the 1980s*. Washington, D.C., 1980.

————. *Tax Incentives for Historic Preservation*. Gregory E. Andrews, ed. Washington, D.C., 1981.

North Carolina Division of Archives and History. *Conservation and Historic Preservation Easements to Preserve North Carolina's Heritage*. Raleigh, N.C., n.d.

Pennsylvania Bar Institute. *Federal Tax Incentives for Historic Preservation*. Harrisburg, Pa., n.d.

Reed, Richard Ernie. *Return to the City: How to Restore Old Buildings and Ourselves in America's Historic Urban Neighborhoods*. New York, 1979.

Urban Land Institute. *Adaptive Use: Development, Economics, Process and Profiles*. Washington, D.C., n.d.

Warner, Raynor H., Sibyl McCormac Groff, Ranne P. Warner, with Sandi Weiss. *Business and Preservation: A Survey of Business Conservation of Buildings and Neighborhoods*. New York, 1978.

Ziegler, Arthur P., Jr. *Historic Preservation in Inner City Areas*. Pittsburgh, Pa., 1974.

Ziegler, Arthur P., Jr., Leopold Adler II, and Walter C. Kidney. *Revolving Funds for Historic Preservation: A Manual of Practice*. Pittsburgh, Pa., 1975.

NATIONAL PARK SERVICE PUBLICATIONS

*The Secretary of the Interior's Standards for Rehabilitation with Guidelines for Rehabilitating Historic Buildings.*
*Tax Incentives for Rehabilitating Historic Buildings.*

U.S. GOVERNMENT PUBLICATIONS

*Catalogue of Federal Domestic Assistance*. Annual.
*Where to Look: A Guide to Preservation Information.*

## HISTORY AND DEVELOPMENT

1.   E. Digby Baltzell, *Philadelphia Gentlemen* (Glencoe, Ill., 1958). The term is used to describe the wealthy and fashionable families whose homes surrounded Rittenhouse Square.

2.   Thomas Fleming, ed., *Benjamin Franklin, A Biography in His Own Words* (New York, 1972), pp. 90–91.

3.   Morgan Edwards, as quoted in Martin P. Snyder, *City of Independence: Views of Philadelphia before 1800* (New York, 1975), pp. 83–84.

4.   Figure 3 is a detail reproduced from Benjamin Latrobe's personal copy of Hills's map in the collection of the Historical Society of Pennsylvania. Latrobe added his waterworks at Center Square, the engine house, and the Chestnut Street tunnel through which water was pumped to Center Square. (*Plan of the City of Philadelphia and Its Environs, Showing the Improved Parts, 1796* [Philadelphia, 1797]).

5.   Native Philadelphians often refer to Penn's large blocks as squares. The custom may have begun in the eighteenth century when there were many undeveloped squares west of the built-up city, but it was continued to describe the blocks bounded by the major east-west streets and numbered north-south streets of Penn's gridiron plan, even after the squares contained solid blocks of buildings and were cut through by secondary streets.

6.   Schuylkill Sixth Street is the present Seventeenth Street. Streets west of Broad Street were numbered east from Schuylkill Front (Twenty-Second Street) until the late 1850s. Twenty-First Street was Schuylkill Second, Twentieth Street was Schuylkill Third, continuing to Fifteenth Street, which was Schuylkill Eighth.

7.   Before 1825 the boundaries for Locust Ward were Walnut to Spruce streets, Fourth Street to the Schuylkill River (*Genealogy of Philadelphia County Sub-divisions*, 2d ed., rev., Philadelphia Department of Records, 1966). The information cited concerns only the portion of Locust Ward west of Broad Street. It was compiled by Temple University students under the direction of Phillip Yanella and Meredith Savery.

8.   Total population for the four wards was 9,005 in 1800, 15,930 in 1810, and 23,175 in 1820. The eastern and western boundaries of the four wards were Fourth Street and the Schuylkill River. The northern and southern boundaries were: Middle Ward, Market to Chestnut streets; South Ward, Chestnut to Walnut streets; Locust Ward, Walnut to Spruce streets; Cedar Ward, Spruce to Cedar (South) streets (U.S. Census Records, *Genealogy of Philadelphia County Sub-divisions*, rev. ed., Philadelphia Department of Records, 1966).

9.   John F. Watson, *Annals of Philadelphia and Pennsylvania* (Philadelphia, 1844), vol. 1, p. 485.

10.   Thrum is the fringe of warp threads left on the loom after the cloth has been removed. Thrum also refers to a mat or rug made of canvas through which the thrum has been pulled.

11.   Meredith Savery, "Rittenhouse," unpublished essay.

12.   *Niles' Register*, vol. 48, June 6, 1835, p. 235 as quoted in William A. Sullivan, *The Industrial Worker in Pennsylvania, 1800–1840* (Harrisburg, Pa., 1955), p. 153.

13.   The presence of workers' housing near the wharves in the 1830s is traced in unpublished research by Phillip Yanella, Temple University, which associates the three Bonsall Street houses with the coal trade.

14.   David Kennedy, "Goosetown," box V–36c, Historical Society of Pennsylvania.

15.   *A View of a Hundred Years: 1875–1975 at Trinity Memorial Church, Philadelphia* (Philadelphia, 1975), p. 3.

16.   There was a textile mill on part of the site of the present Graduate Hospital and two more were located below Lombard Street in the 2000 block of Naudain and Rodman streets. Others were at the southwest corner of Twenty-First and Pine streets, and at the southwest corner of Uber (formerly Elm) and Pine streets (*Maps of the City of Philadelphia Surveyed by Ernest Hexamer and William Locher, Volume 3, Comprising the Seventh and Eighth Wards* [Philadelphia, 1858]).

17.   The population continued to grow. Ten years later in 1850, after Cedar Ward was divided into three wards, Pine, Lombard, and Cedar, the total population was 21,358, an increase of over 9,000 persons (*Genealogy of Philadelphia County Subdivisions*, 2d ed., rev., Philadelphia Department of Records, 1966).

18.   The 1841 State Tax Assessment Ledgers enumerated 941 workers west of Broad Street in Cedar Ward: 415 unskilled, 183 semiskilled, 170 skilled, 114 engaged in trade, 40 proprietary, and 19 clerks.

19.   Jacqueline Saylor, unpublished research. Saylor relied on 1840 U.S. Census records, 1841 State Tax Assessment ledgers, and the 1838 and 1848 Census of Philadelphia Blacks undertaken by the Pennsylvania Abolition Society and the Society of Friends. The latter two are in the manuscript collection of the Historical Society of Pennsylvania.

20.   *Maps of the City of Philadelphia Surveyed by Ernest Hexamer and William Locher, Volume 3, Comprising the Seventh and Eighth Wards* (Philadelphia, 1858).

21.   George B. Tatum, *Penn's Great Town* (Philadelphia, 1961), p. 83.

22.   A committee of Presbyterian laymen, formed in 1850

while St. Mark's was under construction, planned the new Presbyterian church. Banker John A. Brown, Sr., chaired the committee, and Henry White, Edward S. Whelan, John Gulliver, Matthias Baldwin, James C. Donnel, Joseph H. Dulles, and Thomas Fleming were members. The plan selected was by John Notman "in the early Gothic Style." An illustration of the church (now demolished) and newspaper descriptions of its dedication in the fall of 1853 are contained in Constance M. Greiff, *John Notman, Architect* (Philadelphia, 1979), pp. 173–74.

23. Edwin Wolf 2nd, *Philadelphia: Portrait of an American City* (Harrisburg, Pa., 1975), p. 180.

24. Frank Willing Leach, *The McCrea Family*, reprinted from the *North American*, Philadelphia, December 17, 1911, p. 11.

25. Ibid.

26. When McCrea subdivided the 2000 block of Delancey, he created a variety of lot sizes, none less than 22 feet, and reserved the widest lot, 43 feet, for his home at 2000–02. His son James lived at 2004, and his son Charles at 2008.

27. The Philadelphia *Public Ledger* of October 21, 1864, carried the following advertisement for Maule's Lumber Yard, 2500 South Street: "Spruce joists, 14 to 32′ long. Veneers— Walnut & Rosewood. Seasoned walnut, poplar, cherry, ash, mohogany, red cedar, oak. Flooring of all descriptions. Lumber for undertakers, A fine assortment always on hand."

28. Philadelphia Deed Book, R.D.W. 16, pp. 407, 411.

29. The Harrison mansion, designed by Samuel Sloan, is at the far left in figure 14. The painting gallery was probably in the two-story wing. Cohen states that the second floor of the brownstone house at the corner also contained a picture gallery. This corner house was built in 1854 before Harrison purchased the entire block. It has been attributed to John Notman or the contractor for the tower of St. Mark's Church, Charles Lacy. It served as St. Mark's rectory in the early 1850s and was later occupied by Harrison's son. The house on Locust Street directly to the east was built in the early 1870s for Harrison's daughter. (See Charles J. Cohen, *Rittenhouse Square: Past and Present* [Philadelphia, 1922], pp. 265–66; Greiff, *John Notman, Architect*, p. 241.)

30. The William West Frazier home at 250 South Eighteenth, designed by Frank Furness in 1881, replaced the 1849 house of William Divine. In 1887, Frank H. Wyeth hired Theophilus P. Chandler to remodel his home at 1912 Rittenhouse Square. The George W. Childs Drexel mansion (now the Curtis Institute of Music) was built in 1894 by Peabody and Stearns, a

Boston firm. The home of Alexander and Sarah Drexel Van Rensselaer at 1801 Walnut Street was also designed by Peabody and Stearns in 1898. It replaced a mid-century house. Thomas Wanamaker turned to the New York firm of McKim, Mead, and White, to design his new house at 1900 Rittenhouse Square around 1901. It replaced the Drexel-Lankenau house of the 1850s.

31. The discussion that follows describes in some detail the post–Civil War development west of Rittenhouse Square. This area was chosen because its streetscapes and residential blocks remain essentially intact after more than a century. It maintains a unique architectural integrity and cohesiveness because it has not experienced the business and commercial intrusions that have transformed other residential sections of the community.

32. Nathaniel Burt and Wallace E. Davies, "The Iron Age, 1876–1905," in *Philadelphia: A 300–Year History*, ed. Russell F. Weigley (New York, 1982), p. 474.

33. Moses King, *Philadelphia and Notable Philadelphians* (New York, 1902), p. 46.

34. The University of Pennsylvania retains the name School of Fine Arts, one of the few American universities to retain "Fine Arts" in its description of its architectural program. And like its European prototype, the departments of Painting, Sculpture, Architecture, and Landscape Architecture are within the school, as are the departments of City Planning and Urban Design.

35. Walter Cope (1860–1902), John Stewardson (1857–96), and Emlyn Lamar Stewardson (1863–1936). The Cope and Stewardson architectural firm was established in 1885.

36. A few years later, the firm designed the College of Physicians of Philadelphia at 19 South Twenty-Second Street, dedicated in 1908. Elsewhere in Rittenhouse, their designs include the Lady Chapel at St. Mark's, 1631–33 Locust Street for A. C. Harrison, 1630 Locust Street for the Markoe family, and 1718 Locust Street.

37. Philadelphia *North American*, May 28, 1897.

38. Kahn had three architectural offices in Rittenhouse from 1947 to 1974: 1728 Spruce Street, 2001 Walnut Street, and 1501 Walnut Street.

39. Richard Webster, *Philadelphia Preserved: Catalog of the Historic American Buildings Survey* (Philadelphia, 1976), p. 105.

40. Anonymous newspaper article, 1923, Charles J. Cohen notebooks, 1925, vol. 5, p. 3, Historical Society of Pennsylvania.

41. The site of Frank Miles Day's Art Club is now a parking

garage. The Shubert Theatre replaced Horticulture Hall, also designed by Day. The Hershey Hotel occupies the site of the Walton Hotel and the Broad Street Theatre. The Atlantic Richfield Building (now Anderson Hall of the Philadelphia College of Art) replaced the Beth Eden Baptist Church.

42. Anonymous newspaper article, 1923, Charles J. Cohen notebooks, 1925, vol. 5, p. 3, Historical Society of Pennsylvania.

43. *Telegraph*, February 24, 1913.

44. Wayne Andrews, *Architecture, Ambition and Americans: A Social History of American Architecture* (New York, 1978), p. 144.

45. The R-10A zoning classification allows single-family residential use of buildings with a height of 35 feet or three stories. R–10 and R–15 classifications cover multiple-family dwellings where the number of units permitted is determined by a formula based on size of the floors in the structure and minimum lot and yard areas. (See *Philadelphia Zoning Code*, Department of Licenses and Inspections, City of Philadelphia, Chapter 14–200, Residential Districts.)

## STYLES

1. An exception is John McArthur's Lombardic-Romanesque Tenth Presbyterian Church at 1700 Spruce Street, of 1854.

2. Asher Benjamin, *The Practical House Carpenter*, 2d ed. (Boston, 1830), p. iii.

3. Andrew Jackson Downing, quoted in Wayne Andrews, *Architecture, Ambition, and Americans*, rev. ed. (New York, 1978), p. 102.

4. John Ruskin, *The Stones of Venice*, vol. I, "The Foundation" (New York, 1882), p. 347.

5. David Van Zanten, "Second Empire Architecture in Philadelphia," *Philadelphia Museum of Art Bulletin* 74, no. 322 (1978), p. 9.

6. Ibid., p. 22.

7. The principles of the Beaux-Arts continued in the evolutionary Art Deco style that emerged in the 1920s. They can be seen in the Rittenhouse Plaza Apartments at 1901 Walnut Street.

8. The World Columbian Exposition of 1893 in Chicago mesmerized thousands of visitors with the grandeur of its planning, which linked buildings with landscape, lagoons, and canals.

## GLOSSARY

1. Sources for Glossary illustrations are as follows: The Parthenon, American Technical Society, *Cyclopedia of Architecture, Carpentry and Building*, 10 vols. (Chicago, 1908), vol. 8. Anthemion, Boss, Half-Timbering, Palladian Opening, Pediments, The Colliery Engineer Co., *A Treatise on Architecture and Building Construction* (Scranton, Pa., 1899), vol. 5. Finial, ibid., vol. 3. Quoin, ibid., vol. 2.

# HISTORIC RITTENHOUSE, INC.

Historic Rittenhouse, Inc., is a nonprofit educational organization, whose purpose is to promote understanding and appreciation of the architectural environment and historic significance of the Rittenhouse neighborhood of Philadelphia, Pennsylvania.

It encourages preservation, conservation, rehabilitation, quality urban design, and appropriate development, zoning, and land use planning which will promote civic pride, improved property maintenance, economic growth, tourism, and investment in the Rittenhouse neighborhood.

## LIST OF CONTRIBUTORS

Funds for this publication were provided by
Atlantic Richfield Foundation
The National Endowment for the Arts
Mellon Bank
SmithKline Beckman Corporation
The Glenmede Trust
CIGNA Foundation
The Dietrich Foundation
Sun Company, Inc.
Bell of Pennsylvania

and the following Sponsors, Supporters, and Patrons

*Sponsors*

The Garden
Latham Hotel
Rittenhouse Plaza
Robert Sheridan and Partners
The Gordon Stouffer Foundation

*Supporters*

1830 Rittenhouse Square
Edmund N. Bacon
Barclay Hotel
Fidelity Bank
William H. Moennig III
Joe Moss
Mr. and Mrs. Bernard Newman
Otto Sperr
Spencer Wertheimer, Esq.

*Patrons*

1845 Walnut Street
Earl P. L. Apfelbaum, Inc.
Mr. and Mrs. David Bergman
James and Barbara Bodenheimer
Jeffrey L. Braff and Hope A. Comisky
Building Owners' and Managers' Association of
    Philadelphia
Robert A. Capps
Center City Association of Proprietors

Dr. and Mrs. Charles W. Charny
Louis Cissone
The Commissary
Commonwealth Land Title Insurance Co.
Continental Bank
Dr. and Mrs. John L. Cotter
Curran, Mylotte, David and Fitzpatrick
Mr. and Mrs. Harry Dannenbaum
Mr. and Mrs. Antelo Devereux, Jr.
David and Beatrice Doret
Nan Duskin, Inc.
Mr. and Mrs. Wesley Emmons
Betty Fitzgerald
Joseph Fox Books
Kenneth Frank
Jack Freeman
Bernard Friedman
William A. Hamann III
Clay W. Hamlin III
Mr. and Mrs. James Harper
Jack and Mary Anne Hunter
IVB Bank
Paul James and Charles Gilmore
Sarah Jordan
Kaiserman Enterprises
Mr. and Mrs. Charles Kanev
Janet S. Klein
Harvey Leibovitz
C. Benson Lewis
H. Reed Longnecker
Nikki X Marx, Esq.
Drs. Anna Meadows and Alfred Knudson
Midtown Realty
Bill and Lenore Millhollen

Nelson Monteleone
George Patton
Philadelphia Ethical Society
Plumer-Levit Real Estate
John Randolph, A.I.A.
Rittenhouse Claridge Apartments
Rittenhouse Foundation
Mrs. E. Florens Rivinus*
Rodin Enterprises
Arnold Rosenberg, Esq., and Joel Prybutok
Milton A. and Miriam F. Rothman
Betsy Salandria
Mr. and Mrs. Gordon F. Schwartz
Drs. T. F. McNair and Dwight Scott
Robert Shatzer*
Robert J. Shusterman, Esq.
Melvin G. Smith
Dr. Stanton and Sara Kay Smullens
Solo Realty
E. Barnett Steinmetz
Jay Robert Stiefel, Esq.
Stolker and Company
Dr. and Mrs. Luther L. Terry
Urban Outfitters
Henry and Audrey Walters
Warwick Hotel
Mr. and Mrs. Jerome B. Weinstein
Joseph H. Weiss, Esq.
Wellington Apartments
Tama Williams
Dr. John F. Wilson


* Deceased